# CREATION IN SPACE

## fundamentals of architecture

# CREATION IN SPACE

## a course in the fundamentals of architecture

### Volume 1: ARCHITECTONICS

Jonathan Block Friedman

**KENDALL/HUNT PUBLISHING COMPANY**
2460 Kerper Boulevard  P.O. Box 539  Dubuque, Iowa 52004-0539

To my family

Drawings page 23 from *The Power of Limits* by Gyorgy Doczi, © 1981. Reprinted by arrangement with Shambhala Publications, Inc., 314 Dartmouth St., Boston, MA 02116

Photo page 34 and drawings on page 35 from Tange, Kenzo and Kawazoe, Noboru. *Ise: Prototype of Japanese Architecture*, MIT Press, Cambridge, 1965.

Drawing lower left corner, page 38, from Mainstone, Rowland. *Developments in Structural Form*. MIT Press, Cambridge, 1975.

Drawings pages 106 and 107 from Aladar Olgyay and Victor Olgyay, *Solar Control and Shading Devices*. Copyright © 1957 by Princeton University press. Figs. 52, 53, 78, 79, 91, 93 reprinted with permission of Princeton University Press.

A complete list of figure credits given on page 185.

Printed in the United States of America

10   9   8   7

## CREATION IN SPACE

Now we enter space
where astronauts wear
halo and wings
like human angels
standing free
with unpressed soles.
Now we may dwell in light
radiant beyond clouds
hard-edged, clear,
uncompromised
by ground or macrogravity.

Now we discover earth
our home is full in space.
Now we find plan in mind
and room in living heart.

# CONTENTS

*Ingres is said to have created an artistic order out of rest; I should like to create an order from feeling and, going still further, from motion.*—Paul Klee, September 1914

## PREFACE: ABOUT THIS BOOK

This book is for students of vision, grown-up children who once built castles and cities from blocks and who now dream of palaces for the human spirit. This course of study in the fundamentals of architecture is for people who have not yet mastered (three-dimensional) space as the medium of architecture as well as they have mastered words and numbers as media for thought and communication. This is a mindbook rather than a handbook. It is not merely a commentary on works already made, nor a guide to simple techniques of production. Rather it is a companion to the studio experience, the living environment in which works are created. Like a book of musical *etudes*, it is organized as a sequence of easy pieces, incremental studies demanding both greater technique and deeper insight. If you *play,* and not just look at, the notes in a book of piano pieces, you learn the material through practice. Practicing the exercises in this book is one way to learn the fundamentals of creation in space.

Too many of our houses are badly planned. Too many rooms are long and narrow and dimly lit; too many yards have no privacy whatsoever; and too many garages get the southeast corner and best light of the house. Our spaces are often ill-fitting or aimed the wrong way, as if builders, owners, and town officials conspired to have a collective spatial stupidity. These no doubt well-meaning people learn from our frontier-mentality culture to assume that space is "just there" to be filled in or used up, but rarely to be planned or organized. In Holland, where every square inch must be won from the sea, and in Japan and Italy, where climate, light and topography are intense, the space between buildings often has more presence and character than the buildings themselves. Our buildings too often sit not in splendid but lonely isolation, in suburbs and even cities. It is as if we are spacially illiterate. We need to cultivate the important part of our brain which thinks in three dimensions and makes spatial order. If we have an internal medicine to care for the spaces in our bodies, we need an *external* medicine for the spaces in the environment around us.

As far as I know, there are few texts for an introductory studio course in architectural design. This is understandable, since such courses usually seek to be original, but a standard course may actually foster rather than inhibit creativity. There are books which tell you how to use a pencil, choose paper or draw a perspectve, and there are "coffee table books" to guide us through the great chateaux and castles. But the curious and motivated reader senses a gap between these two types. The search is not only for "how to" but also "why to", which means to find and pursue an *idea* through the difficult and exacting medium of three dimensional space. This book is intended to be a companion and guide through that lonely search. Examples from world architecture and from the work of previous students are included to illustrate provocative questions rather than answers, because each serious and valid plastic work redefines the field of its inquiry. If Picasso had never lived, we would not have missed him. But the works he made changed forever the way we look at the world. The same is true for each project illustrated herein— if it had not been made, we would not know such a solution is possible. This book is presented in the spirit in which it was conceived—not to promote any one approach to architecture, but to introduce difficult material in a direct and clear way. The sequence was designed to teach architectonics, and has been tested by many beginners and professionals . . . above all, the sequence *works.*

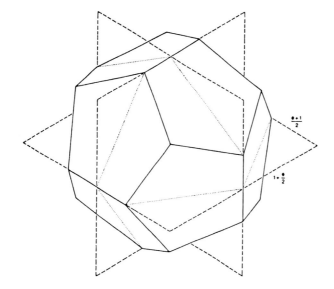

$\frac{\phi + 1}{2}$

$1 + \frac{\phi}{2}$

# ACKNOWLEDGMENTS

Many people helped make this book possible. Foremost are the New York Institute of Technology Design Fundamentals students who from 1983 to 1988 participated in the development of this course; second are the faculty, whose instructions and insights helped to translate words on paper into spatial realities; third are my fellow Design Fundamentals coordinators, Bill Walther and Warren Winter, whose tile projects provided the first point of departure for a portable interactive design sequence in many dimensions, and Michele Bertomen, whose talent for teaching and making spirited, and graceful architecture is especially demonstrated in Study 7; and finally is Dr. Julio San Jose, Dean of the School of Architecture at NYIT, whose constant support and guidance through these years has been instrumental and inestimable. I am also indebted to Alan Sayles, William Gati, and Michael Schwarting for background materials, and above all to Paul Amatuzzo for help in preparing the notes in the Visual Glossary, for lessons in competence, and for friendship in vigilance.

Maria di Natale, exceptionally talented in architecture, gave vital help in research and layout design. Linda Manz, Kathy Chesnowitz, and Alex Eng also provided valuable assistance in these areas. Lindsay Shapiro edited the text, saving us all from the murkiest passages. Abigail Sturges made useful suggestions for the book design. The NYIT office staff at Ed Hall, including Irma Roby, Jean Lambert, Joan Bassin, Carol Alper, Anne Zollo, Pat Joyce, Lisa Sylvestri, and Bill Diehl, were always there when needed. Jeanne Reilly was especially helpful in obtaining permissions. Jean-Louis Schulmann, Todd Class, Kurt Kalafsky, and Leo Exconde helped with computers. I was indeed fortunate to encounter these good people. Since book space is limited, only a very few of the hundreds of students who took the course are represented, and only a very small part of their work is illustrated. A few deserve special mention. Trevor Wisdom, Andrew Tychaz, Anthony Hatzionnou, John Pavlou, John Angelos, and Paul Anderson were pioneers in the first development of some of these ideas who did so well that they inspired me to continue. Older articulate and curious students including Mark Abrahamson, Juliane Tomiser, Nancy Bretzfield, Michael Lodespoto, Harriet Gettleman, Michael Gordon, and Andrea Kaplan, were honestly baffled by the arcane and obscure expectations of the normal design studio milieu, where learning is often assumed to occur by osmosis. They have lived long enough to know that there is really no time to waste. In many respects, I have written this book for them.

And there were many people whose voices I heard and whose visions I beheld as I wrote and designed this book. They have guided me to insights I sought to articulate throughout these studies. They include: Robert Slutzky, Anthony Eardley, Tony Roccanova, Ken Schiano, Len Wujcik, Bev Wujcik, Jody McKee, Charles Graves, Jose Oubrerie, Jullian de la Fuente, Sheldon Reaven, Jeff Kalban, Judy Sheine, Ernie De Maio, Clay Smook, Steve Badanes, John Ringel, Roger Bone, Evan Mawdsley, Dick Gaulton, Mark Skolnik, Reuben Katz, Richard Etlin, Emilio Ambasz, Paul Segal, Mike Pribyl, Tod Williams, Bob Geddes, Anthony Vidler, Michael Wurmfeld, Ken Frampton, Doug Kelbaugh, Jon Dyer, Robinson Brown, Alan Wexler, Mike Webb, Peter Carl, Danny Liebeskind, John Hejduk, Peter Eisenman, Michael Graves, Charles Gwathmey, Michael Kalil, Richard Meier, Bill Gordon, Martin Garfinkel, Richard Painter, Sam Paul, Sy Jarmul, John Dyer, Janis Richter, George Segal, Chris Chimera, Joe Snyder, Michelle Judge, David Lenson, Jim Kostman, Tim Wood, Jim Swan, Jim Weisenfeld, Mills and Suzanne, David Chorlian, Greg Martin, Sue Aronson, Ellen Stavitsky, Lee Fawkes, Susan and Wayne Cohen, Steve and Helen Chernicoff, Iris Orens, Susan Jacoby, Susan Gallagher, Linda and Eric Sallee, Quentin Munier for discussions on soldier courses and Bill Serra for coloring books—

Beyond all these are my mother Bernice, my brother Jeremy, and Lisa, Lindsay and Caroline, and Aubrey, Penny, Amy, Nancy, Jeff, Norman and the kids, the Turtz clan, Elsie, Izzy, Iris, Judy, Len, Tracy, Jennifer, and Linda, Jennie, Sam, Kate, and those who watch from afar . . . Dad, Minnie, Howard, Jimmy, my grandmothers, matriarch and dentist, and my grandfathers, chemist and musician.

I give special thanks to my wife Marilyn whose constant wisdom, patience, support, and love through thick and thin has kept me going and taught me love. And to Charlie who gave me life and continues to give me the world. . . .

**FOREWORD**
**by Robert Slutzky**

This book has been designed for students who seek a college-level knowledge of architecture fundamentals. As such, it admirably succeeds. Yet it is not merely a beginner's guide. Like Bach's pedagogic preludes and fugues (Magdalena) intended for the beginning student of music, the six or seven 'easy pieces' forming the backbone of this architectural primer can also be 'played' by the initiated, the practitioner, the teacher, the artist, and all other visualizing minds who derive pleasure from articulated and intelligent 'problems' or, if you will, *etudes*.

Beyond the content of this 'primer' is its very manner of construction as 'book', making its organization a metaphor for architecture. Being a 'house' of information inhabited as well by profound architectural 'spirits' within (rooms) that textually and illustratively interchange thought and concept (like Le Corbusier's free plan, *le plan libre*), it is also an architectural promenade, both mindful and mind-filling. But the 'path' is anything but linear. Jostled by quantum-like insights that periodically rescramble our perceptions, the book becomes an intricate mini-palace of architectural culture. To cite an example: in the Introduction, a full-page blank square (verso) drifts through its opposite of pre-ambling text (recto) to reappear on the following page (verso) as a diminished *blanc* canvas sitting nearly centered within an ornately defined studio interior by Picasso. This in turn emerges as the very centered Laurentian Library pedimented portal photographed in absolute frontality, followed by yet another full page (verso) photograph of a sharply 'pedimental' mountain backdrop to Machu-Picchu frontally nestled beneath it and in deep perspective (a tipped and warped urban grid) which reappears as the absolute frontality of an urban metaphor as painting (Mondrian's *Broadway Boogie Woogie*), which then dissolves into the next verso full-page photograph of that marvelous synthesis of hyper-styled othogonality pedimented . . . the Parthenon!

Next stop . . . Ise! And so on . . . producing a veritable Baedecker of cross-related imageries, probed by reflective texts, some of which are descriptive, some presciptive, still others citatory.

Still more examples of this pervasive 'connectedness': Rose Windows are recalled by Mandelbrodt fractals (another reading of the Gothic?), Stonehenge expands the meaning of 'sticks and stones', the Parthenon of the 'kit of parts', Ise of Piranesi and more . . . seemingly infinite relationships unfold within the reader's stimulated brain, exercises of associative perception calculated to hone one's retinal intelligence.

Continuing the book-as-architecture metaphor, we sense an unorthodox cladding of the front and rear cover plates. Are they facades? Are they deliberately dematerialized through the content of illustration to suggest the fracturing of traditional edifice walls? This is a bound book 'unbounded' by a pictorialization of boundless space! The cover presents a placental darkness levitating an icon-like postured astronaut (McCandless—candle-less, newly sprung fetal spaceling) bouyant in his hermetic life-support suit untethered (umbilical cord cut!) astride a mini-vehicle (the new aedicule?) called MMU (anagram for MUM . . . reflecting the awe-filling silence of his endless black surround? Or perhaps an affectionate recall of MOM, or a mocking arch-typical pharaonic MUMMY, that earth-bound double-encased royal corpse centered within its inaccessible and utterly compressive pyramid tomb!).

The rear cover plate shows a space-station awaiting further growth, articulated as a bifurcated double-square linear truss, symmetrical along its sectioned axis which in turn is affixed and appendaged by planar and volumetric geometries (a seemingly random composition of points, lines, planes, and volumes recalling the non-objectivity of Malevich, Lissitsky, and Tatlin) that cluster and pattern according to the rules of a scientific rationalism (no picturesque Constructivism here!). Glistening in an unatmosphered sunlight, a crystallized PROUN unencumbered by earth-born statics, it portends the architecture of outer-space (really unpretentious space-engineering?) and summons *Vers une Architecture* . . . 'Eyes that do not see' . . . part II.

Architecture, like art, cannot be taught. But it can and should be cultivated. The technology of 'building' and the means of its graphic articulation can be taught. Architecture, as the art of building, demands the skill of building, yet it also preserves for itself the freedom to disengage from the purely functional pragmatic 'program'. As an art it draws sustenance not only from the other spacial and temporal arts but from any and all realms of concept, idea, and imagery. It is privileged to comment not only on itself but the world at large. It is the touchstone of more than tradition and memory . . . it might even suggest dreams that defy materialization. It is rooted in revelation; its flower is metaphor. If 'building' remains mundane in the perjorative, architecture becomes mundane in the celestial as well as the earth-bound sense. From momentaneous perception to thoroughly familiarized ones, architecture transcends the vicissitudes of daily existence by endowing them with insight and intensity. The enemy of architecture is the 'obvious', its nemesis is boredom. It must never cede its beckoning power, that silent yet irresistable force. Born from esthetic sensibility, architecture can only be realized by the mastery of its formal means of expression. These means can be taught. *Creation in Space* generates that special and appropriate pedagogic environment within which the mind remains provoked as the hand develops it skills. As it stresses model-making, with its attendant flexibility to research space and structure, and particularly drawing (that suggestive word both noun and verb, whose etymology relates to *education* . . . educe . . . to draw out from . . . translated to French *dessin,* Italian *disegno,* back to English as design), this architectonics primer celebrates the eye and hand as it extols the language of architecture.

*Give me extension and motion
and I shall construct the universe.*
Rene Descartes

## INTRODUCTION: A FOUNDATION

### STUDENTS OF VISION

We are all architects as children. A five-year-old's fresh imagination can transform wood blocks into castles, ships, or palaces and discover caves, dens, and nests beneath tables and behind dressers. Youthful visionaries climb trees and discover vistas to new horizons. Inhabiting these spaces new minds may dream of making homes and cities.

At these tender ages we are each also linguists, mathematicians, and natural scientists. By the time we graduate high school we have advanced these skills with perhaps twelve full years of formal instruction. But public education rarely offers any parallel twelve year course in the study of spaces, so our ability to make space and realize our youthful dream worlds hardly grows at all. Even high school technical drafting and "architecture" courses often teach only how to depict inherited spacial conventions without investigating the sources of those forms. (How few of us learn that the "ranch house" was essentially invented by Frank Lloyd Wright in his Prairie Houses!) As a result, most adults who begin to study architecture lack any mature capability to understand or invent even simple creations in space, let alone to realize and express ideas through the difficult and exacting medium of architecture.

This book therefore presumes that the reader has spacial ideas and visions but lacks the means to express, improve, or evaluate them. It presumes no previous training, knowledge, or experience in the field of architecture (except that of any normally curious person with the equivalent of a typical high school education). It sets a course of study to help recover each person's creative spirit for designing space. The studies in this book will show how to formulate spacial inventions and study them in two and three dimensions. The "how-to" part of *form-making* in architecture is relatively easy to learn. It involves techniques of making drawings and models to communicate sizes, scale, materials, structures, etc. of proposed spaces. But the "how-to" part of *meaning-making* in architecture is more subtle. More properly it should be called "why-to". So this book emphasizes not so much "how-to" as "why-to"; not only a "handbook", it is also a "mindbook" about how to think in the medium of architecture. The combination of built work by masters and student designs presents architecture as a living tradition where every work is part of a process of becoming.

This book is for the person who seeks to understand the fundamentals of making meaningful architecture. It considers both the *form and idea* of creation in space from solid foundation to springing vault. It is based on the premise that as words can become literature or notes can become music, the order of spaces (mass and volume) in light is a medium that can become architecture. Whereas building is a question of making shelter, architecture concerns the human heart. It is an ancient but still primary means for expressing our deepest feelings.

To make space well, one must cultivate *vision*, the ability to foresee events in the three dimensional world and act on that prescience. Whereas poets are students of language, playwrights are students of drama and comedy, and opera singers are students of voice, architects are students of vision.

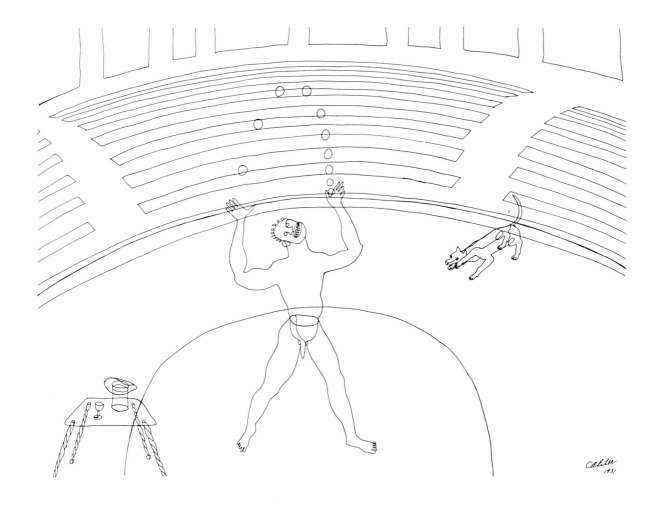

## VISION IN SPACE

In childhood each of us mastered creation in space. Playing with blocks is intuitively close to the central act of making architecture. Whereas children position solid forms to make their castles, the architect composes volumes which may be either solid or void. This study of design picks up where we as children left architecture—with blocks of special shape and dimension, coordinated so that complex ideas of spacial order can be expressed directly and eloquently. The first geometry presented is simple to draw and easy to make. As methods of depicting spacial ideas with these forms are mastered, increasingly complex forms and geometries are introduced.

Space is the medium of architecture. Working directly in this medium gives the architect an advantage in visualizing the effects of a design. Since architects often must manipulate given elements like the rooms, parking spaces, or access corridors a client or code may require, they must be proficient in the composition of given elements in many dimensions simultaneously. Thus the architect is often more like a juggler than a sculptor. Whereas a sculptor shapes clay or stone into any desired form, the aim of the juggler is to keep given elements in the air. What matters to the juggler is not so much what the elements are but their relationships in space and time. Recognizing and solving problems about the ordering of patterns are skills of great value to an architect. Like contestants in the early TV show called "Beat the Clock" who rearranged a scrambled set of words into a well-known phrase, the architect must unscramble a chaos of masses and volumes into an ordered set of spaces. It is not simply the contents, but the rhythm of relationships that is important to the architect.

### Architectonics

The intentional arrangement of mass, space, and light to communicate human values is called *architectonics*. Curiously, the Oxford English Dictionary defines "architectonics" as both the science of architecture and (in metaphysics) the science of the systematic arrangement of knowledge. Architectonics explores the relationship between volumes in three dimensions, both solid and void, as a medium for human creation in space.

### Graphics

The study of the relationship between figure and field in two dimensions is called *graphics*. What architectonics is to three dimensions, graphics is to two dimensions. Sharp contrast can be made vivid through careful graphic design. We see white on black as lights in space. Black on white is the common form of ink on paper. This medium is simple, yet so rich in communicative potential that all human ideas can be expressed through it in images or symbols. A single width of ink line in Alexander Calder's drawing *Juggler With Dog,* describes a man in action, barking animal, props, seats, and the space of a circus. Some phenomena, like music, space, and love are difficult to capture in this two-dimensional medium, yet the very fact that you are reading the words "music, space, and love" and associating them with your own experience reveals the power of graphics.

## EIDETIC VISION

Children "build" drawings. Child psychologists have identified the process whereby an image is built up of elements, each of which represent an idea, to make a whole picture. Thus a face is made of eyes, nose, mouth, hair, etc. The image is not copied directly from life. Rather it is drawn from the mind's understanding and memory of significant elements and relationships between them. This is how five-year-olds see. This primordial union of architectonics and graphics is called *eidetic vision*.

"Eidetic" comes from the Greek term *Eidos* which denotes the form or shape of a figure, and which is akin to *idein,* meaning to see, hence idea. This connection implies that the form and idea of a thing are the same. The sense that meaning can be communicated through the form of a thing is one that both artists and engineers understand. This book is based on the proposition that *the **idea** of a work of art **is** its **form.*** As the writer James Baldwin put it, "The form *is* the content." Meaning resides in the work's unique order of concrete elements that compose it. Thus for example the particular combination of notes, silences, tempos, rhythms, harmonies, and melodies of Beethoven's Ninth Symphony *is* its meaning. The form of this work *is* how Beethoven thought through the medium of music.

Eidetic vision depends on imagination, which in one sense is the capacity to create visions of what may be. The ability to previsualize complex three-dimensional designs can be cultivated even in adults. Certain projections in descriptive geometry, including plans and perspectives, help to make this easy, but working directly with solids makes this even easier. As a designer gets to know the project better, its spacial qualities become ever more vivid in mind and can be plotted ever more vividly in model or on paper. The poet William Blake was said to possess a very strong eidetic vision; he wrote as if he were seeing his images complete before his eyes. Certainly Picasso had a remarkable capacity to draw whatever he wished and to invent spaces complete in every detail of light, form, and anatomy. Some psychologists have claimed that eidetic vision is innate in children and lost in most adults, but we have found, and we believe that the examples in this book show, that eidetic vision *can* be recultivated. Aristotle said, "The soul never thinks without an image." The cosmologist Steven Hawking, holder of the same Lucasian Professorship at Cambridge once occupied by Sir Isaac Newton, has said, "People have the mistaken impression that mathematics is just equations. In fact, equations are just the boring part of mathematics. I attempt to see things in terms of geometry."

Working directly in the medium of space cultivates eidetic vision. Seeing what you propose actually develop in three dimensions, and drawing what you have created in two dimensions, strengthens the ability to synthesize form. The sequence of plastic investigations you will encounter, the specially designed sets of tiles and Kit of Parts you will make, and the rubber cement you will use for assembling compositions fosters an ease and fluency with understanding how to order space. Rubber cement allows you to "sketch" directly in and with space, so that every model is both a preliminary and final study. Coordinating the everyday tools of hand, eye, and brain can transform them into an instrument of infinite expression, so that every view of space may become an eidetic vision.

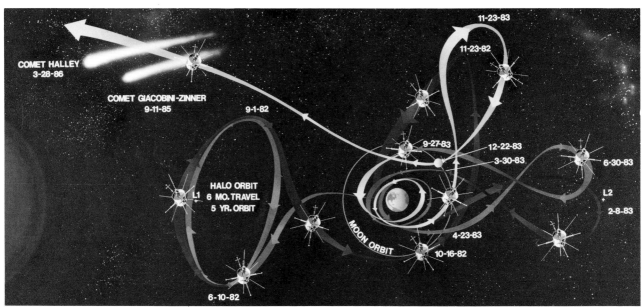

## DRAWING IN SPACE: AN INSTRUMENT OF VISION

A point has no dimension, but the extension of a point describes a line. Whether that point is the tip of a pencil, a flashlight in the dark, or a spaceship intersecting a comet, its free travel in space generates the first dimension—line. Translation of line creates plane, or structure in two dimensions. And when a point can move freely and independently in 3 dimensions it describes and creates space. While Matisse created his wonderful paper collage of Icarus by "drawing directly with a scissors", Picasso could draw figures in space with a flashlight. This book's emphasis on architectonics may encourage people to draw directly in space not just with lines and surfaces, but with masses and volumes.

### Precision and Freedom

Picasso's flashlight drawing is freehand. The similar fluid curves of the ICE cometary explorer are the product of the most mechanical drafting processes available to aerospace technology. Both approaches achieve beautiful intelligent curves through a balance of freedom and precision. Although some drawings are made with tools to assist geometric precision, all *vision* is "freehand". The drawing hand is only free when the eye sees clearly. Freehand drawing exercises are presented to cultivate hand/eye coordination, and temper abstraction with realism, but the "how to" of this activity is outside the scope of this book and is well documented (see Bibliography). The "why" of freehand drawing should be clear by the contents of the suggested exercises.

Simple drafting has as little to do with the real practice of architecture as penmanship has to do with the practice of law. Making precise drawings to describe one's spacial ideas, on the other hand, is as necessary to architects as a command of the language is to lawyers. Too many high schools (and colleges) teach *only* the conventions of drafting, belying the name of architecture. The drafting technician is not trained to make decisions about space that affect human values. Since computerized drafting systems already do much of the automatic work needed to translate a spacial idea into a building (including dimensioning, rendering, detailing, specification writing, energy calculations, and cost control via spreadsheet analysis), the question arises, "what does the architect really do?" Just as the Impressionist and Cubist painters sought a deeper role for art after the advent of photography, so too must we penetrate to the essence of architecture stripped of its superficial aspects.

### Tools and Instruments

What an architect does is to generate, explore, test, and realize visions of creation in space. How this is accomplished is as important as why it is done. Technique is only the means to a more human end. A tool performs its task reliably. We expect a hammer to swing with constant arc so that we can drive each nail cleanly home. An instrument, on the other hand, is designed to perform complex combinations of actions without limit. Although there are only 88 keys on the piano, there is no limit to the music it can create. Our senses, with training, can become instruments as well as tools. Just as the voice is an opera singer's instrument, the architect's instrument is the special kind of seeing called *eidetic vision*.

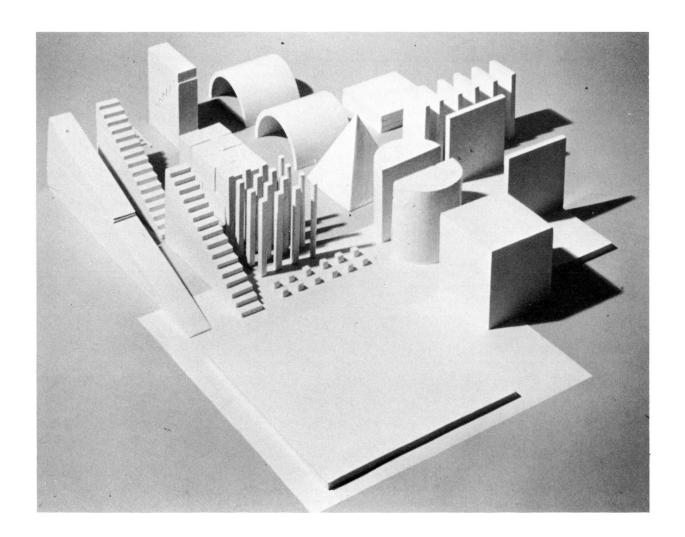

## ARCHITECTONIC VISION

Construction sets are favorite toys. Playing with blocks has often been a basis for teaching architecture. The Kit of Parts you will make is related to the "nine-square problem" kit developed by Bob Slutzky, Lee Hersche, and John Hejduk in Texas and at the Cooper Union School of Architecture, but differs in certain proportions and the way parts are connected. The rubber cement you will use for assembling compositions fosters an ease and fluency with understanding how to order space. Rubber cement allows you to "sketch" directly in and with space, so that every model is both a preliminary and final study, and so that every view of space may reveal an eidetic vision.

The pedagogic and educational program documented in this book was developed from necessity—the difficult constraints of learning and teaching architecture at the School of Architecture at New York Institute of Technology. A lack of permanent studio space, shops, and other facilities, along with a commuter student population required that the study of the fundamentals of architecture become more direct, basic, and generalizable than is normally the case in schools with a great deal of special equipment and support spaces. Like Einstein with his *gedanken* (the thought experiments) it seemed to us possible to be able to speak of architecture directly, in the simplest terms through ordinary means and everyday items. Why then require high technology to pursue a discipline which has at its core a humanistic discourse between people about values, feelings, and ideas? Clear and elegant expression in the medium of plastic form can even communicate a philosophy. The architect Le Corbusier might be said to have spent a lifetime exploring the profound question of how to formulate a cube.

Students do not always master everything equally well. A scheme may be an interesting spacial idea, but conceptually weak or inaccurately drawn. So the reader must be critical. Some examples in this book are brilliant; others are modest. But all merit our respect as attempts and actualities that have been made through honest human work. The museum goer or concert listener, the art "consumer" of contemporary culture, does not always understand what it means to undertake such effort and therefore cannot be truly critical, which may be why so many people do not comprehend what they encounter in galleries. It is easier and more honest to do this after having tried to make work oneself. Then how quickly one appreciates both the achievements and limitations of any work. Then the simple plan becomes miraculous for its elegant solution to many complex problems. The work in this book comes in the two categories of art we face in real life. The first is the "classics"—the great works treasured in museums whose inspiring qualities have grown over time as they reveal depth of human meaning. Classics are easy and comforting to study, because we know they are great (so we hear). The second group is the "unknowns", the new (and perhaps avant-garde) work seen in or out of galleries. Here we must rely on our own judgement, not the pronouncement of experts, and combine training of the eye and formal sensibility with intuition and feeling— the hunch. To say "yes I like this work" is to risk that everyone else will say it is awful. Individual insight may be alone for decades or centuries. Even pure and good works may be unpopular for lifetimes, too plain when the fad is for ornate, too complicated when the fashion is to oversimplify complexity. The purity of a form may only emerge through use, beyond prejudice. The Japanese concept of *shibui,* that a thing which at first appears ugly may grow to be beautiful (the VW beetle is an example) cautions us against overhasty rejection of the new.

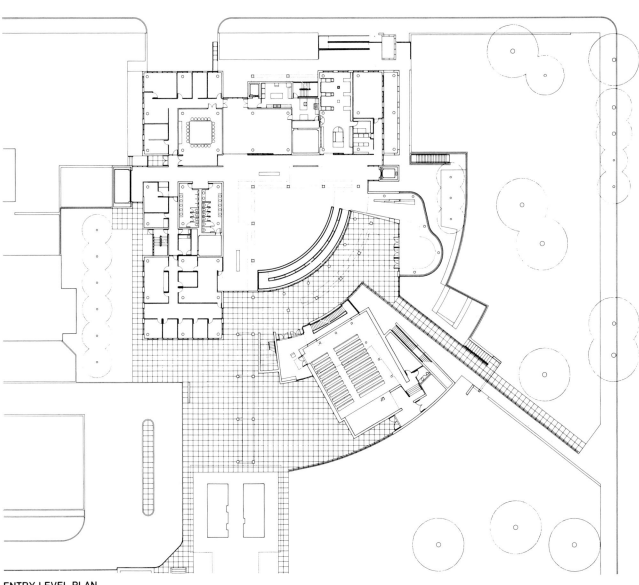

ENTRY LEVEL PLAN

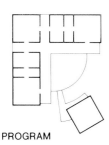

PROGRAM

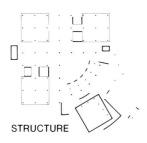

STRUCTURE

CIRCULATION

## PLAN: VISION IN MANY DIMENSIONS

Making architecture requires cultivating the ability to compose form simultaneously in both two and three dimensional space. Space is a medium of multiple dimensions including (but perhaps not limited to) length, breadth, and volume. We always see space ambiguously. It is not possible, for example, to determine whether a given figure is a trapezoid drawn in two dimensions or an image of a square floor seen in perspective as part of a volume in three dimensions. Plans and sections are horizontal and vertical slices through a work that, like X-rays, enable an architect to see throughout an order of created spaces.

*"The plan is the real eye-opener when it comes to understanding architecture." With the plan one may still fail to appreciate a building to the full; without it one may never even begin to. . . . The plan expresses the fundamental organization that underlies everything else. A building that one experiences as an incomprehensible maze when walking through it at ground level may suddenly become intelligible when, for example, one looks down on it from the air. From this vantage-point the halls, courtyards, etc. all fall into place; chaos gives way to order."*
*Henri Steirlin* Encyclopedia of World Architecture

Steirlin links the architectural plan to the myth of Daedalus, the architect of the Labyrinth, palace of King Minos. Daedelus fabricated wax and feather wings for himself and his son Icarus to escape from the king's prison. Soaring into the sky he also escaped his mortal condition, seeing from his "god's-eye view" a whole world revealed in plan. Today we can all be Daedelus, transcending everyday barriers and confusion to find order and clarity revealed to our view from an airplane. Who has not thrilled to the exhilaration of this vision? Like Daedelus we return to earth having read from above the essential source of all architecture, the *plan*.

Icarus flew too high and perished. His tale cautions us to be careful with plans, not to lose sense of what we are doing. Diagrams can be powerful tools as abstractions of plans which help us to understand graphically the underlying spacial order in any set of building instructions. But when a plan is only a diagram, it will create an architecture without a body. Plans and "blueprints" are actually a union of architectonics and graphics. Architecture requires not only the juggler's sense of order and the sculptor's sense of "feel" for mass and volume, but also the painter's eye for composition and arrangement. Like paintings, plans and sections are also graphic works of vivid formal composition. The study of graphics can enhance the architect's ability to organize form in space. The space of Richard Meier's High Museum in Atlanta is described in its plan; the intentions of the architectural ideas are clarified and resolved through its diagrams.

Making plans can mean more than describing three dimensional form in graphic terms. *Planning* also means "to set a strategy"—to propose and carry out a vision for human benefit. By the same token, making projects also has an active mood—*projecting* means "to throw something forward". Projections are systems of drawings that can carry three dimensional information on a two dimensional surface. The studies in this book enlarge the designer's repertoire by demonstrating plan and section, axonometric, shade-and-shadow, perspective, and sun-angle projections. Projecting can create new means for vision.

## CLEAR VISION

Clairvoyance, the power to see what is normally obscured, like the future, is literally "clear vision". Architects' plans propose an everpresent future. Studying graphics cultivates the habit of seeing plans clearly. Two dimensional order is most vivid to the mind as well as the eye; the meaning of what is "graphically clear" is unmistakable. Geometric order in two dimensional space has many lessons for architectonics. Each surface is a study in design. A sequence of surfaces, like the pages of this book, is an unfolding of ideas.

### Beginning Architecture

We cannot see empty volume, but we can see an empty surface. A blank square can be a model of empty space. Beginning architecture is like facing a blank square, confronting an unfilled site, an unoccupied and unordered volume. The waiting potential of the empty field demands a response. The first intuitive mark suggests others, and soon structure emerges. Through doing one can soon learn how form follows form. Explorers in every art unify experience with experiment. Wise children and adult beginners become a culture, a group who share the same language of exploring, stretching, and restating rules and limits through their work and studies. A beginning architectural design studio is such a culture.

Adult beginners need to understand the act of creation beyond merely solving necessity. There are many who, for example, take beautiful photographs but do not regard their family snapshots or travel pictures as creative. Every artist redefines the possibilities of the medium. If Beethoven had never lived, we would miss his music but never know it. The adult beginner is always becoming young. Some easy exercises can also become art at the most advanced level. With a simple piece of music like Bach's *Prelude in C* in the *Well Tempered Clavier,* both a child and a virtuoso like Horowitz can play the notes correctly, but only Horowitz can continue to discover new levels of meaning and human expression in the piece at every recital. So too in the study and practice of architecture one begins, again. And again. . . .

### A Sequence of Visions: Six Easy Pieces

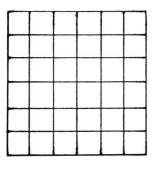

This book is conceived as a series of increasingly demanding studies or *etudes,* like a book for musical instruction. Six chapters, called Studies, present projects, related issues, and new skills for making two and three dimensional form which build on what has already been learned. A seventh chapter takes the student beyond prescribed exercises and challenges the creative imagination to continue the investigations.

Each Study replicates the experience of creating plastic work in studio. The first part of the chapter presents issues on which to focus *thinking.* The second introduces and demonstrates a means of *projecting* spacial ideas as they develop. The third outlines a set of things to be *doing* and shows examples of architectonic and graphic responses to these challenges taken from fellow creators, beginning students who followed the sequence of development outlines in these studies. The fourth part presents some concerns by others working in related areas, and provides a chance for *reflecting* on the work accomplished so far. Like a friendly critic, this book can supply half of a dialog about the work created. Each study is a cycle, spanning perhaps several weeks. When the doing reflects the thinking and the thinking relects the doing, then perhaps there may be a unity of hand, head and heart.

30 III 1956

## THE STUDIO EXPERIENCE

Vision is cultivated in studio, which is both a physical place and a state of mind. Only through facing the real unknown of the blank canvas, empty page, or silent space can one begin to sense the potential of what *may be* made from what *is* made. Only thus can one understand the necessity and virtue of limits that transform intention into realization. Picasso's painting simply entitled by its date *30 III 56* shows a canvas empty of all but possibility surrounded by a fertile universe filled with vibrant actualities. But the empty canvas remains meaningless until filled with the ordering marks of the artist. The sculptor George Segal has written that to be an artist "most of your energy has to be involved with increasing the vividness of your drawings, plans, etc. to the unmistakable state of saying what you most deeply feel." If the activity of an architect is making order in space (where a site, real or imagined, may be like an empty canvas), the work in an architect's studio involves ordering, restudying, and resolving possible compositions of elements and volumes in space. Such work requires both drawings and models to reveal the spacial and visual implications of the work as it emerges.

The first space an architect must make is the design studio itself, a home for the spirit of creation. As a place *studio* is a laboratory for patient research removed from the daily labor of survival, where the human capacity to create artifacts can flower into a cycle of intensive making and extensive reflecting. It must provide room for both actions, allowing the architect to alternate between moving close enough to touch the work and then stepping back to gain perspective and see the results . . . like a painter at her easel. A studio can be in or outdoors, stationary or portable. As a state of mind *studio* is the capacity to experiment with options, to reify (make concrete) the results and develop them to increasingly vivid levels of expression. Sketches, drawings, and models document the investigations and reify the thinking into a growing body of work. The artist Sam Richardson has said "anyone can be an artist if they devote forty hours a week to it." An experimenting artist, like a musician at practice, is devoted to perfecting each study but also seeks meaning in the sequence of developments— not to any predictable outcome, but rather because of a basic curiosity to find what may emerge.

In making architecture, as in any creative act, the end product is unknown at the beginning. The horror of the blank canvas or clean page is real, because the possibilities for filling it are both endless, and at this stage, entirely the responsibility of the designer. Creating a work is not exactly like solving a math problem or a crossword puzzle. Initial insights may be fragmentary. Development of early ideas may progress in what are ultimately fruitless paths. Things are not neat. The mess of an artist's studio is not so much the result of confusion as both source and receptacle for the material elements that permit a plastic idea to come into being. Crumpled old sketches on the floor are like the marble chips a sculptor must remove to find the figure in his block of stone. However, what soon appears, as if by miracle, is a succession of forms that begins to reveal an underlying and almost unconscious intention. After a first try, the question "what if" arises, and some change is made. What if what was in front is now put in back, or black is made white, or round becomes square? The quality of the "what if" question may itself evolve. For example, the Impressionist painters investigated whether shadows are not black but blue or red. Cubist painters explored form from more than one side or view at a time. As more alternatives are created, personal concerns are revealed. Thus *how* a thing is made also becomes *why* it is made. Aesthetic judgement enters into the concern.

## A STUDIO COMPANION

This book is neither a coffee-table picture book nor a simple compendium of technique, rather it is *a companion to the studio experience*, a critical friend to help consider "why" as well as "how" in finding a union between perception, intention, creation, and means. To the extent that architecture is a concrete activity wrought with the hands, this volume is a handbook; but for those who can learn to to truly see and understand, it is also a *mindbook*. The existing buildings and places illustrated in this book are far from each other in time, space, temperament, and culture. Yet all are architecture: human values and ideas expressed through an intentional and simultaneous ordering of space, form, structure, and light. The remaining illustrations are taken from fellow beginners who followed this sequence of studies. Their works show numerous solutions, or rather re-solutions, because in any art every solution also restates the problem. Creativity exists on the edge of the unknown. It takes effort to climb stairs, walk through a door, and enter a new room. Although anyone may casually glance through this book, only those who are motivated will seek and appreciate its true meaning. The reader who practices and executes these studies is invited to share that work with the rest of us in subsequent editions of this book.

### A Humanistic Discourse

This book proposes that the essentials of architecture can be learned through actual doing. Remarks in the text will only become meaningful to the individual who has actually undertaken the suggested design investigations. True understanding cannot be accomplished simply by reading about other people's efforts, yet one of the great joys of architecture is that it is a humanistic discourse with all its practicioners throughout human history. Thus a client's request for a staircase design is also an opportunity to reconsider the fundamental meaning of staircase and vertical movement. The architect discusses the options not only with the client, but also in a sense with Michelangelo, to consider, for example, what the Renaissance master accomplished in his staircase from the entry vestibule to the Laurentian Library in Florence.

An architectural library is therefore an important tool in the design studio, not for copybook sources, but for guides to insight and clarity. Books and architecture have a strange affinity. Edifice and edify are kindred words. The art of memory views the mind as spaces and places to store things to make linked imagery. The vast literature of architecture includes a few classic treatises and many monographs on architects that analyze works through plans, diagrams and background history and theory. Picture books attempt to give the reader the feeling of "being there" in wonderful spaces or explain the meaning of landmark buildings and cities. But between these commentaries on creation in the past (existing architecture) and manuals for creation in the future (textbooks on drafting or structures) there is the need for a companion to creation in the present, a guide to issues and processes that generate design decisions.

"In the end," said Frank Lloyd Wright, "all that matters is a body of work." Since architects often read pictures before words, we have arranged the layout of this book to make it easy for the practiced eye to understand its contents by studying the images of graphic and architectonic designs and scanning or perhaps even ignoring the written text.

The ancient Inca city of Machu Picchu, high in the Andes of Peru, rests easily upon its wild mountain footing, and creates walls, floors, windows and doors as congenial to human needs as the carpentered space of a suburban ranch house. The lofty Incan city in the clouds provides a roost for our dreams and imagination. When a foundation is firm and clear, there is no apparent limit to the heights human creation can attain.

## FOUNDATION

Fundamentals are found at the beginning, at the base of something. The basis of making architecture is the order of form in space. Form is measured through geometry, which literally means "earth measure". Moving through rooms, stepping out of doors, into "plein air", we may discover the moment where the conception of geometry meets the footing or the world. A foundation, the often invisible basis of a building, transforms the uneven conditions of the site's bearing soil and rock into a square, firm, and level base for human constructs. It is said that foundation stones for the cathedrals were cut square even though they were invisible deep below grade. First the architect must learn how to think in terms of space and communicate spacial ideas. Then the complexities of materials, site, structure, program, codes and so on may be mastered.

### What Do Architects Do?

Frank Lloyd Wright called architecture the mother art. He illustrated his idea of "organic" architecture with the fingers of his two hands interlaced, showing how each part of a design depends on every other part. But his demonstration did not explain the means, content, or medium for making architecture. Bernini claimed that sculpture was more difficult than painting, because it must be seen from all angles. Leonardo da Vinci, on the other hand, argued that painting was a more potent medium for expression, because the painter could create any imagined space convincingly. Since the time of the Roman architect Vitruvius, and on through the Renaissance architects Alberti, Bramante, Michelangelo and Palladio, a trinity of concerns generally called "Firmness, Commodity, and Delight" have reminded architects of their responsibility to make their structures strong, spacious, and beautiful, but again these reminders fail to give clear direction as to how this is to be accomplished. Mies van der Rohe said that "architecture is the will of an epoch, translated into space, living, changing, new", but this important reminder to consider societal concerns when designing buildings and cities again leaves us little guidance as to how to accomplish such noble goals.

Le Corbusier has provided what may be the most helpful contemporary working definition of what architects actually do: "Architecture is the correct, masterful, and orderly play of masses [or volumes] brought together in light." This approach makes it clear that the social, religious, psychological or whatever intentions of the architect can only be accomplished through the arrangement of masses in space. Beneath important but ultimately extraneous practical considerations of building codes, budgets, and the like, what all architects do is compose, order, play with, and delight in the creation of form in space.

### Architectural Ideas

Art criticism often purports to explain the "meaning" or "ideas" of a painting or a piece of music. We believe that the "idea" of Mondrian's "Broadway Boogie Woogie" *is* "Broadway Boogie Woogie", and the meaning of Beethoven's Ninth Symphony *is* Beethoven's Ninth Symphony. The particular combination of notes, silences, tempos, rhythms, harmonies, melodies, and organizational strategies *is* how Beethoven thought when he had access to communicating through the medium of music. Critical evaluations of these works, are commentaries about the work, but they are by no means the work in themselves. To truly understand how to arrive at an architectural idea, one must work directly in space, the medium of architecture. The foundation of architecture is the set of ideas that order the formal play of creation in space.

# ARCHITECTONICS

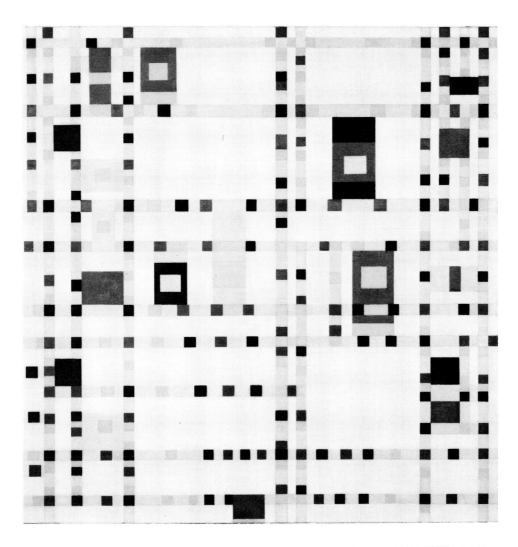

MONDRIAN, BROADWAY BOOGIE WOOGIE 1942-43.
OIL ON CANVAS, 50 × 50". COLLECTION, THE MUSEUM
OF MODERN ART, NEW YORK. GIVEN ANONYMOUSLY.

**1 Unity**

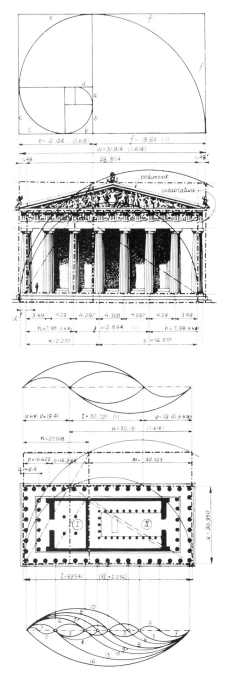

## THINKING

*Beauty is unity in variety.*—Coleridge

To the unperceptive, the world is a chaos. Chaos, without order, is an easy but meaningless unity. Find one thing and the world is no longer only chaos. Everywhere, from the commonest sources, the world offers us treasures, if only we would discover them and contemplate their possibilities. To create unity from many things demands skill, perception, and imagination.

Our whole universe is made of mass, energy, and space. Nature orders cosmic space through gravitational attraction and the stellar fusion which transforms mass into radiance. But the intentional ordering of mass, space, and light is the uniquely human activity called architectonics. Architectonics also applies to metaphysics, where it means the science of the systematic arrangement of knowledge. In these studies, we take architectonics to mean the study of the human, intentional, systemmatic arrangement of spaces.

Architectonics is a means of communication. When the intention is coherent and the medium is clear, unity may be attained. For both the philosopher and the architect, the world is ever a unity and a diversity, where the overall order is at least as beautiful as any element.

The Parthenon, jewel of the Acropolis built 2500 years ago, shines like a beacon high above the modern city of Athens. We sense the unity in its arrangement of forms, profiles, and proportions as a powerful presence of both clarity and passion. The basic organization of the Parthenon, its *parti,* is very simple. A double row of columns surrounds a central room and supports spanning stones which in turn support a triangular pedimented roof. Yet the architects, with daring and astounding precision, adjusted its ideal abstract geometry to deepen our experience of space, order, and light. Each part *and* the whole ensemble were lovingly modelled to intensify our sense of its mass and space. For example, the Doric columns' vertical grooved fluting reveals the roundness of their cylindrical shafts through the shadows cast in the brilliant Greek light. The sticklike columns are actually stacks of carved stone drums, shaped to flowing lines in every dimension. The columns' subtle swelling (called *entasis*) and the slight upward bowing of the *stylobate* and *plinth* that compose the base of the building, correct our eyes' tendency to find straight forms too thin or weak. As a result, the Parthenon rests easily on its base, and seems to leap into the sky.

The columns carry an entablature of clean horizontal stones below panels called *triglyphs* and *metopes* which precisely measure the intervals between them. Yet the triglyphs at the corners are not centered over their columns. These corner columns are closer to their neighbors than the interior ones, because when seen in a diagonal view only the corner columns will have no columns behind them. The column spacing at the corners is reduced to correct our view, so that from the Propylaea entry we see the building as perfectly dense rather than with visually eroded corners. Every stone is cut and placed with an evident passion for order, clarity, and beauty. It is not simply the shapes of sticks or stones that create plastic unity—rather it is the spacial relationships between them from which unity may arise. Architectonic unity can be accomplished with the simplest of means, even just common sticks and stones.

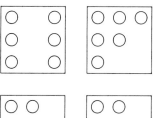

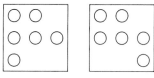

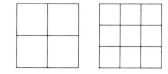

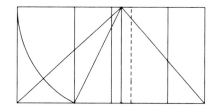

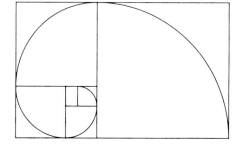

# PROJECTING

### FINDING UNITY

Construction of geometric figures is accomplished with compass and straightedge. While these tools are useful in planning buildings for assuring that walls meet at right angles or determining the radius of an arch, a deeper understanding of geometry enables architects to organize the entire ensemble of elements they are creating. Geometry provides architects with a means to find unity in the order of the parts, the characteristics of the site, and the proportions that relate all elements. Such strategy is not merely aesthetic conceit. Architects continually use geometric analysis to re-solve design problems, so that people and the space they occupy can become one harmonious whole. See the Visual Glossary for more on these topics.

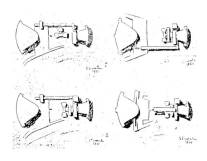

*Parti:* Geometry can suggest strategies for organizing the solids and voids of architectonic space. Such a strategy is known to architects by the French term *parti*. A *parti diagram* can clarify ideas and reveal their esssential ordering principle. Each *parti* has its own logic, and can determine further development of the scheme in detail. When Le Corbusier was studying the organization of assembly chambers, concert halls, and other spaces in the 1931 project for the Palace of the Soviets, he investigated a number of possible arrangements or *partis*. After he had completed a number of houses in the 1920s and '30s, he made a sketch in which he organized them all according to four basic types or strategies of volumetric organization. *Parti* can be both a projective and reflective analytic tool.

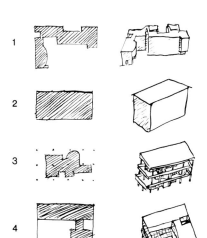

1

2

3

4

*Properties of the Square: Parti* is especially useful when applied to an analyis of the geometric properties of a given site or field. For example, a square is not just a place bounded by four equal lines. Its properties can determine whether an arrangement of elements within it is particularly appropriate or not. Among the many ways of placing six equal elements in a square, the "boxcar" pattern creates three equal zones (two filled, one empty) and shows a different symmetry about each of two axes. Another array of the six elements places them all on one side of a diagonal of the square. This creates two similar zones (one filled, one empty). Now its two different symmetries occur along the diagonals of the square, not the orthogonals. Other arrangements will show no axes of symmetry. In every case, the pattern of the six elements organizes the entire space of the square field, highlighting various properties of its geometry.

*Proportion* establishes the relationship of sub-parts to the geometric order of the whole form. For example a square may be divided into four equal smaller squares, called quadrants, or into nine equal squares, as in the familiar tic-tac-toe pattern, now commonly called a nine-square. The basic proportion of the first form is 1:2, in the other it is 1:3. Other proportional systems are based on geometric rather than number relationships. For example, projecting the diagonal of a half square onto the base of the square will generate a figure of the most fascinating proportions called the Golden Rectangle, whose sides are 1:1.618. . . . Known at least as far back as Classical Greece, this special proportion called the Golden Section, denoted by $\Phi$ (phi), is like $\pi$ (pi) an irrational number which cannot be reduced to whole fractions. Its unique property is that it can divide a line or area into two parts in which the smaller is to the larger as the larger is to the sum of both, that is to the whole. Phi keeps recurring in the most beautiful forms found in both nature and made by humankind. It is the basis for the beautiful logarithmic spiral curve of the nautilus sea shell, and the organizing proportion of the Parthenon.

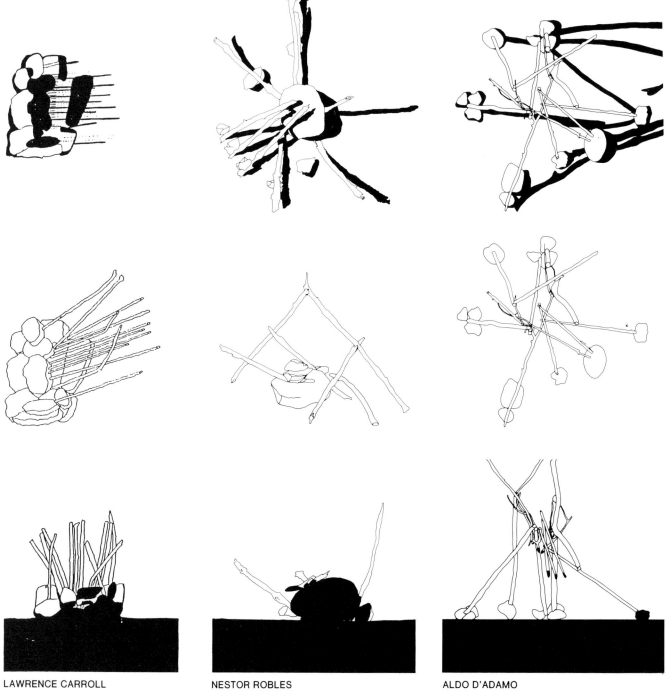

LAWRENCE CARROLL          NESTOR ROBLES          ALDO D'ADAMO

DOMENICO RAUCCIO

TERRY KELLY

DEBBIE HALPERN

## DOING

Go outside and pick up what drops from trees, arises from earth, and blows by in the wind. Consider each element's shape, line, and weight. How can you bring them together to make a new creation in space? What constitutes order? Symmetry and repetition are easy patterns to recognize. Simple symmetry can make unity of paired elements, but what kind of order comes from balancing uneven elements about a center? A checkerboard is an order of repetition, unity without diversity. Sticks and stones can create patterns on a surface, yet the same elements can take full advantage of three dimensions, balancing expectation with surprise, creating unity from diversity. Unity in formal order comes from using what is outside us to express what is deepest within. The following exercises let this happen.

## ARCHITECTONICS

Make anything you want, using 12 sticks and 12 stones. Sticks to be about ⅛″–¼″ diameter, 6″ long, stones to be 2 to 3 oz. each (the weight of 10 to 15 quarters). Explore how solid and void order space; how construction creates drama through balance and line; and how number and group create rhythmic intervals of space. Explore how centered stone masses and linear sticks can create volumes of unique form.

## GRAPHICS

Make anything you want using 12 pieces of paper. Tear a 6″ × 12″ black piece of paper into 12 pieces of any shape, and arrange them on a 12″ white square field. Mount them using rubber cement on a ¼″×12″×12″ foam-core board. Explore above issues in this two-dimensional realm.

## FREEHAND DRAWING

Draw the spaces made by your sticks and stones, keeping the volumes they describe in proper proportion. Be sure to make drawings of clean (not "fuzzy") lines which describe the volumes of the solid shapes of the sticks and stones, as well as the voids between them.

## DOCUMENT

In plan and section, document the space you have made with your sticks and stones. Draw the objects at (1:1) full scale in ink on paper. Use the dimensions you measure to generate the first drawing as a plan and project the other views at the same scale and in related position. Hang the graphics study with the architectural drawings and model and consider the relationship between two- and three-dimensional perceptions. See the Visual Glossary for more on plan and section.

## PREPARE (for an upcoming series of studies)

4—1″ cubes
4—¼″ × ¼″ × 3 rods
1—8″ × 8″ square base,
1—sturdy container with 8″ × 8″ × 4″ inside dimensions.

The rods must be made out of white painted wood (basswood is ideal). The cubes may be made out of white painted wood or "Strathmore" board. Cut the base out of ¼″ thick foam-core. Mount an 8 × 8 piece of ¼″ grid graph paper on one side of the base. Leave the other side blank white. All dimensions must be precise (± 1/64″) and all corners must be exactly 90 degrees. Cut all edges square. See the visual glossary for a guide to making these elements.

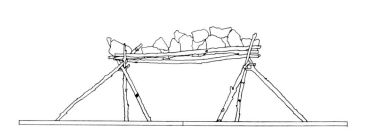

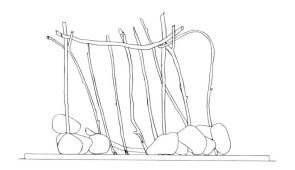

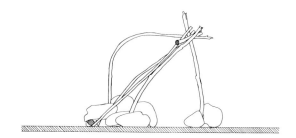

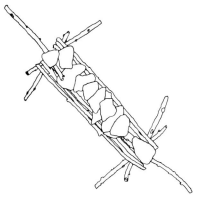

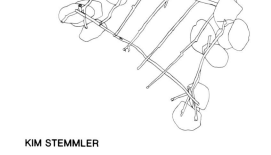

GREG SANZARI

KIM STEMMLER

KIM STEMMLER

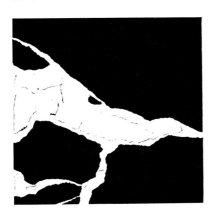

CHRIS FERNANDEZ

GREG MEINDL

## REFLECTING

After work is created in the studio, one can reflect on the deeper, perhaps unconscious, impulses the work reveals. How a work actually apppears is as much its meaning as the original conscious intentions of the creator. Beyond simply "being creative", an *artist* is someone who takes care with every step of a process and makes every element of a form count. The sloppy painter of a screen door will eventually get paint on the screen despite the best intentions. The artist will take care to consider the problem beforehand and will find masking tape to protect the screen. As a result, the artist's brushstrokes will be fluid; her movements will be confident. If you make your cubes and rods carefully, using correct tools and materials in proper sequence, cutting and joining at right angles, and accounting for thicknesses, then three cubes will be exactly as long as one rod, and four rods as wide as a cube, whatever their orientation. Then you can order space with precision. An artist makes UNITY by ordering forms and perceptions at the highest level of attention. "Synthetic inevitability" is architect Christopher Chimera's term for the resolution of design in which formal relationships reinforce each other and the whole, until "by bootstrap" the final work stands as inevitable UNITY.

The following essay, "On the Plastic," by the painter Amedée Ozenfant and the great architect Le Corbusier, suggests how form communicates idea through the impact of its physical properties on the physiology of human perception. "Plastic" was a concept understood in ancient Greece, where it meant "capable of being molded". The word "plastic" is related to "clay" and "play". To know any thing, one must know what it could be but isn't. Hence the first study of form is plasticity. The real issue of the study of UNITY is to discover how plastic space itself can be. What you make of space, even with humble elements, is limited only by courage, imagination, and the willingness to generate and evaluate alternatives. At nineteen, already having designed and built a house, Charles Edouard Jeanneret, later calling himself Le Corbusier, journeyed to "the Orient", that is, the Eastern Mediterranean. At Athens he discovered the Parthenon, which he says "was a shout of inspiration, a dance in the sunlight . . . and a final and supreme warning: do not believe until you have seen and measured . . . and touched with your fingers." He felt its physical presence of forms in light proclaimed a truth that cleared away Academy lies made in its name which had stultified European practice of architecture. To feel, by observing successive results, how space can stretch, twist, or march in perfect cadence is to enter the realm of the Plastic. We participate in creating the universe, ordering even humble materials in subtle ways. As Le Corbusier said, "Passion can create drama out of inert stone". His essay presents a still-controversial position about form in the plastic arts. He demonstrates through the works of two "men of temperament", the painter Cézanne and the sculptor/painter/architect Michelangelo how an internal structure of proportions, rhythms, modules, and regulating lines can create UNITY in plastic form. Le Corbusier spent a lifetime pursuing UNITY in his works. One of his noblest, most visionary creations, the Marseilles Block, integrated 350 apartments having balconies, double-height living rooms, and cross-ventilation with shops, kindergarten, health club, and culture facilities. He called it a "unity of habitation."

## READINGS (see also Bibliography for extended selection)

Le Corbusier, *Notebooks; Towards a New Architecture; Creation is a Patient Search*
Ozenfant, *Foundations of Modern Architecture*
Frank Lloyd Wright, "To The Young Man in Architecture" in *Writings and Buildings*

# ON THE PLASTIC

## 1. Enquiry into Primordial Conditions

The scope of our article does not permit us to treat the conclusions drawn from our experimental investigations into the MECHANICAL ORIGINS OF PLASTIC SENSATION—consequently, into the mechanical origins of plastic beauty—at great length; on this occasion we shall consider only the sensations that are directly perceptible to the eye.

Let us merely say that these sensations seem to us to hinge first of all, and essentially, *on actual movements imposed on the head and principally on the eye itself, through the instrumentality of different forms; the movements are* DIFFERENT, *and* INVARIABLE FOR EACH FORM. *These compulsive movements modify the* MUSCLE *tension of those organs, and the* REGIMEN OF BLOOD FLOW *also, thus introducing a particular physical sensation having pleasurable or painful characteristics, with each primary form.* Contrary to what has been accepted at the present time, the plastic arts, which were thought of as immobile, may find their vital source in motion.

Schematic examples:

*The straight line:* The eye is made to travel in an uniterrupted movement, the blood circulates steadily: continuity of effort, calm, etc., etc.

*The zigzag:* The muscles become abruptly taut and relaxed with each change of direction, the blood is pounded in its vessels, its flow changed: discontinuity, irregularity or cadence.

*The circle:* The eye rotates: continuity, closed recommencement.

*The curve:* Unctuous massage.

With modified primary forms these primary sensations become orchestrated.

A mere allusion to a previously tested physical phenomenon releases the entire play of physico-subjective sensation, together with all its reactions; this admits of certain "abbreviations" in the release mechanisms, in the work of art, and in the alterations also.

The trigger mechanism for physico-subjective *mnemes* (the allusion to experiences that not necessarily everyone has undergone, felt, or taken note of) accounts for the differences in sensation between different individuals viewing the same plastic fact, but actually such differences are trifling; the underlying sensation remains, and practically speaking, the main point is:

LIKE PLASTIC ELEMENTS TRIGGER LIKE SUBJECTIVE REACTIONS, which is what has brought about the universality of the plastic language, the language of the true work of art, and its grandeur.

Hence, since we are considering the primordial conditions for the plastic, we must first understand that if the human value of a work of art resides in the quality of the subjective sensation which it releases, the intermedium between the creative imagination and other men is a system of massage for the eye.

*The painting,* PHYSICALLY, *is a masterly massage appliance.*

\*

\* \*

There will be no discussion here of either genius or aesthetics, but only of metier.

Genius is something fated.

An aesthetic is something that may be conceived.

Metier is acquired.

Metier comprises, on the one hand, the science of composition, and on the other, the technique of execution.

Let us say forthwith that an aesthetic having inadequate technical means at its disposal is soon obliged to confine the conception within the compass of the means of realization. We conceive clearly only that which we are able to execute perfectly.

Clearly, the work of art is valued, in the long run, only for the sake of the genius that it reveals. A half-wit, a man without gifts, despite all the most general and fecund of rules, will never create a work of art.

Sensation can only be released through the selection and the "ordonnancing" [the proper or orderly arrangement of parts] of primary elements.

The work of art is an artifical physical object intended to generate subjective reactions.

\*

\* \*

The work of art is not a useless thing.

The work of art is not a childish game.

The work of art is a natural necessity.

Man creates this physical fact out of his need for order.

At table, when I have satisfied my appetite, I align my scattered breadcrumbs. Why have I done so? When I do it, I do it quite unconsciously; I do it in spite of myself. I meet with that need of order which dominates man, and then, when, recalled to consciousness, I take heed of the figures I have made with my bread-crumbs, I have a sense of well being: I have made a god.

This order is the law of the sentient world:

*The need of order is the most elevated of human needs; it is the very cause of art.*

\*

\* \*

STANDARDS.   In every human being, the horizontal releases an identical primary sensation. In every human being, black releases an identical primary sensation.[1] Nothing mystical about that: physical facts with subjective reactions.

There are physico-subjective facts which subsist because the human organism is such as it is.

I chop off your head; you die.

I build a pyramid; you experience a sensation of stability. I paint a red and the drowsing bull that is within you is stirred awake. I paint a blue; now you are tranquil. Thus were the wild beasts overcome by the music of Orpheus. In every living man on earth I have released the same sensation.

All the arts are built upon these standards.

In every born man, the same primordial sensations, constant, standard, are triggered under the impact of the same physical facts.

It is important to be in agreement on this point.

\*

\* \*

---

[1]Coming into combination through the play of association of primary forms, these primary reactions trigger secondary sensations, tertiary sensations, and sensations beyond these which constitute countless keyboards of elements from which the artist makes his selections and synthesis when he composes: countless subjective inferences with an unquestionably physical radix.

PRIMARY ELEMENTS.   These forms are the primary elements of every plastic work. Their association operates the release of symphonic sensations.

RHYTHM.   This association, always in pursuance of the principle of order, becomes perceptible only through the instrumentality of rhythm; rhythm is the peremptory live rail of the eye, charging it with continual displacement, the source of visual sensation. In every case, the invention of the rhythm is one of the decisive moments of the work; rhythm is joined to the very source of inspiration.

COMPOSITION.   To be plastic, a rhythm must be an equation, in equilibrium, like the self-closing polygon of forces in statics. *That is the object of compostion.* It is based on numbers, on canons. It is not possible to plastically associate forms without a canon, that is to say, without a regulating link, whether *intuitively* or *scientifically* established.[1]

MODULES.   The module is the means of giving regularity to the rhythm conceived; it intervenes at the time of the fabrication fo the work, as a regulator.
The elements being chosen, it remains to associate them according to the appropriate module which will adjust the composition.
This operation, which entails an active imagination, originates to a greater or lesser extent in the intuition or in reason, depending on one's temperament.
The creative emotion has an adumbration of the work; it instigates the selection of elements, as also transmitting the rhythm of this emotion; after that, co-ordination, composition. Thus the emotion is scored into the substructure of the work, which is plastic from now on.

\*
\*   \*

The primary elements are the straight line and the curve.
When incorporated into completelely defined figures, when ordonnanced, in closed figures, each of them bearing individual emotive properties, they produce a direct sensation with specific impact, distinct, immediate and constant, the cause of well-being, a truly plastic sensation.
They bear within them the geometrical constants, the keys to composition.
They are bountiful forms. These forms are the essential components of the plastic work.

CONSEQUENCE.   Cezanne, after all the great masters he may have been acquainted with, has said:
"Everything is spheres and cylinders."

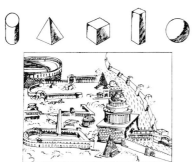

There are simple forms, the triggerers of constant sensations.

Modifications, derivatives, intervene and attend the original sensation from the major to the minor order), with the whole of the intermediate range of combinations. Examples:

Here is the example of a primary cylinder-element systematically modified and releasing a play of subjective sensations.

This is the application and the demonstration:

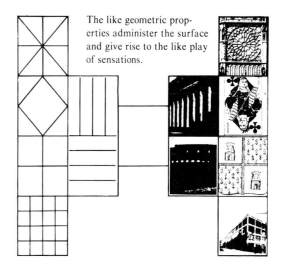

The like geometric properties administer the surface and give rise to the like play of sensations.

[1]Everything the masters have done gives proof that they knew of this extremely well, or very deeply felt it.

If Claude Monet is already out-dated it is because he has disregarded the physics of the plastic. Rodin idem.

BAD
(MONET)

GOOD
(JUAN
GRIS)

GOOD
(SEURAT)

BAD
(RODIN)

GOOD
(NEGRO)

GOOD
(GREEK)

In the erection of the Capitol, Michelangelo applies one of the most austere of canons, the "*positioning of the right angle.*" Among a great many works to which we have found the key, the Capitol strikes us as a typical example, all the more so as Michelangelo is generally depicted as an impetuous intuitive.

Having settled on the proper bulk of the palace in the surrounding landscape and having acknowledged the principle of pavilions and the high basement story with its flights of steps he regulated this decision through the constraint of number:

First setting out:    A.A.A.
Second setting out:   B.B.B.
Third setting out:    C.C.C.

The structure is resolved, a module rules it, unity endows it with life.

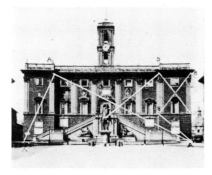

It is the same case with Cézanne, another man of "temperament."

In the positioning of the right angle, the equilateral triangle, the Egyptian triangle, the golden section, so many regulating modules.

All this may seem very commonplace. It is simply the foundation of the plastic work, it is the very stuff of the plastic work.

As to sensibility, our epoch is fraught with it. Indeed, the entire world has sensibility.

And yet after a century of sensibility, and prior to certain CUBISTS, only INGRES, COROT, SEURAT, and the excellent ROUSSEAU also, are taken into account. Why? As we come to know the lives of these artists and as we consider their works, we note the dogged tenaciousness that they have brough to bear to achieve this *foundation*.

Their foundation is identical, as it is identical to that of POUSSIN, of CHARDIN or of RAPHAEL. We are compelled to conclude that all the recent movements based on the glorification of sensibility, on the liberation of the individual and his detachment from contigencies, from the "tyrannical" conditions of the metier (composition, execution) collapse lamentably one after the other. This is because they had renounced, or been blind to the physics of art.

The painters today would appear to seek only to elude the laws of painting, and architects the laws of architecture. Physical and terestrial man seeks to evade the constant conditions of nature, and that is rather ridiculous.

\*
\*   \*

Art is a sane thing and its laws are general.

We do not elude that which exists.

The greats have taken up the things of the earth and have constructed with them.

There are primary elements and derived elements. The whole world feels the jubilation in them. Without that there can be no plastic work.

Before all else, an aesthetic, a work of art, are systems.

An attitude is not a system.

Genius is a separate and fated thing.

Genius gains utterance with the aid of systems.

There is no work of art without system.

A. Ozenfant and Ch.-E. Jeanneret.
"L'Esprit Nouveau" No. 1, 15 October 1920
Translated by Anthony Eardley 1970 Lignter.

GREG SANZARI

# 2 Dialog

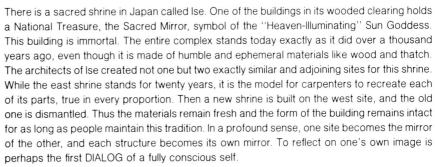

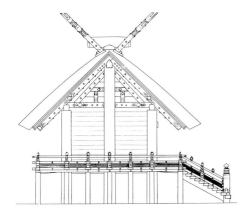

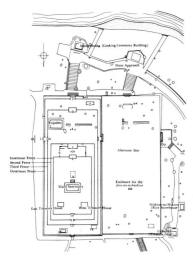

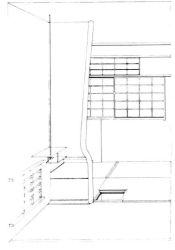

There is a sacred shrine in Japan called Ise. One of the buildings in its wooded clearing holds a National Treasure, the Sacred Mirror, symbol of the "Heaven-Illuminating" Sun Goddess. This building is immortal. The entire complex stands today exactly as it did over a thousand years ago, even though it is made of humble and ephemeral materials like wood and thatch. The architects of Ise created not one but two exactly similar and adjoining sites for this shrine. While the east shrine stands for twenty years, it is the model for carpenters to recreate each of its parts, true in every proportion. Then a new shrine is built on the west site, and the old one is dismantled. Thus the materials remain fresh and the form of the building remains intact for as long as people maintain this tradition. In a profound sense, one site becomes the mirror of the other, and each structure becomes its own mirror. To reflect on one's own image is perhaps the first DIALOG of a fully conscious self.

Ise, the prototype of Japanese architecture, represents an origin of national unity, where diverse ancestral tribes joined to create a collective identity. It is still a place where trees are revered as celestial landings and stones are venerated as abodes of the spirits. The trees and rocks, living sticks and stones, and the buildings they become are images of sacred beings. The architect Walter Gropius wondered over human nature as he compared the deep shadows hanging over Ise to the limitless radiance of the Parthenon. Deep in the woods, Ise's sacred mirror can catch and return sunlight, whereas the Acropolis, the "high city", cuts its profile into the light of the sky. This eternal DIALOG between East and West, acceptance and domination, light and form, and energy and matter still lives within each of us. Animism and abstraction still meet where humanity is both angel and animal, ever filled with wonder. Consider the twelve stones you have, how did they get so smoothly rounded?

The empty space at Ise is filled with the *potential* for a building and a place. Emptiness is the grounding and support for solid mass. For "room" to have meaning, there must also be "no room". To understand the quality of a thing, we must be able to *compare*. A twig is long in comparison to a pebble but short in comparison to a branch. To know ourselves, we must know others. When an artist makes a lump of clay into a ball, the artist knows that its meaning also includes the decision not to make a brick. Plasticity is the quality of a work which reveals the potential of its form in space. An architectural DIALOG is an order of comparisons.

Another Japanese space, the Shokin-Tei Tea House at Kastsura Imperial Villa uses the cool order of its right-angled floor mats and carpentered walls, openings, and corner columns to set off the wilder beauty of the bent post supporting the screen in the middle of the space. At once we can understand what a column once was and what a tree may become. Plastic elements have been combined to produce a simultaneity of experiences. Two have become One: DIALOG becomes UNITY. To know any thing it is also necessary to know what it could be but isn't. The plasticity of space sustains UNITY in form. To know that a present form could have been molded into others is to sense plasticity through DIALOG. "Only those who play can be serious," said Marcel Duchamp.

In keeping with the spirit of the meaning of DIALOG, this study is divided into two parts. Making one of an infinite number of possible distinctions, the parts are called "rough" and "dressed", as are the two types of commonly available lumber, corresponding to such contrasts as free form to meter or the complex shape of a tree branch to the pure geometry of a square. Afterwards, certain common themes may emerge, and a UNITY through DIALOG may be revealed.

## THINKING

*All Arts were begot by Chance and Observation, and nursed by Use and Experience, and improved by Reason and Study.* —Leone Battista Alberti, Ten Books on Architecture, 1443; translated by James Leoni, 1755; reprinted by Joseph Ryckwert, 1955

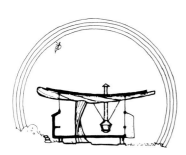

A most powerful means to express ideas through form is by way of *contrast*. Each artistic medium has its own particular means for heightening our perception of contrasts and to organize these perceptions into meaningful patterns.

Tuning a string on a musical instrument can make it taut (sharp) or loose (flat). The same adjustments can be made to a drawn line or an arrangement of forms in space. A form and its variant are already two forms, creating dialog. Heightened contrast emphasizes major differences between two close things. Two sticks may differ from each other but seem identical when contrasted with a stone. All 2 X 4's look alike when compared to a tree branch. Wood and stone are either rough-cut ("rough") or finished ("dressed"). So too can one space seem closed and another open by the careful arrangement of material elements and formal relationships.

Architecture can communicate human meaning through the order of forms and spaces, as well as through material, site, or scale. As such, it may be akin to language, with aspects similar to syntax, grammar, and vocabulary. This can be evident even with the humblest means, like a collection of sticks and stones. By finding their differences, we can establish relationships in which sets of formal elements respond to each other.

This simple dwelling, called the "Leaf Retreat," is full of grace and subtlety. The rough shape of ridgepole and support set the shape of the roof, which is curved in plan and section. Yet the straight line and flat plane are also evident in abundance. The richness of its spacial presence comes not from grandeur in size, or from luxury in materials, but from its DIALOG— the contrasts between horizontal and vertical, large and small, light and heavy, rough and smooth, bright and dark, "wiggly" and straight, between rounded or sharp-cornered, between flat and sloping.

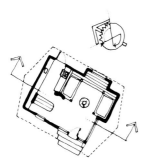

The heavy ridgepole appears to be too much for the twisted and bent main support column. Yet in contrast, it also appears to have levitating energy to spare, since the fireplace actually hangs from it. The spaces near the fireplace seem to be right-angled individual volumes, yet their totality seems to be round. The roof and walls seem to press in on the center of the volum and intensify the sense of cozy enclosure. Yet the eroded glass corner at the entry and the projecting bay window across from it serves to expand the space beyond the boundary of its walls.

Everything in the "Leaf Retreat" holds together. Yet the union is lively rather than inert, since it is built on the tension of contrast rather than on a monolithic and blind uniformity. There is unity in the form of this little building and in how comfortably it belongs to its site, and there is diversity in the range of experiences it promises.

REPRODUCED FROM *ARCHITECTURAL DESIGN* MAGAZINE, LONDON, NO. 7, 1978.

*MAKING PLANS*

*A plan is an organization of spacial elements with respect to the horizontal ground plane. Plans organize human movement as well as structure and reveal the emotional qualities of being in space. A plan is an intersection of gravity and light. Since gravity is the dominant force on earth, movement along the ground plane is far easier than perpendicular to it. Developing layers in depth with tracing paper cultivates plastic imagination. Paradoxically, plans are thus both flat and deep. Making plans raises architectural design to a truly three-dimensional art. This is as true for the designer of a space station or moon base as it was for Byzantine architects 1500 years ago.*

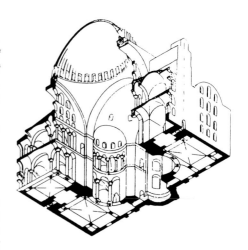

> *"I can't draw a straight line."*
> *"I can't read a blueprint."*

*Nobody can and everyone can. A plan is both a picture of a layout and a call to action. As a drawing, a plan embodies relationships, appeals to the eye, and relates different elements of shape and line simultaneously—like a painting. A plan is a paradox and ambiguity in both two and three dimensions. Whole and present, its two planar dimensions precisely reveal every spatial particular, like an X-ray through solid walls and floors. As a call to action, a plan sets intentions, rules, guidance, and maps for campaigns in our 3D world. A plan is a template for projecting our dreams into space, full of possibility. Plan as strategy can envision hopeful futures. With time, plan embraces a reality of more than three dimensions.*

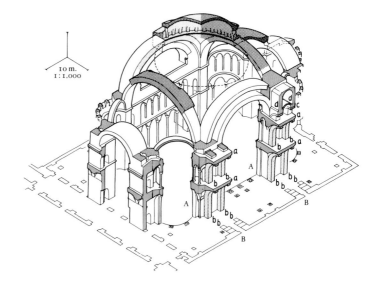

10 m.
1 : 1,000

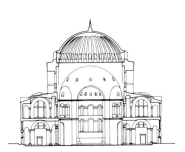

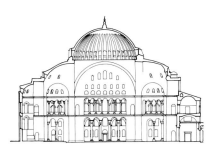

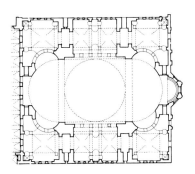

## PROJECTING

Architects make plans. An architect places elements in space to produce an optimum combination of structure, light, materials, and utility to create an order that appeals to both the senses and the intellect. How to do this well is the primary goal of an architect's education. Geometry, composition, and rules of order are the tools. Scale and proportion are the secrets. Together they enable the architect to make plans better than anyone else. Thus great architects are often optimistic, peace loving, constructive champions of both the human and the divine. Thus architecture at the very least must be a kind of external medicine, at the most a concrete embodiment of the living spirit.

Perpendicular views are essential to three-dimensional imagination. A vertical cut through spacial elements is a *section.* An *elevation* is a vertical cut taken outside the structure. In both, heights are measured as direct verticals, and all elements touching the ground sit on a common line, or *datum.* Sections and elevations demand the same sense of order as plans. Learning to think in *plan* (as both noun and verb) requires an ability to move easily between two and three dimensions, to think through the implications of both simultaneously, to see something from many sides, and to see it profoundly. A clear spacial idea has meaning in every dimension. You will discover such unity for yourself as you make plans that organize space and document those organizations. Precise graphic depiction of complex spaces is easy through the planimetric projections architects call plan, section, and elevation.

Planimetric projections denote spacial position in mutually perpendicular planes. Unlike our everyday perspective, where parallel lines like railroad tracks appear to converge at a common vanishing point, planimetric drawings carry no perspective diminution. Dimensions parallel to the reference planes can be taken directly from the original model. A cube can be defined by three squares (top and two sides). The ground plan is a "footprint" of the elements that touch it. Sketching the shapes on a grid while studying the original structure is an easy way to make an accurate plan of even complicated elements. Tracing paper overlays simplify developing plans from one level to the next, generating sections, and preparing clean presentation drawings. They also suggest a way to envision spacial transparencies, through "x-ray" layers of space.

Some common architectural conventions are generally followed throughout this book. Plans are normally taken just above the level being considered, to show the significant elements which organize both structure and movement through space. A plane cutting through solid mass is usually rendered in the drawing as heavy outline or as filled in ("*poche-ed*", from the French word meaning "pocket"). Something seen below the reference plane is drawn in simple outline, so we know that it is *not* being cut through. Anything above the reference plane is shown in dotted outline, indicating not hidden lines but overhangs. It is good to organize drawings for presentation, relating them spacially on the page or wall. Upper above lower plans reads logically. Plans should show orientation when appropriate (north as "up" is most common). Sections should relate to the plans they are taken from (section above plan is common but not inevitable). If the the white space of the drawing field or page and the position of the drawing within it are considered, the result can look balanced and commodious, with enough room for each figure, neither crowded nor empty. See the Visual Glossary for more on planimetrics.

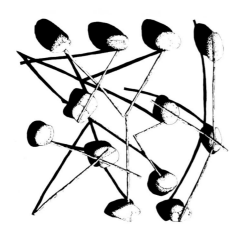

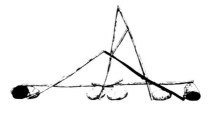

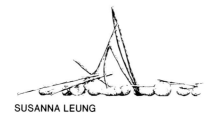

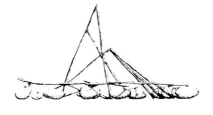

SUSANNA LEUNG

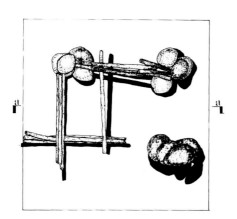

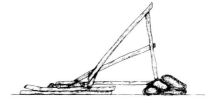

DEBRA HOPKE

SANGITA BHAYAN

MICHAEL SCHETTINO

MIKE ROMANI

# DOING

## ARCHITECTONICS

Using your twelve sticks and twelve stones, create two spaces in DIALOG that respond to the geometric properties of your 8″ square base. Note that each element has its own characteristics: for example, STICKS are essentially linear and extended; STONES are essentially central and dense. Consider the properties of the square field and the proportions between the elements and the spaces they create as you develop your *parti*. Explore the dialogues between STICK and STONE, center and edge, orthogonal and diagonal, horizontal and vertical, number and geometry, mass and space, solid and void, object and field, and figure and ground. These properties can suggest likely strategies for the plan, giving character to the total organization through both similarity and contrast.

## GRAPHICS

The extreme contrast of black and white creates a visual dialog that clarifies all other contrasts. That big is not little, that center is not edge, that inside is not outside, that square is not linear, all become explicit in the powerfully expressive medium of graphic form.

Organize an 18″ square field to create a DIALOG of form and space. Use black and / or white paper. Only tear the paper. Do not cut it. Explore the properties of the square field in a visually vivid way.

## FREEHAND DRAWING

Set your toolbox in the sun or a strong light and draw it as areas of black and white planes.

In your newsprint pad, make two half-hour studies of your architectonic creation, from at least two different angles, showing in black and white the spaces your arrangement creates.

## DOCUMENT

In plan and section, document the space you have made with your sticks and stones. Carefully draw the differing size and shape of each stick and stone, as well as the spaces between them in each projection. Draw the objects at (1:1) full scale, in ink on paper. Hang the drawings with the model nearby, as well as the graphics study, and consider the relation between two- and three-dimensional perceptions.

## PREPARE

12—1″ cubes
12—¼″ × ¼″ × 3″ rods

Reminder: All dimensions must be precise (± 1/64″) and all corners must be exactly 90 degrees. All paper constructions must be glued sturdily with white glue. Work carefully, because these elements will be used in all subsequent studies.

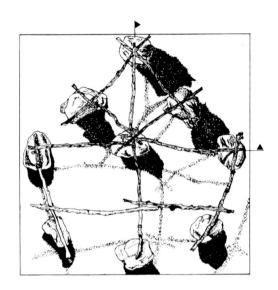

TOM SCAVO

# REFLECTING

Square, triangle, and circle may be simple figures, but their geometric interrelationships are rich and complex. Designing a window might seem to be a simple questiom of sufficient light and proper hardware, but the architecture of wall and opening only begins with such mundane matters and can progress to deeper issues concerning inside to outside, solid to void, light to dark, and the implicit geometries of circles found within squares. After a long period of experimentation, the Gothic architects evolved the magnificent form of the great circular stained-glass light filters called Rose Windows. As the following excerpt shows, these functional lighting elements were also the opportunity to provide an essay through form of a glimpse of the Infinite. The reflections, ramifications, and unfolding relationships of their structural geometry were seen as Divine Embodiment, just as light was seen as Divine Illumination.

The great wheel of a Rose Window, the circle at the heart of an orthogonal composition, could set the whole of a cathedral facade in rotary motion while holding the center still and serene, like a compass setting bearings in a turbulent sea. The Rose Window at Amiens Cathedral, for example, shows human figures rising and falling around its perimeter as it turned, representing the Wheel of Fortune. The rose was a medieval symbol of beauty and ideal love, and it was only natural that the Rose Window became an image of messianic as well as earthly love. The play of male and female, of virginal mystic flower supported and framed by virile masonry, of earthly horizon to solar disc, are dialogs which can be endlessly elaborated.

From within the nave, the circle of the Rose Window presented a complete figure, a halo of heavenly light transformed into a luminous brocade of deep color. It was an image of the Universe, of the celestial sphere, replete with prophets, apostles, saints, signs of the zodiac, and the human manifestations of virtues and vices. Commonly divided into twelve segments, it could be both almanac and calendar. In the calculus of Gothic numerology twelve was the number of the universal church; it was the product of three (Trinity and Spirit) and four (the Elements and Material) representing the infusion of matter with spirit. The following excerpts from Painton Cowen's book *Rose Windows* show how complex geometric, spacial, and symbolic interrelations can become.

# READINGS

Kenzo Tange and Noboru Kawazoe. *Ise: Prototype of Japanese Architecture*
Mircea Eliade, *The Two and the One, Sacred and Profane, Cosmos and History*
*AD Profiles # 14*, 7/78 "Hand Built Hornby"
Frisch, *Animal Architecture*
Brown, *The Laws of Form*
Paul Klee, *The Thinking Eye*
Francis Ching, *Architecture: Form Space and Order.*
Wittkower, *Architecture in the Age of Humanism*, especially part IV,
  "The problem of Harmonic Proportion in Architecture"
Le Corbusier, *Le Modulor*
Painton Cowen. *Rose Windows*

SUSAN LORENTZEN

## ROSE WINDOWS
### from *Rose Windows,* by Painton Cowen

### GEOMETRICAL SCHEMES

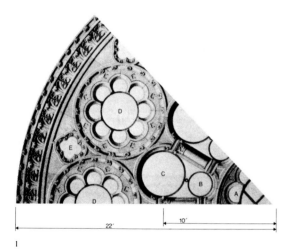

1

## Divine geometry

As the geometer his mind applies
　To square the circle, nor for all his wit
　Finds the right formula, howe'er he tries,

So strove I with wonder – how to fit
　The image to the sphere; so sought to see
　How it maintained the point of rest in it.

Thither my own wings could not carry me,
　But that a flash my understanding clove,
　Whence its desire came to it suddenly.

High phantasy lost power and here broke off;
　Yet as a wheel moves smoothly, free from jars
　My will and my desire were turned by love,

The love that moves the sun and the other stars.

(Dante, *Paradiso,* xxxiii.1.133–45,
translated by Dorothy L. Sayers.)[55]

The almost obsessive interest that medieval architects and theologians showed in geometry goes back at least to St. Augustine and his concern with Pythagorean and Neoplatonic number mysticism as an expression of divine proportion. He talks about the anagogical function of music and geometry, of beauty realized through figures and proportions. At Chartres, Chancellor Thierry's preoccupation with numbers manifested itself in his geometric representation of the Trinity and led to a trend of almost reducing theology to geometry that disturbed a later chancellor, John of Salisbury. Nevertheless, geometry is at the basis of all Gothic cathedrals, everything being created from basic relationships. The means of proportioning elevation from plans using regular polygons—particularly the square—was a carefully kept secret until the fifteenth century, when Matthew Roriczer of Ravensburg made the knowledge public.

Geometry and the use of polygons in setting proportions is fundamental to all rose windows: every one of them involves extremely careful calculation and precise construction. It operates in different ways in different windows, and in the greatest of them the satisfaction is more than visual—it is intellectual and even cosmic in its implications. Four of the greatest windows are analysed here, in order to give an insight both into how the windows were conceived and into the other, secondary geometric relationships that emerge from any perfectly designed window.

This classic rose window on the west facade of Chartres is more than a triumph of design: it is a 'tour de force, where five separate systems of proportion rhythmically pulse across the wheel, dividing the whorls from the vortex'.

This quotation is from John James' article on the geometry of this window, a superb analysis which will act as the basis of this account. Working from the best drawings and measurements available, James rarely accepted an error of more than plus/minus 2 cm in the work of establishing the relationships within this immense rose. He found it to be built up on two units, measured as shown above [left] in Roman feet of 29.6 cm: one of 3 feet and another of 10 feet, which reduces to ⅔ and ⅓ to give 6⅔ and 3⅓ feet (an expansion of the number 3, and a division by 3, being a neat echo of Thierry's preoccupation with the geometric configuration of the Trinity). Here are the main features of this extraordinary construction:—

## Figure 1

A segment of the rose from Lassus' drawing of 1842 shows that the 10-foot unit gives the line of centres of the middle row of lights, and the 6⅔-foot unit that of the inner twelve medalions. (The twelve petals of the central rose lie on the 3⅓-foot circle.) These outer two circles also define the masonry joints at each end of the pillar.

Figure 2

The twelve large rosettes D are defined from the 3-foot unit by creating 6 squares of side 12 feet about the centre, and expanding them to a
24-pointed star which then creates the centres and the points of contact of
the rosettes.

Figure 3

By interconnecting the centres B to form three squares the inner
cornice is defined, and when the squares are expanded into a 12-sided star
they meet at the centres of the small outermost lights E. This same star is
also tangential to the rosettes and to the middle row of medalions C. Finally
a hexagon around the star defines the perimeter of carved leaves, and, as
John James says, 'With an elegant precision the Master placed the leaf that
adorns the centre of each capital on the intersection of the arms of a star.
Thus in a splendid consistency the thirds fix both leaf forms, and the three
concentric rings of circlets that look like a sunflower.'

Figure 4

There is one final construction from the 3-foot unit that generates
the outer circle. Around the 3-foot centre four equilateral triangles are drawn,
and the three squares that enclose them are expanded into a twelve-pointed
star which arrives at the perimeter on the axis of little lights.
John James takes the analysis even further, finding that a series of
'expanding pentagons' from the central 3-foot unit confirm certain points in
the structure, although I find this less convincing. James finds many more
subtle inter-relationships and the use of a second unit, the *pes manualis,*
6/5 Roman foot; between the two units, every minor element and every
moulding relects one or another of the basic measures. In careful geometry
everything is made a part of everything else; nothing stands alone. Thus it
was with God's universe, thus it should be in man's efforts in praise of him.

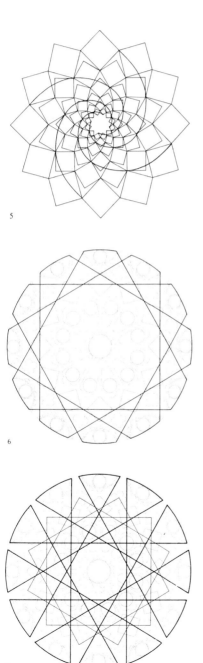

5

6

7

## CHARTRES NORTH

The glorious Rose de France in the north transept of Chartres had been used in this book to illustrate many differing aspects of rose windows; its divine geometry is amongst its finest glories. Everything in the window is generated from the properties of the square within the circle.

The twelve squares set at angles to the radii are the most striking features of this window. They can easily be related to three interpenetrating squares that contain the smaller ones; the eye can pick these up unaided. These squares suggest that there is a very subtle underlying geometry that is based on the spiral, and the eye seems to sense the window's sunflower form that spirals out of (or into) the centre. In fact the set of squares that creates the true spiral geometry is more closely related to the outside stonework. It is the centres of the small outer circular lights that create a geometry of expanding and diminishing squares that takes in the square lights. By joining every second and every third of these the sequence of squares can be drawn, and they very neatly focus down to the central rosette with its twelve little petals (see figure 5).

This series of squares can also be related to the Golden Section, for the intersecting points of the two sets of squares lie on a spiral whose points are governed by the Fibonacci series (a series in which each term is the sum of the two preceding ones). The underlying geometry and mathematics of this relationship is explained in Peter S. Stephens' Patterns in Nature. Briefly, the points through which the spiral passes are laid out so that the circular arc between any two consecutive points is 137.5 degrees, which is 360 degrees $\times$ $(3 - 5)$ divided by 2, or 360 degrees $\times$ $\Phi 2$, where $\Phi$ is the golden section 0.618. 'In terms of the Fibonacci series it approximates 360 degrees times one term in the series (1,2,3,5,8,13 etc.) divided by the term directly after the next succeeding one.'

It is this system that governs the system of growth in a number of flowers—notable the sunflower, daisies and in a related but more complex way the rose. Certainly the Golden Section must have been known to the School of Chartres through their studies of Euclid. Fibonacci (Filius Bonaci—'son of good nature') published his work in Liber abaci in 1202—some thirty years before this window; it was, according to H. E. Huntley, widely known and may well have come to the attention of the Chartres mathematicians.

In this window at Chartres there are twelve groups of spirals following this law, four of which are drawn in figure 5. Thus the lights of the prophets on the outer circle bind into the key points in the structure, pass through the twelve kings, angels and doves to give birth to the Logos at the centre. The Creative Logos of the universe, the law of nature, is followed by man to give perfect beauty.

There are three other structural relationships in this window, independent of this sunflower arrangement. The first two are in figure 6, which demonstrates the network of equilateral triangles built up from the semicircles around the edge. They create three interlocking squares around the centre, the corners of which define the centres of the twelve innermost circles. Another system of squares interlinks the twelve quatrefoils—shown by the light lines in figure 6. In figure 7 another system of squares interconnects the outer semicircles to the diagonals of the twelve little squares—yet another demonstration of the subtle nature of this remarkable rose. Further studies on this window may well reveal that, like the west window in the same cathedral, it is built up from units of measure which are equally subtle and ingenious.

Figure 8 shows a scheme for the south rose window at Chartres. Doubtless there are other schemes more subtle than this, but this one shows some interesting relationships that the eye probably picks up unconsciously. The semicircles around the edge suggest a 'focusing mechanism' which leads the eye to the centre: the thin lines in the diagram drawn from the extremities of each of the outermost semicircles to a point at the centre of the opposite semicircle define perfectly the central medallion that encloses Christ. (And each one picks up the little quatrefoils en route, thus defining their centres.) Any line drawn from the centre of one semicircle to that of another, five windows away, is tangential to no less than four of the twelve central medallions—a remarkable alignment! Furthermore, a set of the three squares inscribed in the rose is tangential to the middle row of the largest windows. This same system of three squares may well generate further subtle relatiuonships built up from the properties of three squares; but this will have to be the subject of another study.

**Geometry and number** combine with light and colour in this classic north rose at Chartres—the 'Rose de France'. It is entirely dedicated to the Virgin Mary, who at the centre is surrounded by doves, angels, and thrones from the celestial hierarchy. In the twelve squares are the kings of her ancestry—the line of David, as recorded by St. Matthew. Beyond are the twelve last prophets of the Old Testament. The fleurs-de-lis are traditional emblems of the Annunciation and of royalty; the window was given by Blanche of Castille, Queen of France. But also we must 'consider the lilies of the field'; for this window is in fact constructed through the number and geometry of the Fibonacci series which undelies the growth of many flowers.

**Perfection.** The doves descnding to the Virgin are in fact only one dove, seen from four different directions—above, below, and from each side; it symbolizes the omnipresence of the Spirit that 'loves and guides all created matter.'

8

9

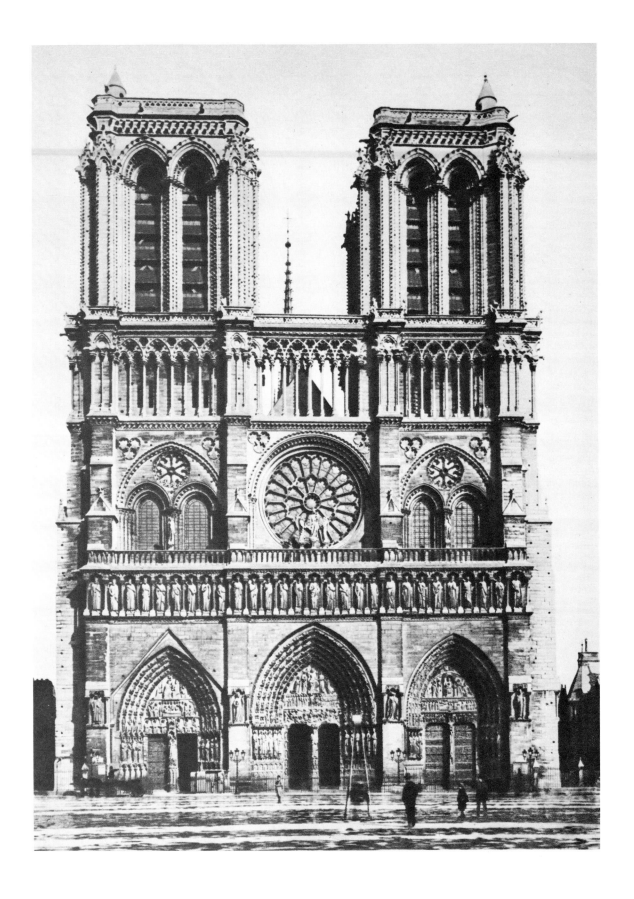

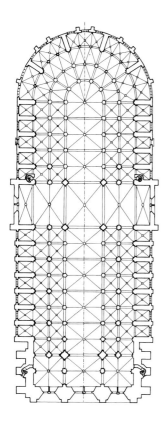

## THINKING

The foundation stones for Gothic cathedrals like Notre Dame were cut perfectly square and smooth on all sides, even though buried deep in the ground. The dressed stones made a solid base for the daring structure above. The geometry of Pythagoras and Euclid gave order to both the hidden masonry and the organization of the visible spaces. Notre Dame's facade, composed of rhythmic intervals of squares, circles, and golden rectangles is a symphony of geometric satisfaction. The square described by the side buttresses, ground and base of the towers intersects an equal square that starts at the Gallery of Kings and rises to the top of the towers. Three entry portals pierce the otherwise solid and massive base. As Allan Temko suggests, the wall seems to rise through a dense band of force in the Gallery of Kings and continues up through the completely open upper gallery, whose colonnetttes, twice the height but half the density of those below, stand with airy grace. The difference in line and mood of the two galleries send the facade springing into the sky. The crockets in the towers mark stone courses giving texture and scale even to those parts too high for the eye to see. Yet this soaring structure is 207 feet high, less than a modern twenty story building. The scale is both human and grand. The great Rose Window, thirty-two feet across, harmonizes the whole composition. Essential dialogs of vertical against horizontal, perpendicular against round, central against peripheral, and dense wall against open screen emerge as the afternoon sun reddens the facade, and the Rose glows. The towers hold the last light of the sky until, in Temko's words, moonlight "seeks the galleries and wanders among the colonnettes."

Harmony is the joining together of elements. Cut stones can become one great Rose Window. But when rough stones or torn papers are placed as close together as possible, there are still gaps; whereas finished rods, cubes, or cut paper squares can abut so that the common edges and surfaces of discrete parts disappear to create what looks like a seamless unity. Systems of elements that can completely fill a given surface or volume are called *close-packing*. With such an order, space itself can seem to be made of related form. Equilateral triangles and regular hexagons, as well as squares, will close pack in two dimensions. Dressed lumber (2 × 4's), shipping cartons, ordinary rooms, and city blocks all belong to the same three-dimensional, close-packing system of cubes and rectangular solids (properly called right rect-angular parallelipipeds). Regular tetrahedrons and octahedrons will also close pack in three dimensions. Recently new crystals of aluminum alloy have been discovered which close pack around icosahedrons (20-sided volumes).

It is possible to arrange elements so that space seems to rotate around a center like a pin-wheel, or shear in two as if a scissor had cut it. Diagonals can become important, or the circle found in every square can seem to appear. Each of the six square faces of a cube carries these geometric properties to qualify the total volume.

The precision with which space can be carved is a skill architects cultivate for both practical and poetic reasons. When inches count, for example in designing a city high-rise, the careful coordination of door swings with cabinetry, of stair headroom with zoning heights, of wall thickness with plumbing diameters, is what may make both room and city comfortable instead of cramped. This is what architects do best. But even for a temple in an open field or a cathedral on a city square, where spacial demands seem "loose", using the elements to unify, align, shear, rotate and otherwise relate spaces can make simple schemes magnificent.

NOTRE DAME, PARIS (1163-1235)

## THE DIAMOND THESIS

Figure 3

*When a diamond form in plan is projected by isometric it becomes a square. This may appear to be a self-evident truth, but such projections, that is, the projections of diamond forms into isometrics, had not appeared in architectural drawings prior to these explorations. The converse has been in existence and use, that is, the square drawn in isometric which becomes a diamond.*

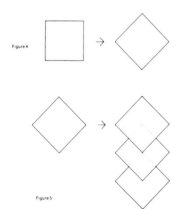

Figure 4

Figure 5

*When a square form in plan is drawn in isometric it appears to the eye as a three-dimensional projection. When more than one floor plan is projected in isometric, it builds up quite naturally and still appears as a three-dimensional representation. When the diamond is drawn in isometric and has a plan of more than one floor, a very special phenomenon occurs. The forms appear two-dimensional; the stories overlap each other in a primary two-dimensional vision. The forms tip forward in isometric towards the picture plane; they are three-dimensional, yet a stronger reading of two-dimensionality predominates. A meshing together of two-dimensions pushing forward is the phenomenon we are most aware of.*

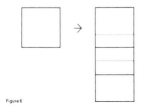

Figure 6

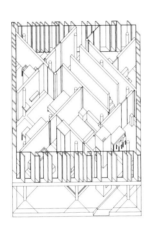

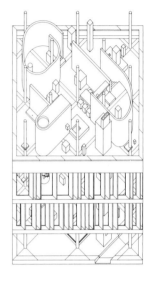

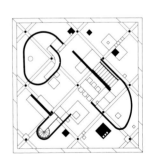

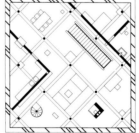

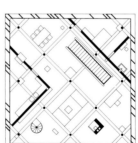

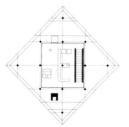

## PROJECTING

### THREE DIMENSIONS ON PAPER

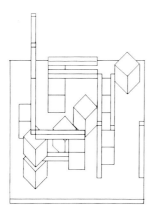

The frontal photograph of the facade of Notre Dame reinforces our sense of the two-dimensional picture plane and frame of the page. When compared with the oblique view of the Parthenon and the Ise shrine, the space of the Gothic image seems "flatter," while the others seem deeper, more three-dimensional. Yet the strong visual satisfaction we find in the cathedral photograph indicates the special union between the worlds of two- and three-dimensional perception, of surface and space.

It is impossible of course to actually create three-dimensional space on paper, that is, in two dimensions. (An amusing investigation of a geometrically consistent two-dimensional world, complete with planar mechanics, optics, human anatomy, aesthetics, and architecture is described in A. K. Dewdney's *Planiverse*. Edwin Abbott's classic *Flatland* is also relevant). Yet since architecture is a spacial, three-dimensional medium, architects and others have developed projections less cumbersome than orthographic projections for simultaneously describing the significant aspects of a work in all three dimensions.

### A WAY TO DRAW SPACE

A plan may be thought of as a "footprint" of a solid object sitting on the ground, as a slice through a solid object, or as the template through which solid form is extruded. We can plot this extension by projecting the third dimension as a vertical onto the two-dimensional surface of a drawing. The general term, *isometric* projection, describes all drawings in which measurements for three dimensions are projected along three axes. Engineers often draw isometrics with three axes at equidistant 120° angles. A particularly useful version for architects, called an *axonometric* projection, maintains both size and shape of plan elements. In an axonometric drawing, the true plan is set on the page at some convenient orientation, and then verticals are projected up from the plan. The top of an axonometric cube remains square, whereas an isometric cube is drawn as three rhombuses. Since a square plan remains square in axonometric, a building drawn this way will show the plan true in both dimension and shape, along with true heights and a sense of the overall spacial configuration. (See the Visual Glossary for more on how to draw axonometrics.)

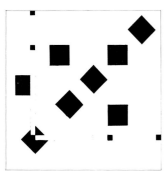

The architect John Hejduk applied a curious discovery about axonometric projections called "the diamond thesis" to architectural drawing. The notes on the preceding page taken from his book *The Mask of Medusa* describe what he found. Where he uses the more general term isometric, his illustrations are in fact what we have been calling axonometrics. If a square is set in plan like a baseball diamond at an acute angle to the reference field before following the normal procedure for axonometric projection, the resulting rotation of the diamond back into a square in the picture plane will create a *frontal* axonometric projection, in which both the front and top of a cube would be square. Although the form is actually three-dimensional, it appears very strongly two-dimensional. It preserves the flatness of the two-dimensional surface far more than the more "normal" oblique axonometric. The "diamond thesis" sets up a fascinating tension and dialog between the two- and three-dimensional sense of form in space.

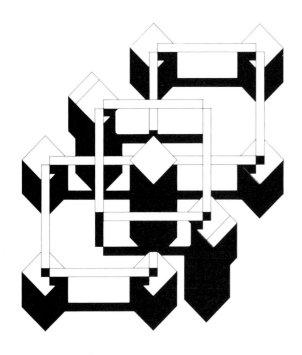

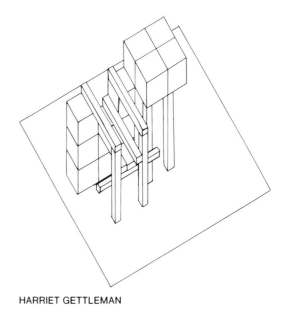

HARRIET GETTLEMAN

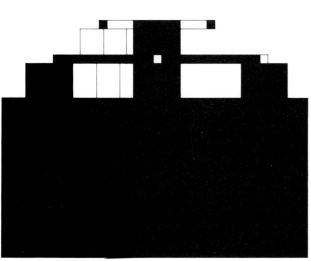

ANTHONY ZARA

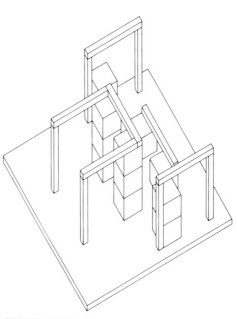

GEORGE GRENIER

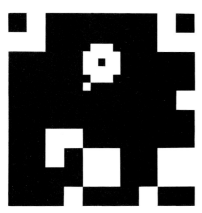

MICHAEL MOTTA

JAMES MOORE

BARBARA HALLER

## DOING

The sides of the cube, the ends of the rods, and the square base in your Kit of Parts share a host of geometric properties. These were hinted at in the article of Rose Windows, and in Hejduk's Diamond thesis. The *parti,* or general strategy for organizing elements within their field, and plan, or detailed order of solids and voids to create space can become more precise with you newly crafted geometric elements. Now every quarter-inch of your base counts! One *parti* may suggest many possible plan configurations. *Reminder: parti,* the properties of the square, plan, and axonometric are described in detail in the Visual Glossary.

## ARCHITECTONICS

Using your accurately made RODS and CUBES, create a series of spaces which explore the dialog between solid and void. Develop a clear and well-proportioned *parti* that uses the given elements and field to investigate the spacial implications of number, order, and the geomtric properties of the square. Explore the language of form suggested in John Hejduk's remarks at the end of this chapter. Note that each element has its own characteristics: RODS like STICKS are essentially linear and extended, CUBES like STONES are essentially central and dense.

## GRAPHICS

The seemingly neutral shape of a square embodies many forces that generate form. The right angles and parallel sides imply an orthogonal grid, while the equal strength of opposite corners imply diagonal flow. A circle is tangent to each side of a square, so the square suggests both sharp and round, repose and rotation. These factors become the simple notes of a music whose symphony can emerge as a plan, a tile, or a Rose Window.

Cut squares of various sizes from black and white construction paper and arrange them on an 18″ square field to explore the properties of the square in a visually vivid way.

## FREEHAND DRAWING

In your newsprint pad, make two half-hour studies of a prepared still life arrangement of three boxes and three cylinders, from at least two different angles. At least one should be in line only, while one should be in tone only. See the work of painters who were great masters of three dimensional form, such as Vermeer, Zurbaran, Morandi, Cezanne, Gris, and Picasso.

## DOCUMENT

Hardline in ink on paper at 1:1 scale, a plan, section, elevation and axonometric of your 3D RODS and CUBES study which show the significant architectural or spacial ideas in your work. Show through simple diagrams the essential organizational strategies of your *parti.* Hang the drawings next to the model and the graphics study, and consider the relationship between two and three dimensional perceptions.

## PREPARE

A new set of rods and cubes of improved precision to replace the original ones, if necessary.

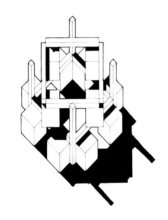

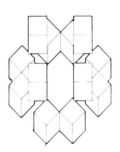

STEVEN WALLSTEDT

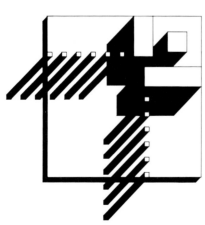

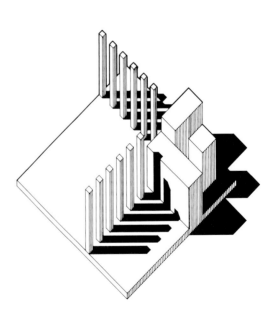

GREG SANZARI

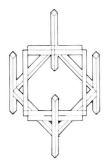

## REFLECTING

What does making dwelling space involve? Lloyd House, the designer of the Leaf Retreat believes the answer lies in nature all around us. This position dates back at least to the French theorist Abbé Laugier, who in 1753 proposed a temple of branches as the original "primitive hut" and protoype for Architecture. Karl von Frisch's studies of animal homes and Joseph Ryckwert's speculation about the possible house of Adam and Eve continue this line of inquiry. But is it enough to enclose a room with plaster and wallboard and say, "Live here"? Or can the relationship of one space to other spaces through geometry, orientation, and form create meaning? To walk outside each morning through a door on the east is to face the sun, to walk out one on the west side is to face an illuminated earth. The builder of the Leaf Retreat had no great affection for "professional" architects. His remarks argue for the virtues of intuition and respect for materials as found. But not all architects are so out of touch with the client's needs nor the meaning of dwelling as he implies. Some have found in the abstraction of geometry very poetical aspects of life.

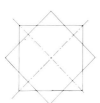

John Hejduk's Wall House raises questions about the meaning of walls in human experience. Hejduk takes as nature a world which includes the most profound mysteries of *human* nature, our capability to reflect, to question, to make meaning. When these capacities, usually reserved for the poet and the philosopher, are allowed to operate in the realm of architecture, space itself can become a poetic medium. This realm includes the work of such architects as Michelangelo, Borromini, and Alvar Aalto. Contemporary architects following this path include Richard Meier, Emilio Ambasz, and Paul Amatuzzo. How does the vertical plane of a wall in continuous space create new worlds on either side of it? How can functions like eating or sleeping be affected by the shapes of the volumes they are in? Walls can make facades (faces, masks), marking planes for passage through life. The central portal in the West Facade of Notre Dame depicts the Last Judgement, reminding the souls who enter that life itself is but a passage through the walls of birth and death. This planar and perforated facade suggests both exclusion and inclusion. In this sense Notre Dame itself is a kind of Wall House.

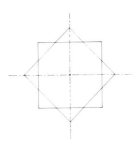

Hejduk's remarkable paragraph on "the form of a vocabulary" and his unusual concept of a "Half-House" suggest some of the distinctions that arise in architectural design, whether of a hut or a palace. Architects as artists depend on making distinctions between things into heightened perceptions. The Leaf Retreat and the Wall House present distinct points in a broad spectrum of possible ways of making a house, the most common yet most elusive problem in architecture. This book takes no position endorsing or rejecting either of the two views presented. We present such clearly opposing views, both reasonable and inspiring, so that the reader must personally rethink these issues, to understand that what a house may be is a limitless proposition. The following selections present two sides of a debate that is an ever-living DIALOG.

## READINGS

Allan Temko, *Notre Dame of Paris*, "The Facade: A Total Architecture 1200–1250"
Summerson, *The Classical Language of Architecture*
Heidegger, "Buidling Dwelling Thinking" in *Poetry Language Thought*
Ryckwert, *On Adam's House in Paradise*
Colin Rowe "The Mathematics of the Ideal Villa"
Hejduk, *The Mask of Medusa*, and *A + U July 1986*

## LEAF RETREAT
### by Lloyd House, from *Architectural Design,* July 1978

This series of drawings explains a very special little house and its definitive building process. Built in 1970 by Lloyd House as an island retreat for two university professors, it displays his unusual care and understanding. Materials, landscape, space, and emotional response are all treated with equal love and respect by this builder.

From a conversation

'This is a forest retreat built seven years ago—right after Wayne's studio,' says Lloyd.

The post was first. Six months before I started this house I wanted to use that post. I knew where all the good wood was. The beach is like a mill-yard and a supermarket to me—a temptress—as I walk along it says 'Take me'—and a bit further on, 'hey Lloyd, change your mind and use me' . . . and so on down the beach, through the wood.

This house is essentially a fallen leaf, just settling in the forest. The ridge log had to be that shape, that curve. The log is the leaf's stem.

The ridge log turned up on the beach the morning it was needed . . . but I didn't accept that it was the one, and spent three days—three days of beach walking before I finally settled on that log.

You soon realise that found lumber building is not cheap unless time is your own. And there's danger to building with found parts. It usually leads to a collage rather than the harmony of a whole. The character has to be right and continuous throughout the house, and this ridge log had to be just right. . . .

The ridge and the roof are balanced on the single post, but there was too much tension in it. I purposely didn't put any mullions in the glass gables so it would be obvious the roof was balanced—it was too obvious and so tense it was unsettling, so those two sticks were put in.

The roof is three laminations of ½in cedar boards, the bottom layer from ridge to eave and the other two diagonally opposed to each other. The compound curve of the ridge and the roof planes form a structural shell . . . a little bit of gymnastics.

Have you noticed the frayed edge of the eaves—remember the leaf.

It seemed a light roof was needed to compensate for the heaviness of the forest. Built the roof first; then the floor, last the walls. To me roofs have become umbrellas that say anything can happen here. When the roof is finished, you can stand under it—feel the space, be in touch with the house—love it.

Trying to anticipate the space, and your reactions to it, before it is formed is a bit like masturbation in comparison.

When the house is there, you can feel where to open walls and where to close them. I used to be very frustrated when trying to build doors and windows; and then I realised I wasn't actually considering what feeling and size I was after, but rather industrial sizing and my ruler—now I use my eyes and a stick to determine dimensions. I think that's one thing that's so appealing about peasant architecture—lack of industrial sizing.

This house is a 16ft × 18ft box, but that's hard to imagine. The projecting alcoves for storage and beds really seem to break up the simple box—the sweep of the roof helps too.

It seems that the new hand-built houses really have eliminated tradition—until they establish their own, of course. They borrow from everywhere, anything . . . spontaneous . . . free.

No, I haven't any formal architectural schooling. Started as a carpenter. I worked on enough custom-built houses to feel something was wrong—generally the architects, and most architecture seems humanly bankrupt. Architects have no affection for the users and owners. The actual building seems secondary to their professional trip.

The experience of building should be *joy.* If it isn't in the construction you can't expect to feel it in the finished building. A building shoud act as a touchstone and source of nourishment.

Oh, back to the windows—you have to do them inside and out at the same time. If your windows aren't right, the house loses its balance in the landscape and you don't feel comfortable with it. You leave part of you outside. The greater the discomfort, the more you leave outside.

And remember, you can't build a good space if there is animosity in the process!!

From a conversation with the authors, 1976

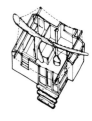

'THE EXPERIENCE OF BUILDING SHOULD BE JOY. IF IT ISN'T IN THE CONSTRUCTION, YOU CAN'T EXPECT TO FEEL IT IN THE FINISHED BUILDING. A BUILDING SHOULD ACT AS A TOUCHSTONE AND AS A SOURCE OF NOURISHMENT.'

REPRODUCED FROM *ARCHITECTURAL DESIGN* MAGAZINE, LONDON, NO. 7, 1978.

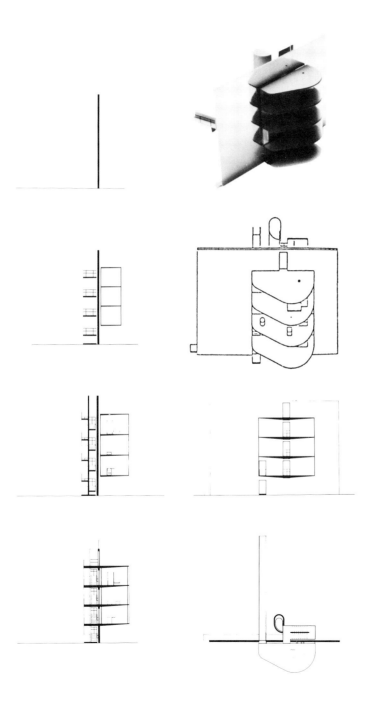

## THE POETICS OF ARCHITECTURE
### from *Mask of Medusa,* by John Hejduk

I was interested in the poetics of architecture, in that which only the architect can give. Everyone else can give everything else, but it's the one thing they can't give that interests me. I'm not an ambiguous architect; I deal with fabrications, with clarities . . . the forms are there, they don't have double meanings, they're singular, anyone should be able to look at them. The wall itself is the most "present" condition possible. Life has to do with walls; we're continuously going in and out, back and forth, and through them. A wall is the quickest, the thinnest, the thing we're always transgressing, and that is why I see it as the "present," the most surface condition. The painter starts with the real world and works toward abstraction, and when he's finished with a work it is abstracted from the so-called real world. But architecture takes two lines. The architect starts with the abstract world, and due to the nature of his work, works toward the real world. The significant architect is one who, when finished with a work, is as close to that original abstraction as he could possibly be . . . and that is also what distinguishes architects from builders.

Wall House 1 was a new discovery. On one side of the wall (the past), the circulatory elements—ramp, stair, elevator—were placed. They were volumetric, opaque, monochromatic, in perspective with the structure grounded. The color was white, grey, black; the materials reinforced concrete, steel and cement. Once the single inhabitant passed through the wall he was in a space overlooking a landscape (trees? water? earth? sky?) which was basically private, contemplative and reflective. There were three suspended floors cantilevered from the collective elements. The materials on this side of the wall were glass and reflective metal; a fluidity was sought after. Whereas the collective side was hard, tough, concrete, the private side was inwardly reflective, a light shattering into fragments, mirror images moving along the polished surfaces of metal.

A duality could be seen. Each function was separated on different floor levels. Level 1 entry and dining, Level 2 living and study, Level 3 bath and sleeping. One had to go in and out of the single opening in the wall to function. The new space was that space which was the quickest, the most fleeting, the most compressed, the shortest distance, the present. It was meant to heighten the fact that we are continuously going in and out of the past and future, cyclical. We never stop to contemplate the present for we can not; it passes too quickly. I poured all the mulitiple meanings I could into this small structure; it was a direct confrontation and challenge to a society that in architecture only celebrated the third dimension. In a way, ironically, this house had to do with the "idea" of the present, the celebration of the two dimensional; it was leading and condensing to a point. It had to do with time.

The wall is a neutral condition. . . . It's the moment of greatest repose, and at the same time the greatest tension. It is a moment of passage. The wall heightens that sense of passage, and by the same token, its thinness heightens the sense of it being just a momentary condition. . . . The sociological aspect of the work, the narrative . . . story-telling. . . . I felt the necessity that the wall be freestanding, acting as a tableau upon which the biomorphic elements should be suspended. The element should float, up in the air playing off the geometric flat wall.

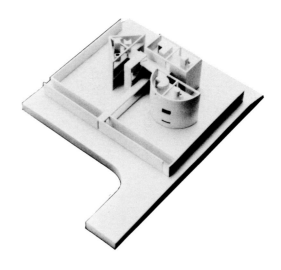

You can be in a volumetric situation which is "encompassing." Architecture is the only art where you can have *that* experience, which is very curious. Or else you can be a distance away, a block away from a house on a hill somewhere, and you can look at that distant thing as an object, whatever your perspective is. You approach it, you move toward it, the object is upon you, there is a moment—and I'm talking not only about the physical but also the mental moment—when you cross a threshold and you're no longer outside the object. You are in it. Now in painting, you are always the observer. While you can mentally "go into" a painting—your mind gets "caught" in it and you mentally proceed through—you cannot physically go into it. Sculpture is similar, it's external to you; very seldom can you go into it. That's why I have an objection to the sculptors who pretend to be dealing with architecture; their interiors are empty. I'm a functionalist in that sense; I believe architectural space has to have a function. To walk into the empty space that some sculptors make doesn't do anything for me—I walk in, I walk out, nothing. Architecture has the double aspect of making one an observer or voyeur externally, and then completely "ingesting" one internally. One becomes an element of the internal system of the organism.

"The problems of point-line-plane-volume, the facts of square-circle-triangle, the mysteries of central-peripheral-frontal-oblique-concavity-convexity, of right angle, of perpendicular, of perspective, the comprehension of sphere-cylinder-pyramid, the questions of structure-construction-organization, the question of scale, of position, the interest in post-lintel, wall-slab, vertical-horizontal, the arguments of two dimensional-three dimensional space, the extent of a limited field, of an unlimited field, the meaning of plan, of section, of spacial expansion—spacial contraction—spacial compression—spacial tension, the direction of regulating lines, of grids, the forces of implied extension, the relationship of figure to ground, of number to proportion, of measurement to scale, of symmetry to asymmetry, of diamond to diagonal, the hidden forces, the ideas on configuration, the static with the dynamic, all begin to take on the form of a vocabulary."

JOHN HEJDUK

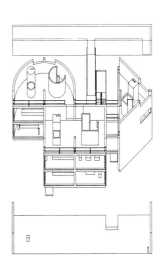

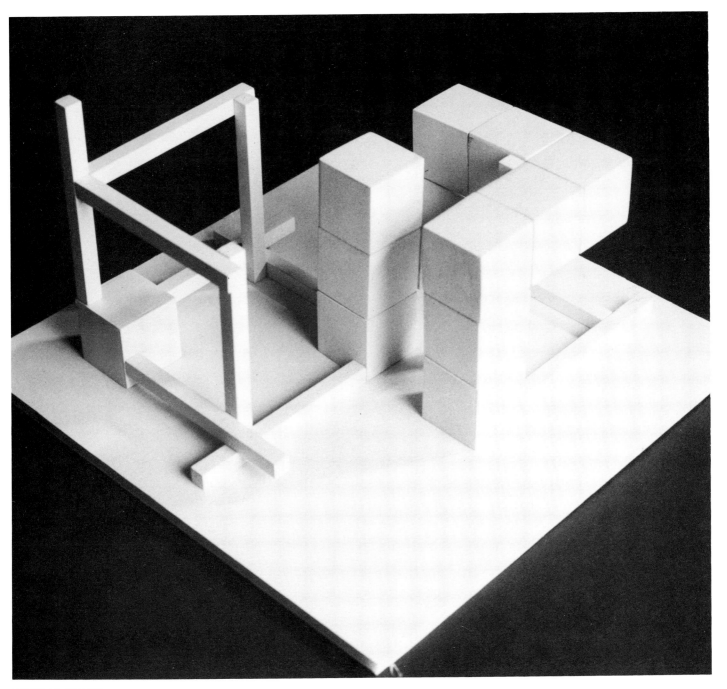

DOUGLAS WILKEN

## THINKING

*The reality of a room is to be found in the space enclosed
by roof and walls, not in the roof and walls themselves.*
Lao Tzu, China, 600 BC

Architects always seek to make spaces. But they are not always successful in actually creating VOLUME. When "empty" space feels solid, we can become conscious of the hollow that makes room to receive us. The dialog between solid and void creates VOLUME.

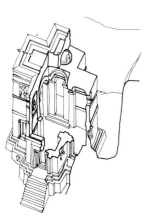

The monolithic churches at Lalibala, Ethiopia are directly carved out of the bedrock of the planet. The creators of these wonderful spaces, like careful and heroic scuptors, excavated the tufa rock beneath their feet, cutting upper-storey windows to be able to open inside and outside at the same rate of descent. Interior and exterior were modeled by chisel rather than hammer and nail and saw. The remaining carved monolithic stone outcrop became roof, wall, buttress and molding all at once. The building is a single piece of stone that has never been cut or moved. Plan and section are rich in spacial presence, because we can see equally well both the figure made and the ground created to hold and reveal that figure. Both stone and surrounding space seem solid and very three-dimensional.

Lalibala makes present to us the strongest possible sense of VOLUME. We are aware of the rock mass removed, of the space thus made. Just as the building is a homogeneous unity of continuous mass, so is the space in and around it a homogeneous unity of continuous void. Since we can perceive that the rock is all of one piece, we sense where rock is missing as an almost tangible presence. Void can begin to feel solid. The comments on Lalibala show the power of such architectural skill:

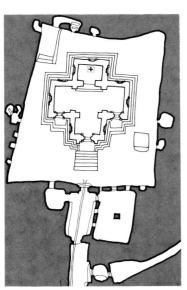

"[To discover] . . . the overruling genius of this organism in the rock, let the visitor only subject himself to the shafts and galleries, courts and halls, tunnels, gateways, and terraces! No need to heed the choirboy tales of secret passages and chambers—the labyrinth is labyrinthine enough as it is. Surprises lurk in every corner. Without any warning, the visitor suddenly catches sight of a church below, crouching at the bottom of a pit. Or else, crawling through an insignificant hole in the rock he finds himself equally unprepared, at the foot of a church towering up to heaven. From inside come song and drum-beat—the rock itself seems to be singing and booming. . . . The churches put to the test those two gifts of the born architect—the ability to see around corners and to think for the future. The churches of the same group have a three dimensional relationship to each other: you leave the courtyard of one monolith at ground level and walk out on the roof of the next." George Gerster *Churches in Rock*

When a piece of pie or corner of a cube is missing we still can perceive the overall form or *gestalt* of the whole. The missing part of the original form is present as space, amplitude, void—VOLUME. The other parts set the bounds in which that form appears. How large a piece or corner can be removed before the original form disappears? Is there volume between the columns of the Parthenon? Between the walls of Ise? The skillful architect can make the sense of VOLUME present even when the original material is separate pieces that must be added together.

LALIBALA, ETHIOPIA

*There is a story, perhaps apocryphal: Once an architecture professor at Cornell was thinking about space and momentarily reversed his perception, so that the space between him and the nearest tree felt solid, while the volume of the tree trunk felt empty. He couldn't move for some time.*

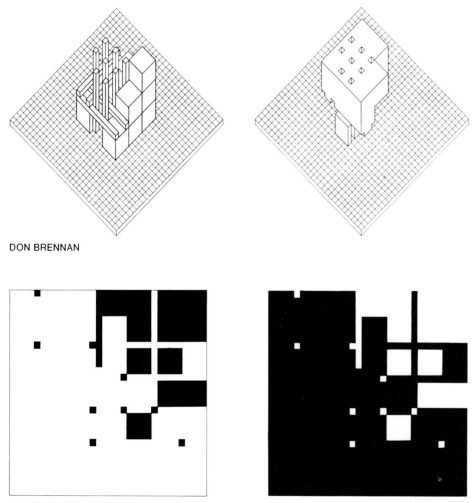

DON BRENNAN

KATHY CHESNOVITZ

*There is an art to making what is ''in between'' things become foremost in our consciousness.*

LINDA MANZ

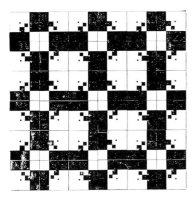

DOMENICO RAUCCIO

JAN MILLER

## PROJECTING

### FIGURE AND GROUND

It is possible to arrange a figure in a contrasting field so that the background becomes the figure to our perception. A further refinement of the phenomenon is to make figure and field (or ground) appear roughly equal; the result can be an ambiguity (often called "figure/ground ambiguity") which is fascinating to behold.

The words and letters of this sentence are black figures on the white field of this page. By increasing the proportion of black area to white area in a given section, we can make the white area appear to be a figure on a black field or (back-) ground. If we carefully adjust the shapes and areas of black and white, we can create an image wherein it is not clear which is figure and which is ground, that is, whether white is on black or vice-versa. This is called figure-ground ambiguity. Graphic design abounds in figure-ground ambiguities.

### SOLID AND VOID

It is possible to so arrange masses that the space between them seems to be "solid". Think of the following three dimensional extension of the figure-ground phenomenon: Buildings are made of rooms which are defined by walls, roofs, floors, etc. These definers are generally made of solid materials like wood, brick, and stone, which we usually think of as objects or figures in our field of perception. If we are at all conscious of the spaces in which we live and work, it is usually as the ground for these material objects. But consider that the floors and walls might be so arranged that we are most aware of the space of the room itself, and that its volume is a figure against the ground of its containing objects. Bramante, Frank Lloyd Wright, Louis Kahn and other great architects have mastered this in their designs.

It is also possible to make space and mass relations ambiguous, so that space is alternately perceived as figure and ground. Negative space can be drawn as solid to reveal this effect (see Hagia Sophia on page 38). Certain wonderful architects have achieved this in some of their designs, including Michelangelo in the Laurentian Library in Florence, the Campidoglio and Saint Peter's in Rome, and Le Corbusier at his churches at Ronchamp and La Tourette. In these the balance between space and mass is so delicate and precise that we may speak of "solid-void ambiguities." The Visual Glossary has more on figure/ground and solid/void relationships.

### SHADE AND SHADOW

Masses in light cast shadows in space. The geometric construction of shade and shadow reveals the play of solid and void. Using both plan and section together, shadow (the absence of light) and shade (the absence of direct illumination) can be plotted. Both altitude and bearing of the light source must be used. A simple triangle makes this information relatively easy to plot graphically in axonometric projection. It is important to understand the three-dimensionality of the spaces plotted: hidden surfaces may cast shadows. Parallel lines cast parallel shadows on parallel surfaces, but other forms may result on inclined planes such as roofs, folded planes such as stairways, and the like. See the Visual Glossary for more on shadow-casting, or consult one of the many handbooks available.

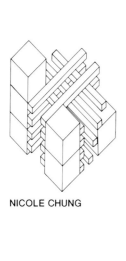

NICOLE CHUNG

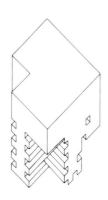

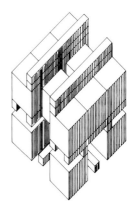

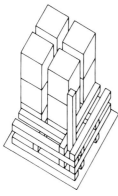

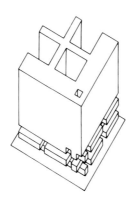

MARTIN SOMERS

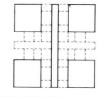

TOM KISPERT

## DOING

To consciously make space is a high achievement. How can it be that we can create something from nothing! Within the dimensions of a cube there can be many volumes. Within the boundaries of a square, there can be many areas. Both area and volume are *spaces*. The forces within a space can extend beyond its boundaries. Assembling many individual squares can create a larger square field of charged graphic organization.

## ARCHITECTONICS

Using your 12 RODS and 12 CUBES define a 3″ × 3″ × 3″ cube so that a solid/void ambiguity results. Use rubber cement to assemble the elements, which must form one contiguous mass.

## GRAPHICS

Using the double-square graphics template shown on page 24, with tracing paper find a 3″ square to use as a prototype for a tile. From this create a black and white 3″ square tile which exhibits a figure/ground ambiguity. Make a set of 36 identical tiles to it. Arrange them on an 18″ square field which respects the properties of the square, creates figure/ground ambiguity, and exhibits a hierarchy of graphic organization.

## FREEHAND DRAWING

In your newsprint pad, make 2 half-hour studies of negative space. Use one half-hour to draw the negative space found between the rungs of upturned drafting stools or chairs piled on top of each other. Use the second half-hour to draw the negative space between the leaves of a plant. Line only.

## DOCUMENT

A full set of architectural presentation drawings depicting your study of VOLUME. This should include, in ink on paper, all necessary plans, sections, and elevations. Draw at least one axonometric view of the finished project. Cast shadows on all drawings where appropriate, especially on elevations, and axonometric drawings. Display the model with the drawings at final presentation. Draw an axonometric projection showing the negative space as a solid (within a 3″ cube).

## PREPARE

| | | |
|---|---|---|
| e. | 1 | 3″ × 3″ × 3″ cube |
| i. | 2 | 3″ × 3¼″ × ¼″ angle forms |
| j. | 6 | 1½″ × 3″ × ¼″ panels |
| k. | 3 | 3″ × 3″ × ¼″ plates |
| l. | 12 | ¼″ cube joints |
| m. | 12 | ¼ × ¼ × 3″ rods |
| o. | 16 | 1″ cubes, including 4 new ones |

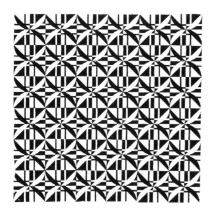

PETER JOHANNES

MIKE KENNEDY

TOM NEJEZCHLEBA

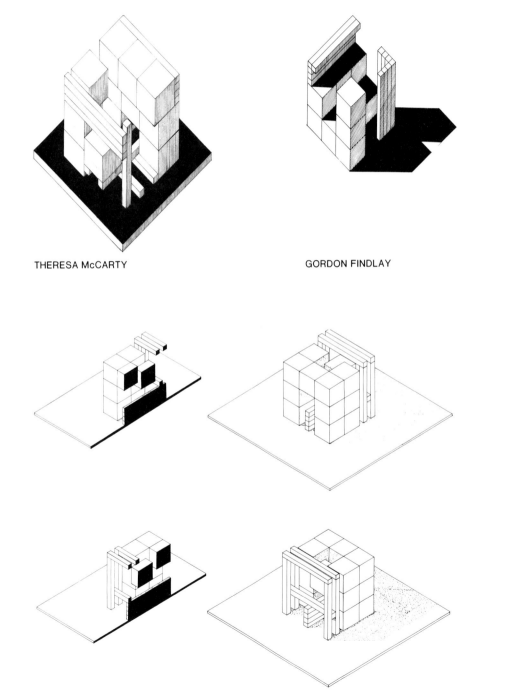

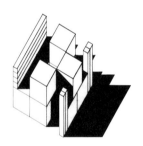

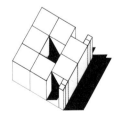

THERESA McCARTY

GORDON FINDLAY

JOSEPH HUMMEL

LINDA MANZ

VINCENT LAINO

ROBT. DE RICO

TED PUPILLA

## REFLECTING

How is it possible to communicate space through the two dimensional medium of the pages of this book? Actually experiencing a space without being there is admittedly impossible, but as Bruno Zevi argues in "*The Representation of Space*" on the following pages, through practice in reading plans, persectives, blueprints and so on, architects come to understand and imagine moving through spaces the way an accomplished musician can hear a score by simply reading it.

Zevi's essay comes from his book *Architecture as Space,* which also includes the wonderful chapter, "Space Through the Ages". His marvelous photos and commentary capture much of what is best in many great works of architecture, but still they pale before the real thing. High fidelity reproduction of music has become a commonplace in our time. We can listen to a good recording of Beethoven's Ninth Symphony and be aware of subtle nuances of musical structure and interpretation that Beethoven himself, who was deaf when he wrote it, never physically heard. Ever improving electronic sophistication has made musical reproduction relatively transparent, which is to say that there is little interference between the intentions of the musicians and the listener. On the other hand, the reproduction and dissemination of architecture remains at extremely low fidelity. We can imagine interactive 3D computer models of the volumes of the Taj Mahal, Mont Saint Michel, or even unbuilt projects like Boullee's Cenotaph for Newton or Le Corbusier's Radiant City. Such high-fidelity "volumes" would allow us to walk anywhere and anytime through them, taking sections as desired, hearing their acoustic reverberations, seeing them in afternoon light and local color, set in their current or historical climate and vegetation. At least until such "volumes" are as commonly available as books and audio recordings are now, the medium of space will only be transmissible through thought and vision.

The discovery of space can take place at all scales. Note how because of the limitations and requirements of this architectonic project the same 12 rods and cubes as used before were forced to create volume. Now if one imagines oneself to be 1'' or 1/4'' tall, then these cubes become holy shrines of monumental scale and power. If the cubes were hollow at this scale, space within as well as between masses would create chambers for habitation. How to study the effect of filling the chamber and articulating its volume in various ways may begin in plan, as the article by Zevi suggests. Thus the graphic fullness of figure and ground ambiguity can become a means for the architect to understand in two dimensions the space to be built in three dimensions. The plan as footprint, extrusion template, or horizontal section through space is descriptive; the plan as diagram of an idea is a generator of organization and form.

## READINGS

Zevi, *Architecture as Space*
Neumann, *The Archetypal World of Henry Moore*
Le Corbusier, *Oeuvre Complet (Complete Works)*
Hejduk, *The Mask of Medusa*
Gerster, *Churches in Rock*
Choisy, *Histoire de l'Architecture*
Chillida, *Chillida*
Aalto, *Synopsis*

## THE REPRESENTATION OF SPACE
### from *Architecture As Space*, by Bruno Zevi

One day, sometime in the 1430's, Johann Gutenberg of Mainz conceived the idea of engraving the letters of the alphabet on little pieces of wood and of putting them together to form words, lines, phrases, pages. He invented printing and so opened up to masses the world of poetry and literature, until then the property and instrument of a restricted class of intellectuals.

In 1839, Daguerre applied his knowledge of photo-chemistry to the problem of reproducing images of an object. He invented photography and marked the passage from the aristocratic to the collective plane of a vast amount of visual experience hitherto available only to the few who could afford to employ an artist to paint their portraits or who could travel to study works of painting and sculpture.

In 1877, Edison invented a cylindrical apparatus and succeeded for the first time in recording sound on a sheet of tin-foil. Forty-three years later, in 1920, the first radio broadcast took place. The art of music, previously at the exclusive command of limited groups of connoisseurs, was by means of the phonograph and the radio made accessible to the great public.

Thus, a continuous scientific and technological progress made possible the large-scale diffusion of poetry and literature, painting, sculpture and music, enriching the spiritual heritage of an ever increasing number of people. Just as the reproduction of sound has by now almost reached perfection, so the progress of color photography indicates that the next few years will show a distinct elevation of general education in chromatic values, a phase of visual experience in which the average level of understanding is still much lower than it is with regard to drawing and composition.

Architecture, however, remains isolated and alone. The problem of how to represent space, far from being solved, has not as yet been even stated. Since up to now there has been no clear conception or definition of the nature and consistency of architectural space, the need for its representation and mass diffusion has consequently not been felt. This is one more reason for the inadequacy of architectural education.

As we have seen, the methods of representing buildings most frequently employed in histories of art and architecture consist of (1) plans, (2) facades and elevations and (3) photographs. We have already stated that neither singly nor together can these means ever provide a complete representation of architectural space. But, in the absence of thoroughly satisfactory methods, it becomes our concern to study the techniques we have at hand and to make them more effective than ever. Let us discuss them in detail and at length:

1) *Plans.* We have said that a plan is an abstraction entirely removed from any real experience of a building. Nevertheless, a plan is still the sole way we have of evaluating the architectural organism as a whole. And every architect knows that the plan, however insufficient in itself, has a distinct primacy in determining the artistic worth of a building. Le Corbusier, speaking of the "plan generateur," does nothing to advance the understanding of architecture; quite the contrary, he is engendering in his followers a sort of mystique of the "esthetic of the plan," scarcely less formalistic than that of the Beaux Arts. However, his concept is based on fact. The plan

is still among the basic tools in the representation of architecture. The question is how to go about improving it.

Let us take, for example, Michelangelo's planimetric design for St. Peter's in Rome. Many books reprint Bonanni's plan (fig. 1), partly because of a snobbish vogue for old prints and drawings (a vogue which plays no small part, particularly in the history of city planning, in increasing the general confusion) and partly because the authors of the books do not bother to investigate the problems involved in the representation of architecture. Yet no one after some thought can say that Bonanni's plan is the most satisfactory representation of Michelangelo's spatial conception for the young man who is beginning his study of architecture or for the general reader who is naturally asking the critic and historian to help him understand architectural values.

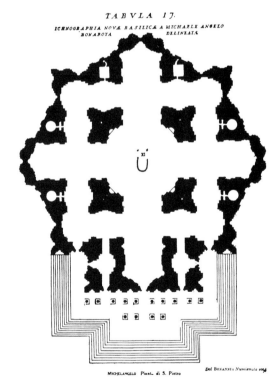

FIG. 1. MICHELANGELO: DESIGN FOR ST. PETER'S, ROME (CA. 1520). PLAN (BY BONANNI).

To begin with, this plan shows an abundance of details, a minute marking of every pilaster and every curve, all of which may be useful in a later stage of the critical commentary (when it becomes our concern to ascertain whether the spatial theme is given a consistent elaboration in the decoration and plastic treatment of the walls), but which is confusing, at this point, when all our efforts should be directed toward illustrating the spatial basis of the architectural work.

A professor of Italian literature does not give his students a complete, unannotated text of the *Divine Comedy,* saying, "Here is the masterpiece—read and admire it." There is first a long phase of preparatory work—we learn about Dante's subject matter from the summaries in our school texts on literature—we accustom ourselves to the language of the period and poet through selections in anthologies. Literary pedagogues devote a considerable part of their labors to simplifying the material, whereas the analogous problem is for the general public. To be sure, it is unnecessary to summarize a sonnet from the *Vita Nuova,* or any brief poetic fragment; similarly, a small villa or country house can readily be understood without a simplified plan. Michelangelo's St. Peter's, however, is a work no less complex than the *Divine Comedy,* and it is difficult to understand why it should take three years of study to analyze and enjoy Dante's epic, when St. Peter's is disposed of in a hasty reference in the course of a lesson on High Renaissance architecture. The gross lack of proportion between the time spent on literature and the time devoted to the explanation of architecture has no justification in criticism (it takes longer to understand Borromini's S. Ivo alla Sapienza than Victor Hugo's *Les Miserables*) and has ultimately resulted in our general lack of spatial education.

Before the performance of a tragedy, the Greeks listened to its plot summarized in a prologue and so could follow the denouement of the play without that element of curiosity which is alien to contemplative serenity and esthetic judgment. Moreover, possessing the theme and substance of the play, they were better able to admire its artistic realization, the value of every detail and modification. In architectural education some method of graphic summary is undeniably necessary, even if limited to the technique of representation offered by the plan. The whole, after all, precedes its dissection, structure comes before finishing touches, space before decoration. To aid the layman in understanding a plan by Michelangelo, the process of criticism must follow the same direction as Michelangelo's own creative process. Figure 2 shows a summarized version of the plan in figure 1 according to one interpretation (any summary implies an interpretation). Although a hundred better versions might be drawn, what matters is that every historian of architecture should consider it his duty to work out this norm of instructive simplification.

We now come to a far more significant matter. The walls, shown in black on the plan, separate the exterior or urbanistic space from the interior or properly architectural space. Every building, in fact, breaks the continuity of space, sharply divides it in such a way that a man on the inside of the box formed by the walls cannot see what is outside, and *vice versa.* Therefore, every building limits the freedom of the observer's view of space. However, the essence of architecture and thus the element which should be underlined in presenting the plan of a building, does not lie in the material limitation placed on spatial freedom, but in the way space is organized into meaningful form through this process of limitation. Figure 2, no less than figure 1, emphasized the structural mass, that is, the limits themselves, the obstructions which determine the perimeter of possible vision, rather than the "void" in which this vision is given play and in which the essential value of Michelangelo's creation is expressed. Since black attracts the eye more readily than white, these two planimetric representations (figures 2 and 3) may appear at first sight to be just the opposite, the photographic negative, so to speak, of an adequate representation of space.

Actually, this is a mistake. If we look at figure 3, we shall see that it is no improvement on figure 2; it is still the walls, the limits, the frame of the picture, not the picture itself, which are brought out. Why? For the simple reason that interior and exterior space are not distinguished from each other in the representation and no account is taken of the absolute and irreconcilable contradiction which exists between the two kinds of space. Being in a position to see the one means being unable to see the other.

By now the reader will have understood where we want to go. In figures 4 and 5 he will find two planimetric representations of Michelangelo's conception. Figure 4 gives the interior space at the spectator's level; it presents the space in terms of a man walking around inside the building. Figure 5, on the other hand, shows the exterior space, which is defined by the outer walls of the basilica, and which, of course, means nothing in itself, since urbanistic space is not shaped around a single building, but is realized in the voids bounded by all elements, natural and constructed—trees, walls, and so forth—that surround them.

Figure 4, particularly in comparison with the characterlessness of figure 1, may strike us as interesting, but gives rise to the objection that in representing the entire *void* as one uniform black spot, it fails to give any

FIGS. 2 AND 3. SIMPLIFIED VERSION OF THE PLAN IN FIG. 1 AND NEGATIVE.

idea of the hierarchy of heights within the space. Apart from the fact that it errs in including, though sketched in lightly, the space of the portico, which cannot be experienced simultaneously with that of the church, it does not separate the space determined by the central cupola, which is very high, from the spaces defined by the four small cupolas at the corners, and these, in turn, from the aisles and niches. Figure 4 would be acceptable if the basilica were all of uniform height, but since there are very marked differences in the heights of various parts of the church, and these are of decisive importance in the determination of spatial values, it follows that even in a plan some attempt must be made to project the forms produced by these differences in height. Some books give figure 6, in which the fundamental structures articulating the organism of the church are shown schematically. This projection represents a step in the right direction with respect to figure 1, in spite of the fact that it retains all the defects we have pointed out as contained in figures 2 and 3.

It may also reasonably be objected that stating an antithesis between interior and exterior space, as illustrated in figures 4 and 5, is somewhat

FIGS. 4 AND 5. THE INTERNAL AND EXTERNAL SPACE OF FIG. 1.

arbitrary and polemic. Michelangelo did not first conceive the inside of the basilica, then the outside, separately. He created the whole organism simultaneously and if it is true that seeing the interior space of a building automatically means not seeing its exterior, it is also true that this gap is to a certain extent closed ty the "fourth dimension" of time employed in seeing the edifice from successive points of view; the observer does not always remain on the inside or outside of a building, but walks from one to the other. In a building erected during different periods or by different architects, where one has created the interior and another the facades, the distinction and antithesis established in figures 4 and 5 may be legitimate. But works of unitary conception are marked by a coherence, interdependence and, it might almost be said, an *identity* between interior space and volume; this latter, in turn, is a factor in urbanistic space. The two originate in one inspiration, one theme, one work of art.

With this we come to the heart of the problem of space and its planimetric representation. One author may consider that the most important

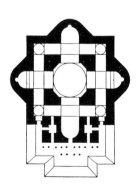

FIGS. 6 AND 7. THE PLAN OF FIG. 1 AS A PROJECTION OF THE FUNDAMENTAL STRUCTURE AND AS A SPATIAL INTERPRETATION.

element to be underlined is the cross-shape of St. Peter's and will draw a plan like figure 7. Another might see fit to underscore the architectural predominance of the central cupola and the square formed by the aisles, as in the interpretation of figure 8. A third might give greater importance to the four cupolas and the vaults, and will produce a plan such as in figure 9. Each of these interpretations expresses a real element in the space created by Michelangelo, but each is incomplete in itself. However, if our investigation of the problem of representing space is broadened along these lines, there is no doubt that although we may never succeed in discovering a method of fully rendering a conception of space in a plan, we shall nevertheless achieve better results in teaching and learning how to understand space and how to look at architecture by analyzing and discussing the means we have than if we merely neglect the problems they offer and limit ourselves to reproducing figure 1.

2) *Facades.* The line of reasoning followed in our discussion of *plans* can be repeated in a simpler way when we deal with *elevations*. Here the

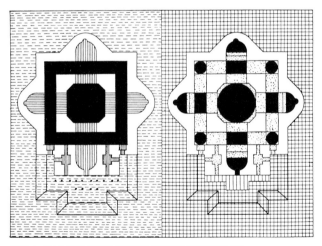

FIGS. 8 AND 9. TWO MORE SPATIAL INTERPRETATIONS OF MICHELANGELO'S PLAN FOR ST. PETER'S.

basic problem is to represent an object which has two, or at most three, dimensions. Skimming through books on architecture, you will find the graphic linear method very commonly used, as for example in Letarouilly's drawing of the facade of Palazzo Farnese (fig. 10) or in the sketched elevation of Frank Lloyd Wright's Falling Water (fig. 11). It would be difficult to conceive a representational method less thoughtful or less fruitful.

The problem of representing the facade of Palazzo Farnese involves only two dimensions, as we are dealing with a wall surface. Therefore our only concern is how to render the voids and the different textures of the materials employed (plaster, stone, glass) and the degree to which they reflect light. In figure 10 the problem is completely ignored. No distinction is made in representing the various materials. A smooth wall, the space surrounding the building, and the window openings are all shown as if they were alike. Although in present-day discussions of architecture much em-

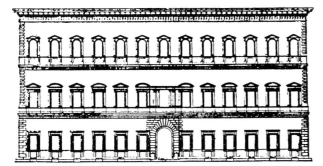

FIG. 10. A. DASANGALLO AND MICHELANGELO: ELEVATION OF PALAZZO FARNESE, ROME (1515-30). DRAWING BY LETAROUILLY.

phasis is placed on the counterpaly between solids and voids, this kind of drawing is still pointed to as a model of clarity. We have rejected the 19th-century pictorial and scenic sketch of a building in the name of greater precision, but on the other hand we have lapsed into an abstract graphic style which is decidedly anti-architectural. In fact, as we are dealing here with a problem clearly sculptural in nature, a representation of this sort is equivalent to rendering a statue by drawing nothing but its outline on paper.

Figure 11 shows a building in which the structure, rather than being confined to a simple stereometric form, is developed with extraordinary organic richness in projections and returns, in planes suspended and intersecting in space. Here we see that the method of representation in figure 11 is hopelessly inadequate to the subject. No layman, not even an architect, highly skilled in visualizing an architectural conception on the basis of its drawings, could ever gather from this design what Falling Water really looks like.

Reproducing the drawing of a facade in its photographic negative is of no more use than it was for us in the case of a plan. Figure 12, the negative of figure 10, has the same shortcomings as its positive. The solution must be something on the order of figure 13, in which the material entity of the

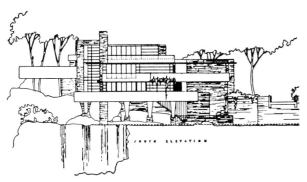

FIG. 11. F. LI. WRIGHT: ELEVATION OF FALLING WATER, BEAR RUN, PENNA. (1936).

building is detached from the surrounding sky, the relatively transparent voids of the windows are distinguished from the opaque wall surfaces, and the various materials are distinguished from each other.

Nothing can be done, however, greatly to improve figure 11. It would be absurd to try to clarify the representation of Frank Lloyd Wright's volumetric play by adding light and shade. Figure 14, in which this has been done, is little more effective than figure 13. It is clear that this technique of representation is entirely incapable of rendering a complex architectural organism, whether it be the Cathedral of Durham, a church of Neumann or a building of Wright. The method of representation must be substantially different. In each of these cases, the box formed by the walls cannot be divided into simple planes or walls independent of each other, because it is a projection of the internal space; the construction is conceived primarily in terms of volumetrics. We are dealing with plastic volumetric conceptions which can be represented only by models. The evolution of modern sculpture, of Constructivist, Neo-Plastic and to some extent Futurist experiments, and of research in the simultaneity, juxtaposition and interpenetration

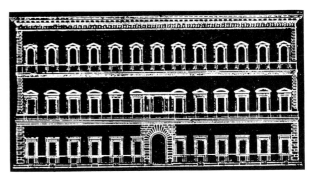

FIG. 12. NEGATIVE OF FIG. 10.

of volumes, all provide us with the instruments necessary for this type of representation.

On the other hand, we cannot say that models are completely satisfactory. They are very useful and ought to be used extensively in teaching architecture. However they are inadequate, because they neglect an element crucial to any spatial conception: *the human parameter*—interior and exterior human scale.

For models to be perfect, we should have to suppose that the value of an architectural composition depended entirely on the relations existing between its various components, without reference to the spectator; that, for example, if a palace is beautiful, its elements can be reproduced exactly in their original proportions, reduced, however, to the scale of a piece of furniture, a beautiful piece of furniture, at that.

This is patently mistaken. The character of any architectural work is determined both in its internal space and in its external volume by the fundamental factor of *scale*, the relation between the dimensions of a building and the dimensions of man. Every building is qualified by its scale. Therefore, not only are three- dimensional models inadequate in representing a building, but any imitation, any transference, of its decorative and compo-

FIG. 13. AN INTERPRETATION OF FIG. 10.

sitional schemes to organically different structures (we have all of 19th-century eclecticism to prove it) turns out to be poor and empty, a sorry parody of the original.

3) *Photographs.* As photography to a large extent solves the problem of representing on a flat surface the two dimensions of painting and the three dimensions of sculpture, so it faithfully reproduces the great number of two- and three-dimensional elements in architecture, *everything,* that is, *but internal space.* The views, for example, in plate 2 [not shown here—ed.] give us an effective idea of the wall surface of Palazzo Farnese and the volumetric values of Falling Water.

But if, as we hope to have made clear by now, the characteristic value of an architectural work consists in our experiencing its internal space from successive points of view, it is evident that no number of photographs can ever constitute a complete pictorial rendition of a building, for the same reason that no number of drawings could do so. A photograph records a building *statically,* as seen from a single standpoint, and excludes the dynamic, almost musical, succession of points of view movingly experienced by the observer as he walks in and around a building. Each photograph is like a single phrase taken out of the context of a symphony or of a poem, a

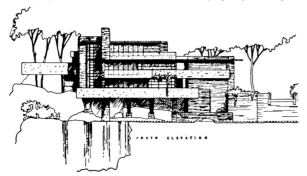

FIG. 14. AN INTERPRETATION OF FIG. 11.

single frozen gesture of an intricate ballet, where the essential value must be sought in the movement and totality of the work. Whatever the number of still photographs, there is no sense of dynamic motion. (See plates 3 and 4. [not shown here—ed.])

Photographs, of course, have a great advantage over three-dimensional models of conveying some idea of scale, particularly when a human figure is included, but suffer from the disadvantage, even in the case of aerial views, of being unable to give a complete picture of a building.

The researches of Edison and the Lumiere brothers in the 1890's led to the invention of a camera geared to carry film forward continuously, so that a series of exposures could be taken in rapid succession, making it possible for photography to render an illusion of motion. This discovery of the motion picture was of enormous importance in the representation of the architectonic space, because properly applied, it resolves, in apractical way, almost all the problems posed by the fourth dimension. If you go through a building photographing it with a motion picture camera and then project your film, you will be able to capture, to a large extent, the spatial experience of walking through the building. Motion pictures are consequently taking their proper place in education and it seems likely that in teaching the history of architecture, the use of films, rather than of books, will greatly advance general spatial education.

Plans, facades, cross-sections, models, photographs and films—these are our means of representing space. Once we have grasped the basic nature of architecture, each of these methods may be explored, deepened and improved. Each has its own contribution; the shortcomings of one may be compensated for by the others.

If the Cubists had been correct in believing that architecture could be defined in terms of four dimensions, our means would be sufficient for a fairly complete representation of space. But architecture, as we have concluded, has more than just four dimensions. A film can represent one or tow or three possible paths the observer may take through the space of a building, but space in actuality is grasped through an infinite number of paths. Moreover, it is one thing to be seated in a comfortable seat at the theater and watch actors performing; it is quite another to act for oneself on the stage of life. It is the same difference that exists between dancing and watching people dance, taking part in sport and merely being a spectator, between making love and reading love stories. There is a physical and dynamic element in grasping and evoking the fourth dimension through one's own movement through space. Not even motion pictures, so complete in other respects, possess that main spring of complete and voluntary participation, that consciousness of free movement, which we feel in the direct experience of space. Whenever a complete experience of space is to be realized, *we* must be included, *we* must feel ourselves part and measure of the architectural organism, be it an Early Christian basilica, Brunelleschi's Santo Spirito, a colonnade by Bernini or the storied stones of a medieval street. We must *ourselves* experience the sensation of standing among the *pilotis* of a Le Corbusier house, of following one of the several axes of the polyform Piazza del Quirinale, of being suspended in air on a terrace designed by Wright or of responding to the thousand visual echoes in a Borromini church.

All the techniques of representation and all the paths to architecture which do not include direct experience are pedagogically useful, of practical necessity and intellectually fruitful; but their function is no more than allusive and preparatory to that moment in which we, with everything in us that is physical and spiritual and, above all, human, enter and experience the spaces we have been studying. That is the moment of architecture.

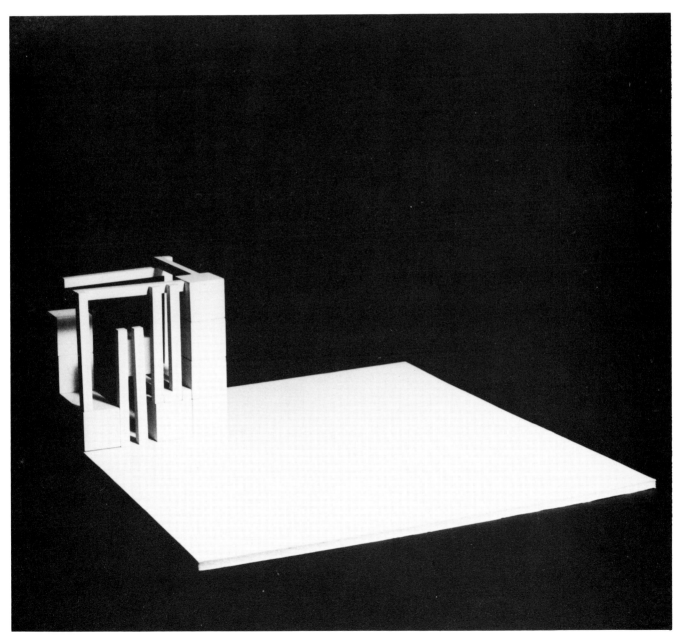

JEFF JAHNKE

**4** Transformation

## THINKING

Plastic form may have ''musical'' qualities. Both music and architecture in essence are expressed through the composition of abstract non-pictorial elements which are ''pure'' notes or shapes that may not refer directly to anything other than themselves. It is the formation, or arrangement, of elements in simple and powerful combinations and then their re-arrangement, or TRANSFORMATION, that can express the progress and development of an idea by the composer or architect. Both music and architecture can develop ideas through the concept of 'theme and variations'. By such means these arts may approach the formal elegance of mathematics.

Between clear contrasts of tense and relaxed (sharp and flat), mass and space, or black and white there exist ambiguities like figure/ground and solid/void. In music between the melody and bass line there can exist inner voices. A proportional constant, like the golden section ($\Phi = 1.618$) can transform a set of numbers or shapes into a harmonic (Fibonacci) series. How transitions are made between the extremes of a continuum can be a formal idea.

A cube filled with void is a box, a hollow volume bounded by surfaces. Most houses are boxes containing boxes of rooms, usually packed as close together as possible for efficiency in layout and use of materials for roofing and siding. Before 1900 Frank Lloyd Wright began to revolutionize that centuries-old way of looking at the forms of buildings by what he called ''exploding'' the box, to create a continuity of internal and external volume. To understand and feel the coherence of the total volumetric unity of these early Prairie Houses and later homes, we must sense the original ''box'' from which these forms ''exploded.'' Wright explodes the box at *Falling Water,* a 1937 masterpiece, where the radiating cantilever slabs seem to expand from a central kernel cube as they leap off their cliff, creating volume between them as they hover in the air above the waterfall. The form of this house is not simply a cube or collection of solids—it is a TRANSFORMATION in space. We can sense where masses once were in the present arrangement that can carry a ''memory'' of an implied earlier form. Just as heat transforms rigid ice into flowing water, a spacial transformation can reveal a structure of order through spacial progress. As the eye and body move through the architecture of the building and site, new aspects are revealed at each turn. But the total unity only be understood as a multi-dimensional phenomenon, a form in the process of becoming—a TRANSFORMATION.

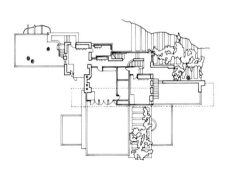

Not only were Wright's houses beautiful and pleasant to inhabit, but also they had a profound influence on European, American, and Japanese architecture, because their spacial flow was the result of a new strategy for transforming basic massing organizations. Wright made plans which are the architectural equivalent of both classical counterpoint and jazz syncopation. The space under deep overhanging eaves would not necessarily be the same as that defined by walls and windows. The sense of closure of a room would not necessarily be felt at corners; one might feel how two spaces were both separate and flowing into each other at the same time. But almost always one could sense the original crossing of horizontal floor plane with vertical ''spike'' of the chimney or the intersection of small scale private (bedroom etc.) volumes with large scale public (living room) spaces. There is no limit to what transformation can become. Before 1920 the Dutch architects like Rietveld and Van Doesburg explored how to make an architecture of pure planes suspended in space. More recently, Peter Eisenman has designed houses whose final forms were meant to reveal an extended set of spacial manipulations.

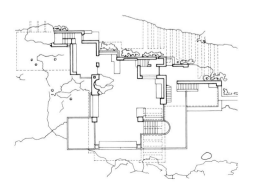

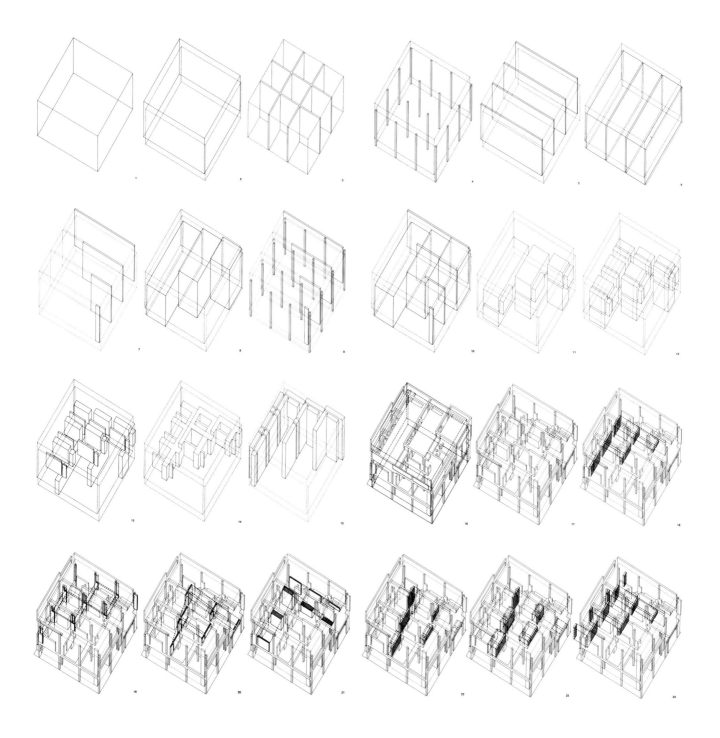

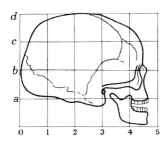

HUMAN SKULL

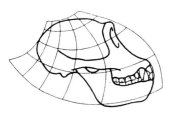

SKULL OF CHIMPANZEE

SKULL OF BABOON

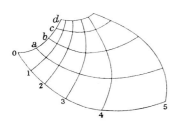

CO-ORDINATES OF CHIMPANZEE'S SKULL,
AS A PROJECTION OF THE CARTESIAN
CO-ORDINATES OF HUMAN SKULL.

## PROJECTING

### TRANSFORMATION

Evolution teaches us that man has evolved from earlier forms of life on earth. Fossil evidence shows clearly how primate skull size has grown to permit increased brain capacity. The steps from baboon to chimpanzee to human can be seen as a geometric transformation of a grid mapped over the skeleton, as D'Arcy Thompson suggests in his book *On Growth and Form.* It is as if living matter itself is a plastic medium. Such graphic demonstration of how genetic material can evolve its form-making instructions is highly suggestive to the architect.

A recent development in mathematical form, called fractals, seems to be able to describe some of the complex shapes of life. Fractal geometries, which exist between standard dimensions, can show transformations at many scales. They seem to describe some forms in nature as clearly and precisely as a compass can describe a circle. Many hitherto seemingly incalculable shapes like trees, foam, mountains, and continents, have been successfully simulated on recent computer graphics programs based on fractals. Through fractals even topography and vegetation might be geometrically generated for the high-fidelity "volumes" discussed in the last chapter.

The fractal "sponge" shown at the end of this chapter is an example of a fairly simple architectonic transformation. The rule is to remove the central cube from each sub-cube zone, and the application is to repeat the process indefinitely. Peter Eisenman has used this kind of thinking to generate architecture which is at once clear in derivation and complex in the resulting form. The fractal sponge is a complex shape but a simple form, whereas Eisenman's House II reveals as much formal complexity as a Classical symphony. He applied geometric transformations in a rational and orderly manner to develop a form everywhere consistent with the implications of the *parti*. What is fascinating about such an approach to architectural design is that it can make homes of a unique plastic order which respond to the site and satisfy the clients. Eisenman's House III, was also designed through successive formal transformations. Despite its problems with leaks, cracked patio tiles, and budget overruns, the client has written:

"I love this house—warts and all—with a passion bordering on obsession. . . . We've been living there three years, and every weekend for me has been pure, simple joy. Living in the house is a *sensuous* experience. I can literally sit for hours in the living room and enjoy the internal views: the sun-strewn pattern of the shadows that cascade on and off the walls, the shape and form of the white beams, the exhilarating feel of space—narrow, then double height, then closing. Architecturally, the house is enormously *interesting,* in the full sense of the word. I find it beautiful, too—every nook, every corner . . . I love the view from my bed, where a solid white beam cuts across the room and rides up against the wall, framing a narrow window; and the view looking straight up from the living room sofa where I can see hundreds of small translucent squares of skylight. . . . It's like living inside a Mondrian painting."

For an architect to think in terms of transformations he or she must discover the formal implications of the *parti* and elaborate those ideas consistently at each level of detailing. This is not easy to do, but the end result can be enormously satisfying to the senses, not only the eye, but also that most sensuous of organs, the human brain.

GEORGE GRENIER          LOUIE BALDINO          GINO LONGO

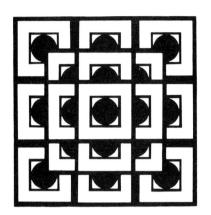

DIANE MORANO

PETER JOHANNES

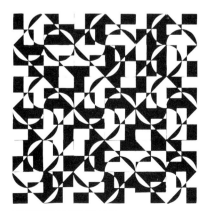

HARRIET GETTLEMAN

## DOING

### ARCHITECTONICS

Transform a 4″ cube into an extended space exhibiting a range of solid/void relationships. Include at least one passage in the form in which void is figure and solid is field. There is no limit to the extension you may make, but all pieces must be contiguous, and the final result must be free standing. (With only rubber cement as "mortar," the mass of the elements and the earth's gravitational field become design factors.) Investigate the meaning of the idea "explosion" using these elements. Use *all* the RODS, CUBES, and other elements from your current inventory. Note that all these pieces together create one 4″ cube with the volume of four additional 1″ cubes added (making 68, not 64 cubic inches).

Advanced project: TRANS4ORMATION
(Conceptually) insert your 3 × 3 × 3″ VOLUME study (from the previous project) into this new study, replacing the 3″ solid cube (element e.) with it. Consider all possible rotations and relations between the two works, and draw the most effective result.

### GRAPHICS

Transform a two-dimensional black and white field into a visual space (2D and 3D) of hierarchically arranged layers, transparencies, figure/ground ambiguity, and depth. Using the graphics template provided, on page 24, make a set of 36 identical tiles, although you may reverse what is black and what is white in some tiles of your choice. Thus you may have a set of both "positive" and "negative" tiles. (However, the more elegant general solution uses only one kind of tile.) Arrange these into an 18″ square field that explores the expressive potential of the visual phenomena of layered space, transparency, and depth.

### FREEHAND DRAWING

Set up group of bottles. In your newsprint sketchpad, draw their volumes, capturing their roundness and profiles. Be sure to accurately depict the spaces between them. Draw the transparencies you see.

### DOCUMENT

A full set of architectural presentation drawings depicting your "explosion" transformation. Include plans, sections, elevations and at least one axonometric projection, in ink on paper. Cast shadows where appropriate, especially on elevations, and axonometrics. Display the model with the drawings together. See the Visual Glossary for more on transformation and on how to cast shadows in axonometric projection.

### PREPARE

| | | |
|---|---|---|
| f. | 2 | 3″ × 3″ diameter half cylinders |
| g. | 1 | 3″ × 3″ × 3″ high pyramid |
| h. | 2 | 3″ × 3″ outside diameter (2½″ interior diameter) vaults |
| n. | 4 | ¼″ dia. × 3″ columns |

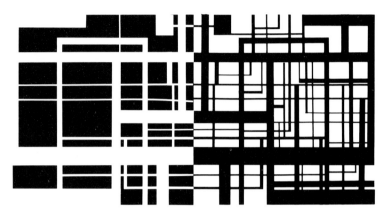

MIKE ROMANI

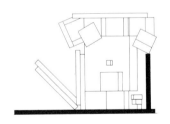
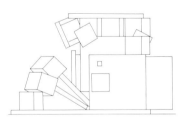

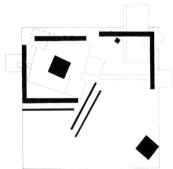
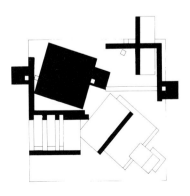
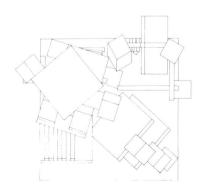

JOSEPH AUTY

MIKE ROMANI

GREG WILLSEY

GREG WILLSEY

## REFLECTING

Wright's early Prairie Houses and buildings like the Unity Temple were published in what were perhaps the most influential documents of early Modern Architecture—the *Wasmuth* volumes of 1910–11. One of the most vivid responses to Wright's call to architects to "explode the box" of their thinking and designs was Gerrit Rietveld's Schroeder House of 1924. Set against a blank masonry wall at the end of a block of rowhouses, like some strange "slender spatial animal" (fellow architect Theo Van Doesburg's description of Rietveld's famous *Red and Blue Chair*), it may appear at first to be a confusing and perhaps random collection of planes "sticking out" of an otherwise normal house. The hovering cantilevered elements seemed to erode the corners of the volume, the site, and whole block of houses to which it was attached. But if we seek the original cube these plastic elements came from, we may read passages of spacial slippage, expansion, and explosion that transform the simple volume of the house. Both Rietveld and Van Doesburg were members of the Dutch De Stijl Movement. As Van Doesburg wrote in his 1924 work, *16 Points of a Plastic Architecture:*

"The new architecture is anti-cubic, that is to say, it does not try to freeze the different functional space cells in one closed cube. Rather it throws the functional space cells (as well as the overhanging planes, balcony volumes, etc. centrifugally from the core of the cube. And through this means, height width, depth, and time (i.e. imaginary four-dimensional entity) approaches a new plastic expression in open spaces. In this way, architecture acquires a more or less floating aspect that, so to speak, works against the gravitational forces of nature."

Such remarks suggest the possibility of a "filmic" or cinematic sense of space. One can imagine moving through and elaborating frames of volume, as Einstein suggested in his discussion of frames of reference in his Theory of Relativity. A continuum of space may sustain the intersection of volumes acting at a distance from each other. Those who are curious and courageous may at this point wish to also read the article in Study #6, in which Colin Rowe and Robert Slutzky explore the possibility of a spacial transparency, where solid masses need not be opaque to the unifying order of separated volumes. These critical ideas presage our own era's fascination with synthesis of new materials and structures, even at the microscopic level. Today the creation of new polymers and the engineering of our very genes is taken for granted as our potential for making TRANSFORMATIONS is extended further into new fields.

## READINGS

Wright, *Writings and Buildings*
Hitchcock *In the Nature of Materials*
Arnheim, *Picasso's Guernica,* and *The Dynamics of Architectural Form*
Peter Eisenman, HOUSE II from *Progressive Architecture,* May 1974; *HOUSE X*
Eisenman, Graves, Gwathway, Hejduk, and Meier, *Five New York Architects*
Mandelbrot, *Fractal Geometry of Nature*
Darcy Thompson *On Growth and Form*
Clark and Pause, *Precedents in Architecture*
Hofstetter, Douglas, "The Music of Frederic Chopin: startling aural patterns
that also startle the eye" *Scientific American* April 1982

## THE DESTRUCTION OF THE BOX
### from *Writings and Buildings,* by Frank Lloyd Wright

I think I first consciously began to try to beat the box in the Larkin Building-1904. I found a natural opening to the liberation I sought when (after a great struggle) I finally pushed the staircase towers out from the corners of the main building made them into free-standing, individual features. Then the thing began to come through as you may see.

I had felt this need for features quite early in my architectural life. You will see this feeling growing up, becoming more apparent a little later in Unity Temple: there perhaps is where you will find the first real expression of the idea that the space within the building is the reality of that building. Unity Temple is where I thought I had it, this idea that the reality of a building no longer consisted in the walls and roof. So that sense of freedom began which has come into the architecture of today for you and which we call organic architecture.

You may see, there in Unity Temple, how I dealt with this great architectural problem at that time. You will find the sense of the great room coming through—space not walled in now but more or less free to appear. In Unity Temple you will find the walls actually disappearing: you will find the interior space opening to the outside and see the outside coming in. You will see assembled about this interior space, screening it, various free, related features instead of enclosing walls. See, you now can make features of many types for enclosure and group the features about interior space with no sense of boxing it. But most important, after all, is the sense of shelter extended, expanded overhead, and which gives the indispensable sense of protection while leading the human vision beyond the walls. That primitive sense of shelter is a quality architecture should always have. If in a building you feel not only protection from above, but liberation of interior to outside space (which you do feel in Unity Temple and other buildings I have built) then you have one important secret of letting the interior space come through.

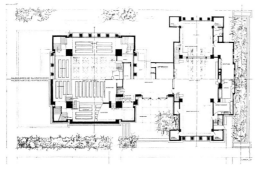

UNITY TEMPLE, OAK PARK, ILL. 1904.

Now I shall try to show you why organic architecture is the architecture of democratic freedom. Why? Well. . .

Here—say—is your box: big hole in the box, little ones if you wish—of course.

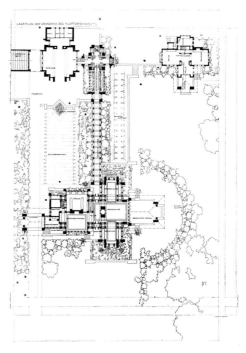

DARWIN D. MARTIN, HOUSE AND ADJUNCTS.
BUFFALO, N.Y. 1904.

What you see of it now is this square package of containment. You see? Something not fit for our liberal profession of democratic government, a thing essentially anti-individual.

Here you may see (more or less) the student architecture of almost all our colleges.

I was never ambitious to be an engineer. Unfortunately I was educated as one in the University of Wisconsin. But I knew enough of engineering to know that the outer angles of a box were not where its most economical support would be, if you made a building of it. No, a certain distance in each way from each corner is where the economic support of a box-building is invariable to be found. You see?

Now, when you put support at those points you have created a short cantileverage to the corners that lessens actual spans and sets the corner free or open for whatever distance you choose. The corners disappear altogether if you choose to let space come in there, or let it go out. Instead of post and beam construction, the usual box building, you now have a new sense of building construction by way of the cantilever and continuity. Both are new structural elements as they now enter architecture. But all you see of this radical liberation of space all over the world today is the corner window. But, in this simple change of thought lies the essential of the architectural change from box to free plan and the new reality that is space instead of matter.

# WORLD ARCHITECTURE

From this point we can go on to talk about organic architecture instead of classic architecture. Let's go on. These unattached side walls become something independent, no longer enclosing walls. They're separate supporting screens, any one of which may be shortened, or extended or perforated, or occasionally eliminated. These free-standing screens support the roof. What of this roof? Overhead it becomes emphasized as a splendid sense of shelter, but shelter that hides nothing when you are inside looking out from the building. It is a shape of shelter that really gives a sense of the outside coming in or the inside going out. Yes, you have now a wide-spreading overhead that is really a release of this interior space to the outside: a freedom where before imprisonment existed.

You can perfect a figure of freedom with these four screens; in any case, enclosure as a box is gone. Anything becoming, anything in the nature of plan or materials is easily a possibility. To go further: if this liberation works in the horizontal plane why won't it work in the vertical plane? No one has looked through the box at the sky up there at the upper angle have they? Why not? Because the box always had a cornice at the top. It was added to the sides in order that the box might not look so much like a box, but more classic. This cornice was the feature that made your conventional box classic.

THEO. VAN DOESBURG. *COLOR CONSTRUCTION: PROJECT FOR A PRIVATE HOUSE* 1923. COLLECTION THE MUSEUM OF MODERN ART, N.Y. EDGAR KAUFMANN, JR. FUND.

Now—to go on—there in the Johnson Building you catch no sense of enclosure whaterver at any angle, top or sides. You are looking at the sky and feel the freedom of space: the columns are designed to stand up and take over the ceiling, the column is made a part of the ceiling: continuity.

GERRIT RIETVELD. *SCHRODER HOUSE* UTRECHT, THE NETHERLANDS. 1924. PHOTOGRAPH COURTESY THE MUSEUM OF MODERN ART, N.Y.

The old idea of a building is, as you see, quite gone. Everything before these liberating thoughts of cantilever and continuity took effect, was post and beam construction: superimposition of one thing upon another and repetition of slab over slab, always on posts. Now what? You have established a natural use of glass according to this new freedom of space. Space may now go out or come in where life is being lived, space as a component of it. So organic architecture is architecture in which you may feel and see all this happen as a third dimension. Too bad the Greeks didn't know of this new use for steel and glass as a third dimension. If they had known what I am trying to describe here, you wouldn't have to think much about it for yourselves today, the schools would long ago have taught these principles to you.

Be that as it may, this sense of space (space alive by way of the third dimension), isn't that sense, or feeling for architecture, an implement to characterize the freedom of the individual? I think so. If you refuse this liberated sense of building haven't you thrown away that which is most precious in our own human life and most promising as a new field for truly creative artistic expression in architecture? Yes, is there anything else really? All this, and more, is why I have, lifelong, been fighting the pull of the specious old box. I have had such a curious, controversial and interesting time doing it that I myself have become a controversial item. Suspicion is always in order.

Now, to go back to my own experiences: after this building of Unity Temple (as I have said) I thought I had the great thing very well in hand. I was feeling somewhat as I imagine a great prophet might. I often thought, well, at least here is an essentially new birth of thought, feeling and opportunity in this machine age. This is the modern means. I had made it come true! Naturally (I well remember) I became less and less tolerant and, I suppose, intolerable. Arrogant, I imagine, was the proper word. I have heard it enough.

From an address to the Junior Chapter of the American Institute of Architects, New York City, 1952. Taped and typed; corrected by Frank Lloyd Wright.

## BETWEEN DIMENSIONS: FRACTALS

Fractals are a curiosity investigated by the mathematician Benoit Mandelbrodt. These notes paraphrase a few of the profound ideas found in his books *Form Chance and Dimension,* and *The Fractal Geometry of Nature.* He explains that there are certain classes of figures which depend on the scale of measurement to determine their size. For example, the coastline of Britain can be measured on a map with a scale rule in which one inch equals 100 miles. But such a measure would seem crude with our actual experience of walking along the seashore, where the edge between water and land curves around each pebble. And even that scale seems crude when compared with the molecular surface of the pebble. A line divided into three segments becoming four segments creates a figure of indeterminate dimension when taken to several iterations. It is more than a line and less than a plane. Mandelbrodt calls these *fractal* dimensions.

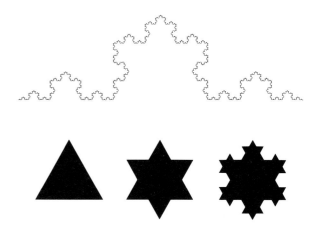

TRIADIC KOCH ISLAND OR SNOWFLAKE
(Coastline dimension D log4/log3 ~ 1.2618)

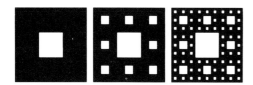

THE SIERPINSKI CARPET (Dimension D ~ 1.8928)

Architects can easily visualize this phenomenon. Consider a 9-square in two dimensions. Imagine a series of operations in which the center square is removed, and the remaining eight perimeter squares each become a 9-square with the center square removed at a smaller scale, the process being repeated infinitely. Mandelbrodt calls this the SIERPINSKI CARPET, after the mathematician who first described it in 1916. The initator, the generator and the next two steps are as shown in the diagram to the left. This carpet's area vanishes, while the total perimeter of its holes is infinite. It is a figure whose intrinsic structure is of a fractional dimension, more than linear (one-dimensional) but less than planar (two-dimensional)—a fractal.

The MENGER SPONGE is the volumetric version of this fractal. At each step of the operation the figure moves toward more surface and less volume, tending toward limits of infinite surface and infinitesimal (zero) volume. Consider 27 identical cubes composing one large 27-cube. This cube has $6 \times 9$ square inches of surface, or 54 square inches. So, $S_1 = 54$, $V_1 = 27$. Next remove one cube from each "face" and center. Now $S_2 = 54 + 18 = 72$, and $V_2 = 20$. Repeating the process leads to $72/54 \times 72/54 = 1.777$ at $S_4$, and $20/27 \times 20/27 = .548$ at $V_4$. Thus the surface area tends to increase while the volume decreases. Just this combination of characteristics is ideal for a sponge which needs to touch as much of the sea or wet countertop as possible using the least amount of material to do so.

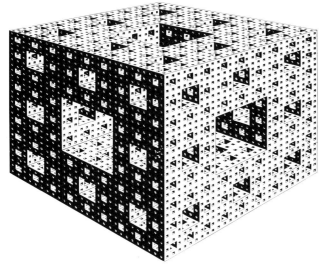

THE MENGER SPONGE (Dimension D ~ 2.7628)

Topologically, every Sierpinski carpet is a plane universal curve, and every Menger sponge is a spacial universal curve. That is, these shapes are respectively the most complicated curve in the plane, and the most complicated curve in any higher dimensional space.

GEORGE HOBEL

# 5 Expression

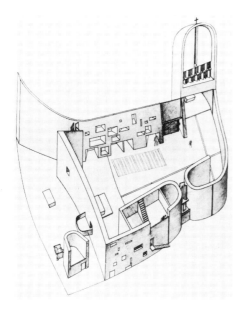

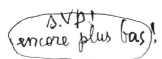

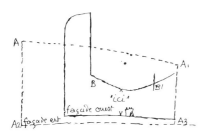

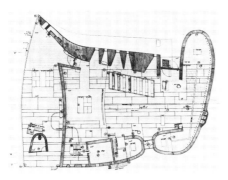

## THINKING

*Nature must be treated in terms of the cylinder,*
*the sphere, and the cone.* —Paul Cezanne

Certain solid forms have expressive potential by virtue of their unique shapes. "Sharp" and "well-rounded" are terms in our daily vocabulary which can even describe intangibles like personality traits. Architects use these forms in designing buildings often for their purely plastic qualities rather than as carriers of symbolic meaning. (Similar to mountain forms the Great Pyramids of Egypt ultimately "symbolize" monumentality, not because they are pyramids, but because they have endured.) Through reasoned and spontaneous combinations of "pure" geometric solids at various scales, truly expressive relationships of masses, contours, and profiles can communicate human emotions. You now have in your architectonic kit of parts new elements which in themselves and in combination make not just mass but space itself. The vaults and the L-shaped forms describe voids within their spans of mass. Columns, beams, and joints can create frameworks enmeshed in space. For the first time, you can compose in three- dimensional volume directly. As introspection and reflection can reveal, the emotional content of spatial qualities is enormous.

Gaston Bachelard, wrote in *The Poetics of Space,* "When one can withdraw oneself into the being of repose . . . then the great stream of simple humility that is in the silent room flows into ourselves." At the level of daydreams, time ceases to quicken memory, and space and light are everything. Certain kinds of spaces attract especially the poetic imagination. These include shells, nests, closets, corners, rooms, and forests—all hollows in their own way. With your new and now enhanced capacity for making space within forms and forms within space, you can consider such deep themes as cave and tree house as they echo in your poetic and plastic imagination. With the given elements, you can now create forms that subtly express your ideas and feelings about such virtually mythic themes.

Le Corbusier sought expressive space in his alpine chapel of Notre Dame du Haut at Ronchamp. Every plastic and architectural element was activated. He found in a crab shell on a Long Island beach the structure for a roof and ceiling that could seem to float on a halo of light, a small, but eloquent, gap between ceiling and walls. He left no major surface a simple plane. The unflat floor follows the natural grade, with the entry "vestibule" at the very apex of the hilltop. The southeast wall is warped, splayed, and angled to make deep truncated pyramids of luminous colored stained glass. The ceiling sweeps low to compress the center while expanding the edges. The swoop to the tall slot at the south and the vertical shear of the three light scoops (a device Le Corbusier found at Hadrian's villa and an image he possibly saw in the hooded costume of the local nuns) create an upward counterpoint to the descending central flow of space. The diagonal pews ride like an ark on an orthogonal sea. Sharp-edged sides contrast with the soft, rounded swells. This church embodies both celestial angelic Mary and robust buxom Earth Mother. Ronchamp on the hill is like a cloud or a house in the treetops, yet inside it is a dark, hollow cave, admitting light only at the fluttering eyelashes of its few openings. No part of this chapel is neutral. Inside and outside form a continuum of space. At the right moment, the pilgrim/visitor may find the moon as a halo behind the wooden image of the Madonna.

[The Carcerii] . . . record the scenery of his own visions during a fever. Some of them . . . represent vast Gothic halls: on the floor of which stood all sorts of engines and machinery, wheels, cables, pulleys, levers, catapults, &c. &c. expressive of enormous power put forth and resistance overcome. Creeping along the sides of the walls, you perceive a staircase; and upon it, groping his way upwards, was Piranesi himself: follow the stairs a little further, and you perceive it come to a sudden abrupt termination, without any balustrade, and allowing no step onwards to him who has reached the extremity, except to the depths below. Whatever is to become of poor Piranesi, you suppose, at least, that his labours must terminate here. But raise your eyes, and behold a second flight of stairs still higher: on which again Piranesi is perceived, by this time standing on the very brink of the abyss. Again elevate your eye, and still more aerial flight of stairs is beheld: and again is poor Piranesi busy on his aspiring labours: and so on, until the unfinished stairs and Piranesi are both lost in the upper gloom of the hall. —With the same power of endless growth and self-reproduction did my architecture proceed in dreams.

Thomas De Quincey, Confessions of an English Opium Eater, 1821

## PROJECTING

Expression through form demands intense personal engagement, a passionate position, a point of view. The axonometric viewpoint often remains abstract. Although designing in axonometric allows a view of all parts in relation to each other, its disadvantage is apparent to the average person: it doesn't look like "the real thing." Our everday way of seeing, in which parallel lines converge at vanishing points, is not the only way of depicting space. Traditional perspective is only one of many geometric methods of spacial projection.

Designing in axonometric does not give us a chance to visualize the sequence of moving from one space to another, which can be done through a sketched series of perspective vignettes. Designing in perspective permits the construction of significant views, at the possible expense of obscuring what happens on the "other side." Perspective can mislead as well as reveal. A bird's eye view of shining glass in a lush and luminous landscape can mask the basic reality: that the new building will be a flat pancake sprawling across an undistinguished field of scrub brush and parking lots. However, many architects have been masters of perspective. Wright's early renderings have the abstract quality of fine Japanese prints and yet look exactly like the finished building. Erich Mendelsohn and Antonio Sant'Elia expressed the drama of modern construction through perspectives taken from especially thrilling viewpoints. A generation before the fall of the Bastille, Giovanni Battista Piranesi made etchings of the fearful and powerful mystery of unexplored spaces in his views of imaginary prisons, *Il Carcerei*. The perspectives construct the architecture, replete with structural ambiguities and spacial contradictions. The rendering of deep shadow and distant, but intense, light and of vaulted halls climbing and extending through imagination into infinity heighten our sense of being lost in a vast place for a very long time. What could be more appropriate for depicting a prison!

Brunelleschi, master architect of *Il Duomo* and progenitor of the Italian Renaissance, was also the modern inventor of the geometric method of visual perspective. His follower, Alberti, codified these findings into the general method still used today. To draw a floor of square tiles in perspective, he suggests that a grid plan of the tiles be imposed on the picture plane as well as a horizon line and vanishing point. On the horizon, to one side of the grid, the viewer's distance to the floor is established. Lines are drawn from this viewpoint across to the base of the grid. Their intersection will establish the depth of successive rows of tiles. Today we normally set a plan of the space on a drawing board at the appropriate angle, draw the picture plane as a line intersecting the plan, establish vanishing points parallel to significant edges of the figure (two for a two-point perspective, one in the center for a one-point perspective, etc.) and project the rays of significant points from the viewpoint onto the picture plane in plan. After the horizon line and a true vertical measurement are set, parallel lines are drawn from the vanishing points to establish depth and complete the construction. Perspective sheets with already constructed spatial grids are also available. See the Visual Glossary for more on constructing perspectives.

The picture plane in perspective presents an intrinsic ambiguity. A trapezoid on the picture plane could be a square floor in perspective. The surrealist painter Magritte made visual puns based on the fact that what we see at any moment may be replaced by a "perfect" image at the picture plane confronting our eyes. The Cubists also exploited this ambiguity.

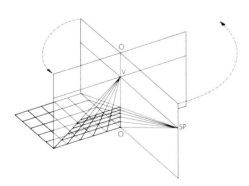

MODERN PERSPECTIVE PROJECTION

TRIMETRIC DRAWING DESCRIBING ALBERTI'S
DISTANCE POINT METHOD.

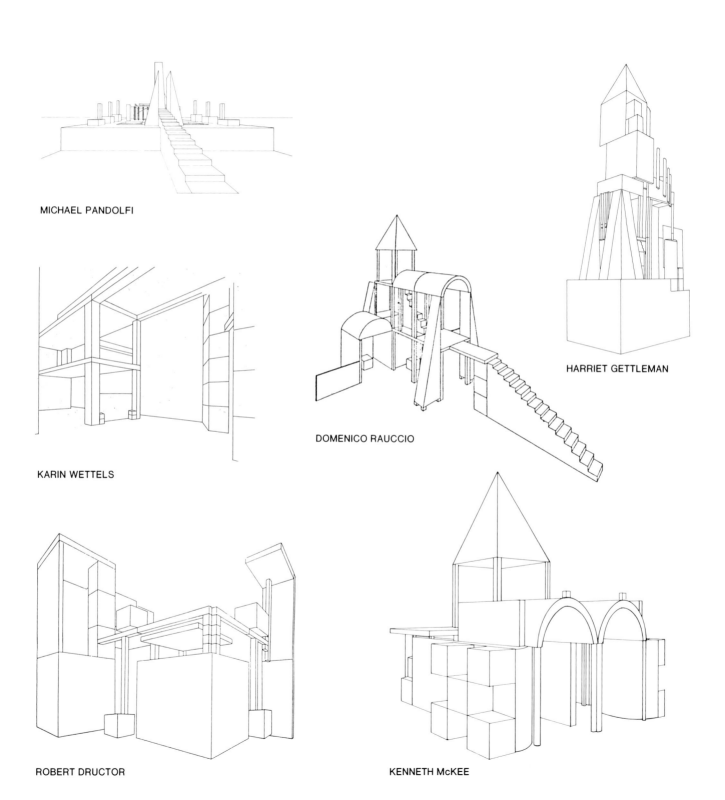

MICHAEL PANDOLFI

KARIN WETTELS

DOMENICO RAUCCIO

HARRIET GETTLEMAN

ROBERT DRUCTOR

KENNETH McKEE

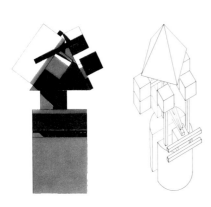

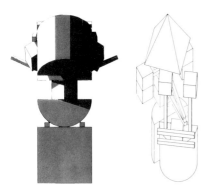

TREVOR WISDOM     ANDREW TYCHAZ

## DOING

### ARCHITECTONICS

Using all the STICKS AND STONES elements made so far (everything but parts $p,q,r,s$ in the inventory), create EXPRESSIVE SPACE. Make the form expressive in both solid and void as well as the play between them. We find expression all around us in the head of an animal in motion, the torso of a person at work, a flowering plant, etc. But the work you make does not necessarily have to be figurative or representational. In fact, it is usually most interesting to the architect to find profound expression directly in the relation of pure forms. (Option: create a special thick base for this project from which volumes equivalent to any of the architectonic elements may be removed.)

### GRAPHICS

Make a 12″ square field of the letters of your name so that the resulting two-dimensional form reads first, before the name, and is also a figure-ground ambiguity (see project 3). Also, if possible, express a characteristic of your personality through the form you make. Use only the Helvetica typeface (the one in which this page is printed). The letter forms may vary in size. Use black and white only.

### Advanced Project: EXPRESSion

Design a record cover that communicates the meaning and feeling of the particular music you choose. Use only found typography, which may be cut out and retraced and/or mechanically enlarged or reduced, so long as all proportions of the letter forms remain constant. Use black and white only. The choice of typeface, qualities of the letter forms, the spaces between them, the dialog between flat and deep space, and the expression of the 12″ square field are all you have to work with.

### FREEHAND DRAWING

In your newsprint sketchpad, make at least four one-hour studies of the human figure in a building or room interior. The person may be a friend, studio mate, or oneself (using a mirror). Quick gesture studies may be helpful when starting these drawings.

### DOCUMENT

Document your EXPRESSIVE SPACE with a full set of architectural drawings. Present all work in ink on paper. The final model should be presentation quality with rubber-cement joints. Include all drawings you prepared for Study Four including plans, sections, elevations, and axonometric. Show shade and shadows as appropriate, This time also draw one architectural perspective (true view drawn to scale, cast shadows optional) of the object.

### PREPARE

| | | |
|---|---|---|
| p. | 1 | 45° stair set with 12 treads (each 8″ at scale of 1″ = 32″) |
| q. | 1 | ladder (8′ high at scale of 1″ = 32″) |
| r. | 1 | 60° stair set with 16 treads (each 12″ at scale of 1″ = 32″) |
| s. | 4 | 1″ × 1½″ × 6″ piece |

PLAN

**SARMA STEINGER**

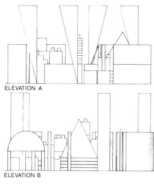

ELEVATION A

ELEVATION B

AXONOMETRIC

**LINDA MANZ**

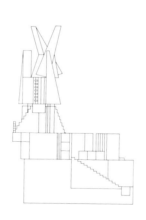

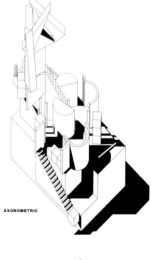

AXONOMETRIC

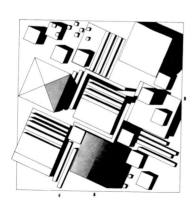

**SARMA STEINGER**

SECTION

ELEVATION B

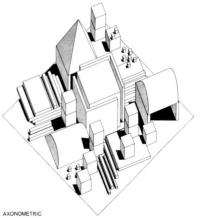

AXONOMETRIC

WILLIAM RECCE

JONATHAN REO

## REFLECTING

When images and symbols carry conventional meanings, expression is easy but shallow. A red octagon is a driver's signal to stop. But this sign cannot help us distinguish between pause, rest, hiatus, break, arrest, or any of the other shades of meaning we use to amplify the general idea of stopping. Human expression depends on subtle distinctions, and referential codes are perhaps the least effective means of communicating such subtleties. The manipulation of abstract elements sets its own rules and structures and is therefore capable of limitless refinements of expression. This is perhaps one reason why music is a medium of such powerful emotional content. Igor Stravinsky, the great 20th century composer and musician, writes in the following excerpt about the necessity of rules and limits to the truly creative act. His thoughts can easily be translated to apply to the composition of space with architectonic plastic elements.

Piranesi, one of the pioneering architectural archaelogists of his time, etched views of Rome which captured the magnificent spaces of Antiquity while suggesting construction and engineering techniques that would make such monuments possible. He illustrated enormous foundations, cyclopean masonry, even the triangular bricks used to hold rubble walls and the cobblestones laid over gravel that made the Appian Way, all in an attempt to demonstrate the power and originality of invention in Roman architecture at the very moment when archaeologists like Winklemann were uncovering the ruins of Classical Greece. Yet even within the realm of fantasy, in his *Carceri,* he still drew as if light and shade, gravity and stone, and the laws of optical perspective were creating an actual place. It is precisely because we feel these ''truths'' to be in play that the sense of massive space, endless volume, and enormous scale play so powerfully on our imagination.

On a less pictorial and more purely architectonic level, the rules of composition demanded in using full and partial domes create the strong spatial rhythms and dramatic lighting of Hagia Sophia, one of the most expressive Byzantine spaces. The Sydney Opera House today presents a similar plastic event: the regular structural order of spherical triangle sections is syncopated in plan so that the shells seem to hover over and around the spaces, enfolding and catching space like billowing sails catch the wind. Here again an order and framework for possible structural configurations is both stated and reinterpreted in the architectural composition. The result, like jazz, communicates both theme and variations in such a manner as to make expression through manipulation of formal elements.

## READINGS

Bachelard, *Poetics of Space*
Wittkower, *Architecture in the Age of Humanism,* especially part IV, ''The problem of Harmonic Proportion in Architecture''
John Wilton Ely, *The Mind and Art of Piranesi*
Stravinsky, *The Poetics of Music*
Ozenfant, *The Foundations of Modern Art,* ''Modalities'', chap. 10
Baldwin, *The Dome: History of an Idea*
Chiang Yee, *Chinese Calligraphy.*
see also the works of the Abstract Expressionist painters, especially Jackson Pollock, Franz Kline, De Kooning, Kandinsky, and Mondrian.

ARTHUR LOMBARDI

# THE COMPOSITION OF MUSIC
## from *The Poetics of Music,* by Igor Stravinsky

We are living at a time when the status of man is undergoing profound upheaveals. Modern man is progressively losing his understanding of values and his sense of proportions. This failure to understand essential realities is extremely serious. It leads us infallibly to the violation of the fundamental laws of human equilibrium. In the domain of music, the consequences of this misunderstanding are these: on one hand there is a tendency to turn the mind away from what I shall call the higher mathematics of music in order to degrade music to servile employment, and to vulgarize it by adapting it to the requirements of an elementary utilitarianism—as we shall soon see on examining Soviet music. On the other hand, since the mind itself is ailing, the music of our time, and particularly the music that calls itself and believes itself *pure,* carries within it the symptoms of a pathologic blemish and spreads the germs of a new original sin. The old original sin was chiefly a sin of knowledge; the new original sin, if I may speak in these terms, is first and foremost a sin of non-acknowledgement—a refusal to acknowledge the truth and the laws that proceed therefrom, laws that we have called fundamental. What then is this truth in the domain of music? And what are its repercussions on creative activity?

Let us not forget that it is written: "Spiritus ubi vult spirat" (St. John, 3: 8). What we must retain in this proposition is above all the word WILL. The Spirit is thus endowed with the capacity of willing. The principle of speculative volition is a fact.

Now it is just this fact that is too often disputed. People question the direction that the wind of the Spirit is taking, not the rightness of the artisan's work. In so doing, whatever may be your feeelings about ontology or whatever your own philosophy and beliefs may be, you must admit that you are making an attack on the very freedom of the spirit—whether you begin this large word with a capital or not. If a believer in Christian philosophy, you would then also have to refuse to accept the idea of the Holy Spirit. If an agnostic or atheist, you would have to do nothing less than refuse to be a *free-thinker.* . . .

It should be noted that there is never any dispute when the listener takes pleasure in the work he hears. The least informed of music-lovers readily clings to the periphery of a work; it pleases him for reasons that are most often entirely foreign to the essence of music. This pleasure is enough for him and calls for no justification. But if it happens that the music displeases him, our music-lover will ask you for an explanation of his discomfiture. He will demand that we expain something that is in its essence ineffable.

By its fruit we judge the tree. Judge the tree by its fruit then, and do not meddle with the roots. Function justifies an organ, no matter how strange the organ may appear in the eyes of those who are not accustomed to see it functioning. Snobbish circles are cluttered with persons who, like one of Montesquieu's characters, wonder how one can possibly be a Persian. They make me think unfailingly of the story of the peasant who, on seeing a dromedary in the zoo for the first time, examines it at length, shakes his head and, turning to leave, says, to the great delight of those present: "It isn't true."

It is through the unhampered play of its functions, then, that a work is revealed and justified. We are free to accept or reject this play, but no one has the right to question the fact of its existence. To judge, dispute, and criticize the principle of speculative volition which is at the origin of all creation is thus manifestly useless. In the pure state, music is free speculation. Artists of all epochs have unceasingly testified to do as they did. Since I myself was created, I cannot help having the desire to create. What sets this desire in motion, and what can I do to make it productive?

The study of the creative process is an extremely delicate one. In truth, it is impossible to observe the inner workings of this process from the outside. It is futile to try and follow its successive phases in someone else's work. It is likewise very difficult to observe one's self. Yet it is only by enlisting the aide of introspection that I may have any chance at all of guiding you in this essentially fluctuating matter.

Most music-lovers believe that what sets the composer's creative imagination in motion is a certain emotive disturbance generally designated by the name of *inspiration.*

I have no thought of denying to inspiration the outstanding role that has devolved upon it in the generative process we are studying; I simply maintain that inspiration is in no way a prescribed condition of the creative act, but rather a manifestation that is chronologically secondary.

*Inspiration, art, artist*—so many words, hazy at least, that keep us from seeing clearly in a field where everything is balance and calculation through which the breath of the speculative spirit blows. It is afterwards, and only afterwards, that the emotive disturbance which is at the root of inspiration may arise—an emotive disturbance about which people talk so indelicately by conferring upon it a meaning that is shocking to us and that eompromises the term itself. Is it not clear that this emotion is merely a reaction on the part of the creator grappling with that unknown entity which is still only the object of his creating and which is to become a work of art? Step by step, link by link, it will be granted him to discover the work. It is this chain of discoveries, as well as each individual discovery, that give rise to the emotion—an almost physiolagal reflex, like that of the appetite causing a flow of saliva—this emotion which invariably follows closely the phases of the creative process.

All creation presupposes at its origin a sort of appetite that is brought on by the foretaste of discovery. This foretaste of the creative act accompanies the intuitive grasp of an unknown entity that will not take definite shape except by the action of a constantly vigilant technique.

This appetite that is aroused in me at the mere thought of putting in order musical elements that have attracted my attention is not at all a fortuitious thing like inspiration, but as habitual and periodic, if not as constant, as a natural need.

This premonition of an obligation, this foretaste of a pleasure, this conditioned reflex, as a modern physiologist would say, shows clearly that it is the idea of discovery and hard work that attracts me.

The very act of putting my work on paper, of, as we say, kneading the dough, is for me inseparable from the pleasure of creation. So far as I am concerned, I cannot separate the spiritual effort from the psychological and physical effort; they confront me on the same level and do not present a hierarchy.

The word artist which, as it is most generally understood today, bestows on its bearer the highest intellectual prestige, the privilege of being accepted as a pure mind—this pretentious term is in my view entirely incompatible with the role of the *homo faber*.

At this point it should be remembered that, whatever field of endeavor has fallen to our lot, if it is true that we are *intellectuals,* we are called upon not to cogitate, but to perform.

The philosopher Jacques Maritain reminds us that in the mighty structure of medieval civilization, the artist held only the rank of an artisan. "And his individualism was forbidden any sort of anarchic development, because a natural social discipline imposed certain limitative conditions upon him from without." It was the Renaissance that invented the artist, distinguished him from the artisan and began to exalt the former at the expense of the latter.

At the outset the name artist was given only to the Masters of Arts: philosophers, alchemists, magicians; but painters, sculptors, musicians, and poets had the right to be qualified only as artisans.

Plying divers implements,

The subtile artizan implants

Life in marble, copper, bronze,

Says the poet Du Bellay. And Montaigne enumerates in his *Essays* the "painters, poets and other artizans." And even in the seventeenth century, La Fontaine hails a painter with the name of *artisan* and draws a sharp rebuke from an ill-tempered critic who might have been the ancestor of most of of our present-day critics.

The idea of work to be done is for me so closely bound up with the idea of the arranging of materials and of the pleasure that the actual doing of the work affords us that, should the impossible happen and my work suddenly be given to in a perfectly completed form, I should be embarrassed and nonplussed by it, as by a hoax.

We have a duty towards music, namely, to invent it. I recall once during the war when I was crossing the French border a gendarme asked me what my profession was. I told him quite naturally that I was an inventor of music. The gendarme, then verifying my passport, asked me why I was listed as a composer. I told him that the expression "inventor of music" seemed to me to fit my profession more exactly than the term applied to me in the documents authorizing me to cross borders.

Invention presupposes imagination but should not be confused with it. For the act of invention implies the necessity of a lucky find and of achieving full realization of this find. What we imagine does not necessarily take on a concrete form and may remain in a state of virtuality, whereas invention is not conceivable apart from its actual being worked out.

Thus, what concerns us here is not imagination in itself, but rather creative imagination: the faculty that helps us to pass from the level of conception to the level of realization.

In the course of my labors I suddenly stumble upon something unexpected. This unexpected element strikes me. I make a note of it. At the proper time I put it to profitable use. This gift of chance must not be confused with that capriciousness of imagination that is commonly called fancy. Fancy implies a predetermined will to abandon one's self to caprice. The aforementioned assistance of the unexpected is something quite different. It is a collaboration which is immanently bound up with possibilities which are unsolicited and come most appositely to temper the inevitable over-rigorousness of the naked will. And it is good that this is so.

"In everything that yields gracefully," G. K. Chesterton says somewhere, "there must be resistance. Bows are beautiful when they bend only because they seek to remain rigid. Rigidity that slightly yields, like Justice swayed by Pity, is all the beauty of earth. Everything seeks to grow straight, and happily, nothing succeeds in so growing. Try to grow straight and life will bend you."

The faculty of creating is never given to us all by itself. It always goes hand in hand with the gift of observation. And the true creator may be recognized by his ability always to find about him, in the commonest and humblest thing, items worthy of note. He does not have to concern himself with a beautiful landscape, he does not need to surround himself with rare and precious objects. He does not have to put forth in search of discoveries: they are always within his reach. He will have only to cast a glance about him. Familiar things, things that are everywhere, attract his attention. The least accident holds his interest and guides his operations. If his finger slips, he will notice it; on occasion, he may draw profit from something unforeseen that a momentary lapse reveals to him.

One does not contrive an accident: one observes it to draw inspiration therefrom. An accident is perhaps the only thing that really inspires us. A composer improvises aimlessly the way an animal grubs about. Both of them go grubbing because they yield to a compulsion to seek things out. What urge of the composer is satisfied by this investigation? The rules with which, like a penitent, he is burdened? No: he is in quest of his pleasure. He seeks a satisfaction that he fully knows he will not find without first striving for it. One cannot force one's self to love; but love presupposes understanding, and in order to understand, one must exert one's self.

It is the same problem that was posed in the Middle Ages by the theologians of pure love. To understand in order to love; to love in order to understand: we are here not going around in a vicious circle; we are rising spirally, providing we have made an initial effort, have even just gone through a routine exercise.

Pascal has specifically this in mind when he writes that custom "controls the automaton, which in its turn unthinkingly controls the mind. For there must be no mistake," continues Pascal, "we are automatons just as much as we are minds. . . ."

So we grub about in expectation of our pleasure, guided by our scent, and suddenly we stumble against an unknown obstacle. It gives us a jolt, a shock, and this shock fecundates our creative power.

The faculty of observation and of making something out of what is observed belongs only to the person who at least possesses, in his particular field of endeavor, an acquired culture and an innate taste. A dealer, and artlover who is the first to buy the canvases of an unknown painter who will be famous twenty-five years later under the name of Cézanne—doesn't such a person give us a clear example of this innate taste? What else guides him in his choice? A flair, an instinct from which this taste proceeds, a completely spontaneous faculty anterior to reflection.

As for culture, it is a sort of upringing which, in the social sphere, confers polish upon education, sustains and rounds out academic instruction. This upbringing is just as important in the sphere of taste and is essential to the creator who must ceaselessly refine his taste or run the risk of losing his perspicacity. Our mind, as well as our body, requires continual exercise. It atrophies if we do not cultivate it.

It is culture that brings out the full value of taste and gives it a chance to prove its worth simply by its application. The artist imposes a culture upon himself and ends by imposing it upon others. That is how tradition becomes established.

Tradition is entirely different from habit, even from an excellent habit, since habit is by definition an unconsious acquisition and tends to become mechanical, whereas tradition results from a conscious and deliberate acceptance. A real tradition is not the relic of a past that is irretrievably gone;

it is a living force that animates and informs the present. In this sense the paradox which banteringly maintains that everything which is not tradition is plagiarism, is true. . . .

Far from implying the repetition of what has been, tradition presupposes the reality of what endures. It appears as an heirloom, a heritage that one receives on condition of making it bear fruit before passing it on to one's descendants.

Brahms was born sixty years after Beethoven. From the one to the other, and from every aspect, the distance is great; they do not dress the same way, but Brahms follows the tradition of Beethoven without borrowing one of his habiliments. For the borrowing of a method has nothing to do with observing a tradition. "A method is replaced: a tradition is carried forward in order to produce something new." Tradition thus assures the continuity of creation. The example that I have just cited does not constitute an exception but is one proof out of a hundred of a constant law. This sense of tradition which is a natural need must not be confused with the desire which the composer feels to affirm the kinship he finds across the centuries with some master of the past.

My opera *Mavra* was born of a natural sympathy for the body of melodic tendencies, for the vocal style and conventional language which I came to admire more and more in the old Russo-Italian opera. This sympathy guided me quite naturally along the path of a tradition that seemed to be lost at the moment when the attention of musical circles was turned entirely towards the music drama, which repesented no tradition at all from the historical point of view and which fulfilled no necessity at all from the musical point of view. The vogue of the music drama has a pathological origin. Alas, even the admirable music of *Pélléas et Mélisande,* so fresh in its modesty, was unable to get us into the open, in spite of so many characteristics with which it shook off the tyranny of the Wagnerian system.

The music of *Mavra* stays within the tradition of Glinka and Dargaomisky. I had not the slightest intention of reestablishing this tradition. I simply wanted in my turn to try my hand at the living form of the opera-bouffe which was so well suited to the Pushkin tale which gave me my subject. *Mavra* is dedicated to the memory of composers, not one of whom, I am sure, would have recognized as valid such a manifestation of the tradition they created, because of the novelty of the language my music speaks a hundred years after its models flourished. But I wanted to renew the style of these dialogues-in-music whose voices has been reviled and drowned out by the clang and clatter of the music drama. So a hundred years had to pass before the freshness of the Russo-Italian tradition could again be appreciated, a tradition that continued to live apart from the main stream of the present, and in which circulated a salubrious air, well adapted to delivering us from the miasmic vapors of the music drama, the inflated arrogance of which could not conceal its vacuity.

23

24

FIGURE 23 IS THE PERFECT VISUALIZATION OF A
PHYSIOLOGICAL FACT: IT SHOWS HOW AN INDIVIDUAL,
UPON AWAKENING, SHEDS THE REMNANTS OF SLEEP.
SHE FLEXES HER BICEPS AND KICKS THE AIR WITH
HER FEET—HER LIMBS ARE LARGEST WHERE SHE
FEELS HEAVIEST. THE *GRAND NUDE* (FIG. 24), ON THE
OTHER HAND, SHOWS A WOMAN WIDE AWAKE, WITH
SHARPLY MODELED FEATURES, A STRONGLY ROUNDED
BODY AND ONLY ONE EVANESCENT FOOT.

I am not without motive in provoking a quarrel with the notorious
Synthesis of the Arts. I do not merely condemn it for its lack of tradition,
its *nouveau riche* smugness. What makes its case much worse is the fact
that the application of its theories has inflicted a terrible blow upon music
itself. In every period of spiritual anarchy wherein man, having lost his feeling
and taste for ontology, takes fright at himself and at his destiny, there always
appears one of these gnosticisms which serve as a religion for those who no
longer have a religion, just as in periods of international crises an army of
soothsayers, fakirs, and clairvoyants monopolize journalistic publicity. We
can speak of these things all the more freely in view of the fact that the
halcyon days of Wagnerism are past and that the distance which separates
us from them permits us to set matters straight again. Sound minds, moreover, never believed in the paradise of the Synthesis of the Arts and have
always recognized it enchantments at their true worth.

I have said that I never saw any necessity for music to adopt such a
dramatic system. I shall add something more: I hold that this system, far
from having raised the level of musical culture, has never ceased to under-
mine it and finally to debase it in the most paradoxical fashion. In the past
one went to the opera for the diversion offered by facile musical works. Later
on one returned to it in order to yawn at dramas in which music, arbitrarily
paralyzed by constraints foreign to its own laws, could not help tiring out
the most attentive audience in spite of the great talent displayed by Wagner.

So, from music shamelessly considered as a purely sensual delight,
we passed without transition to the murky inanities of the Art-Religion, with
its heroic hardware, its arsenal of warrior-mysticism and its vocabulary sea-
soned with an adulterated religiosity. So that as soon as music ceased to be
scorned, it was only to find itself smothered under literary flowers. It succeeded in getting a hearing from the cultured public thanks only to a misunderstanding which tended to turn drama into a hodgepodge of symbols,
and music itself into an object of philosophical speculation. That is how the
speculative spirit came to lose its course and how it came to betray music
while ostensibly trying to serve it the better.

Music based upon the opposite principles has, unfortunately, not yet
given proofs of its worth in our own period. It is curious to note that it was
a musician who proclaimed himself a Wagnerian, the Frenchman Chabrier,
who was able to maintain the sound tradition of dramatic art in those difficult times and who excelled in the French opera comique along with a few
of his compatriots, at the very height of the Wagnerian vogue. Is not this
the tradition that is continued in the sparkling group of masterpieces that
are called *Le Médecin malgré lui, La Colombe, Philémon et Baucis* of
Gounod; *Lakmé, Coppelia, Sylvia* of Léo Delibes; *Carmen* by Bizet; *Le Roi
malgré lui, L'Etoile* of Chabrier; *La Béarnaise, Veronique* of Messager—
to which has just recently been added the *Chartreuse de Parme* by the young
Henri Sauguet?

CAREY PRESS

Think how subtle and clinging the poison of the music drama was to have insinuated itself even into the veins of the colossus Verdi.

How can we help regretting that this master of the traditional opera, at the end of a long life studded with so many authentic masterpieces, climaxed his career with *Falstaff* which, if it is not Wagner's best work, is not Verdi's best opera either?

I know that I am going counter to the general opinion that sees Verdi's best work in the deterioration of the genius that gave us *Rigoletto, Il Trovatore, Aïda,* and La Traviata. I know I am defending precisely what the elite of the recent past belittled in the works of this great composer. I regret having to say so; but I maintain that there is more substance and true invention in the aria *La donna è mobile,* for example, in which this elite saw nothing but deplorable facility, than in the rhetoric and vociferations of the *Ring.*

Whether we admit it or not, the Wagnerian drama reveals continual bombast. Its brilliant improvisations inflate the symphony beyond all proportion and give it less real substance than the invention, at once modest and aristocratic, that blossoms forth on every page of Verdi.

At the beginning of my course I gave notice that I would continually come back to the necessity for order and discipline; and here I must weary you again by returning to the same theme.

Richard Wagner's music is more improvised than constructed, in the specific musical sense. Arias, ensembles, and their reciprocal relationships in the structure of an opera confer upon the whole work a coherence that is merely the external and visible manifestation of an internal and profound order.

The antagonism of Wagner and Verdi very neatly illustrates my thoughts on this subject.

While Verdi was being relegated to the organgrinder's repertory, it was fashionable to hail in Wagner the typical revolutionary. Nothing is more significant than this relegation of order to the muse of the street corners at the moment when one found sublimity in the cult of disorder.

Wagner's work corresponds to a tendencey that is not, properly speaking, a disorder, but one which tries to compensate for a lack of order. The principle of the endless melody perfectly illustrates this tendency. It is the perpetual becoming of a music that never had any reason for starting, any more than it has any reason for ending. Endless melody thus appears as an insult to the dignity and to the very function of melody which, as we have said, is the musical intonation of a cadenced phrase. Under the influence of Wagner the laws that secure the life of song found themselves violated, and music lost its melodic smile. Perhaps his method of doing things answered a need; but this need was not compatible with the possibilites of musical art, for musical art is limited in its experssion in a measure corresponding exactly to the limitations of the organ that perceives it. A mode of composition that does not assign itself limits becomes pure fantasy. The effects it produces may accidentally amuse but are not capable of being repeated, for it can be repeated only to its detriment.

Let us understand each other in regard to this word fantasy. We are not using the word in the sense in which it is connected with a definite musical form, but in the acceptation which presupposes an abandonment of one's self to the caprices of imagination. And this presupposes that the composer's will is voluntarily paralyzed. For imagination is not only the mother of caprice but the servant and handmaiden of the creative will as well.

The creator's function is to sift the elements he receives from her, for human activity must impose limits upon itself. The more art is controlled, limited, worked over, the more it is free.

As for myself, I experience a sort of terror when, at the moment of setting to work and finding myself before the infinitude of possibilities that present themselves, I have the feeling that everything is permissible to me. If everything is permissible to me, the best and the worst; if nothing offers me any resistance, then any effort is inconceivable, and I cannot use anything as a basis, and consequently every undertaking becomes futile.

Will I then have to lose myself in this abyss of freedom? To what shall I cling in order to escape the dizziness that seizes me before the virtuality of this infinitude? However, I shall not succumb. I shall overcome my terror and shall be reassured by the thought that I have the seven notes of the scale and its chromatic intervals at my disposal, that strong and weak accents are within my reach, and that in all of these I possess solid and concrete elements which offer me a field of experience just as vast as the upsetting and dizzy infinitude that had just frightened me. It is into this field that I shall sink my roots, fully convinced that combinations which have at their disposal twelve sounds in each octave and all possible rhythmic varieties promise me riches that all the activity of human genius will never exhaust.

What delivers me from the anguish into which an unrestricted freedom plunges me is the fact that I am always able to turn immediately to the concrete things that are here in question. I have no use for a theoretic freedom. Let me have something finite, definite—matter that can lend itself to my operation only insofar as it is commensurate with my possibilities. And such matter presents itself to me together with its limitations. I must in turn impose mine upon it. So here we are, whether we like it or not, in the realm of necessity. And yet which of us has ever heard talk of art as other than a realm of freedom? This sort of heresy is uniformly widespread beacuse it is imagined that art is outside the bounds of ordinary activity. Well, in art as in everything else, one can build only upon a resisting foundation: whatever constantly gives way to pressure, constantly renders movement impossible.

My freedom thus consists in my moving about within the narrow frame that I have assigned myself for each one of my undertakings.

I shall go even further: my freedom will be so much the greater and more meaningful the more narrowly I limit my field of action and the more I surround myself with obstacles. Whatever diminshes constraint, diminishes strength. The more constraints one imposes, the more one frees one's self of the chains that shackle the spirit.

To the voice that commands me to create I first respond with fright; then I reassure myself by taking up as weapons those things participating in creation but as yet outside of it; and the arbitrariness of the constraint serves only to obtain precision of execution.

From all this we shall conclude the necessity of dogmatizing on pain of missing our goal. If these words annoy us and seem harsh, we can abstain from pronouncing them. For all that, they nonetheless contain the secret of salvation: "It is evident," writes Baudelaire, "that rhetorics and prosodies are not arbitrarily invented tyrannies, but a collection of rules demanded by the very organization of the spiritual being, and never have prosodies and rhetorics kept originality from fully manifesting itself. The contrary, that is to say, that they have aided the flowering of originality, would be infinitely more true."

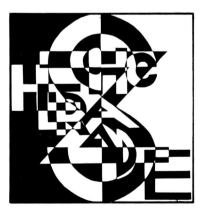

HARRIET GETTLEMAN

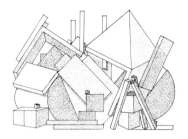
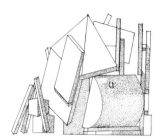
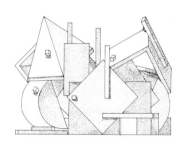
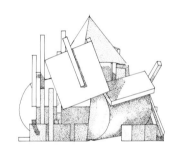
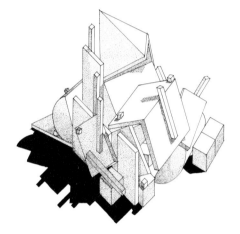
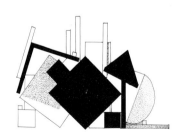

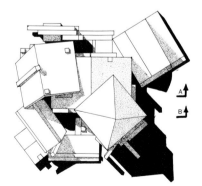

DANA ANDRYSIAK

DANA ANDRYSIAK

# 6 Timepiece

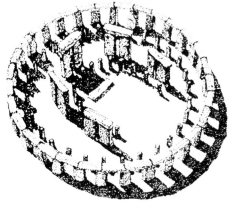

## THINKING

Before Stonehenge, ten thousand years ago, our ancestors hunted beasts to survive. Facing the equivalent of a living jet fighter charging directly at the human heart, the hunter's vision became filled with the dynamic vitality of animal breath and spirit. The beautiful Paleolithic drawings in the caves at Altamira capture the power in such visionary imagination. The discovery of agriculture, a revolutionary development in human existence, challenged the way of the hunting cultures. Since this new method of food-gathering involved planting seeds and harvesting their fruits in a predictable cycle, timing was vital. Where and when the sun, moon, and planets crossed the horizon were clues to the coming of warm weather and the return of winter's cold. These events could be measured. When the awesome, yet magnificently precise, motions of the heavens became comprehensible, the calendar was invented. The sky turning around the axis of the world revealed meaning in existence. Teleology, the study of "ends" is also that part of philosophy concerned with meaning. Its root *teleos,* meaning complete, perfect, an end (to which one moves) also creates the word *wheel.* The imagination of spirit, breath, and nostrils was replaced by an imagination of wheels, cycles, and the rhythm of time. Thus was Stonehenge born, that still mysterious and powerful circle of massive posts and lintels on the Salisbury Plain. Stonehenge has been described by some as a very sophisticated calendar, a watch for the ancients that could tell the times of the beginning of spring, the onset of winter, the advent of eclipses. It was a timepiece on an architectural scale.

The rising midwinter sun flashes for an instant through the sarsen trilithon. The three stones in this gargantuan primordial construction, the largest of which was 22 feet long and weighed 45 tons, were carved where they met to form colossal hidden mortise-and-tenon joints. The lintels of the outer circle of sarcen stones were also fitted with tongue and groove joints connecting them. These rock chunks of our planet, turned perpendicular to their formative sedentary beds, marked space no less precisely than any rods or cubes we may form today. In addition, by framing sectors of the sky and seasons, they made light and time active elements in the architecture. One cannot understand the form of Stonehenge without including the luminous moving spheres of earth and sun in the architectonic composition.

A fundamental concern of architecture is *architectonics,* the arrangement of masses and spaces in light. So far in these studies light has been treated as an abstract point source of illumination fixed in space and time, useful for constructing shade and shadows to graphically reveal volume in drawings. But in our world, natural light is never fixed. Light and shade change as the sun appears to move through the sky during the earth's daily rotation, as the seasons change the angle of the sun's rays, as clouds cool and darken the land, even as we migrate from one latitude to another. The perception of light brings awareness of the cycles of change.

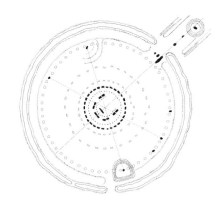

Now we have arrived at the completion of a cycle, a rhythmic interval of unison in the midst of many processes. We have gone from the dark of a new beginning to the height of a season of light. Your set of STICKS AND STONES and their geometric elaborations now fills its designated container. Your constructions can create form in space—and even time. Through such simple acts of ordering plastic elements and intervals of volume, it is possible to express ideas and meaning, ever more vividly communicating what you most deeply feel.

*Swiftly the years, beyond recall.*
*Solemn the stillness of this spring morning.*
—Anonymous Chinese poem, translated by Arthur Waley

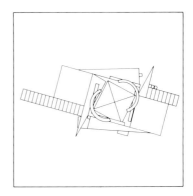

The human mind has two main scales on which to measure time. The large one takes the length of human life as its unit, so that there is nothing to be done about life, it is of an animal dignity and simplicity, and must be regarded from a peaceable and fatalistic point of view. The small one takes as its unit the conscious moment, and it is from this that you consider the neighboring space, an activity of the will, delicacies of social tone, and your personality. The scales are so far apart as almost to give the effect of defining two dimensions; they do not come into contact because what is too large to be conceived by the one is still too small to be conceived by the other. Thus, taking the units as a century and the quarter of a second, their ratio is ten to the tenth and their mean is the whole summer. The repose and self-command given by the use of the first are contrasted with the speed at which it shows the years to be passing from you, and therefore with the fear of death; the fever and multiplicity of life, as known by the use of the second, are contrasted with the calm of the external space of which it gives consciousness, with ther absolute or extra-temporal value attached to the brief moments of self-knowledge with which it is concerned, and with a sense of security in that it makes death so far off.

Both these time-scales and their contrasts are included by these two lines in a single act of apprehension, because of the words *swift* and *still*. Being contradictory as they stand, they demand to be conceived in different ways; we are enabled, therefore, to meet the open skies with an answering stability of self-knowledge; to meet the brevity of human life with an ironical sense that it is morning and springtime, that there is a whole summer before winter, a whole day before night.

I call *swift* and *still* here ambiguous, though each is meant to be referred to one particular time-scale, because between them they put two time-scales into the reader's mind in a single act of apprehension. But these scales, being both present, are in some degree used for each adjective, so that the words are ambiguous in a more direct sense; the *years* of a man's life seem *swift* even on the small scale, like the mist from the mountains which 'gathers a moment, then scatters'; the *morning* seems *still* even on the large scale, so that this moment is apocalyptic and a type of heaven.

Lacking rhyme, metre, and any overt device such as comparison, these lines are what we should normally call poetry only by virtue of their compactness; two statements are made as if they were connected, and the reader is forced to consider their relations for himself. The reason why these facts should have been selected for a poem is left for him to invent; he will invent a variety of reasons and order them in his own mind. This, I think, is the essential fact about the poetical use of language.

—William Empson, *Seven Types of Ambiguity*

In their first, heroic period, modern architects and designers were mainly concerned with arriving at 'the prototypical solution,' that impeccable conceptual model that would lead us slowly but surely from today to tomorrow.

In their quest for that conceptual ideogram that would insure the success of 'the long journey,' they neglected to consider the succession of constant and new experiences, conceptual and perceptual, that occur and recur between today and tomorrow.

Our task, therefore, is to reconcile one time scale with another. One possible approach may be to search for the meanings of the *rituals* and *ceremonies* of the twenty-four hours of the day, and to design the *artifacts* and *spaces* that give it structure.

*Italy: The New Domestic Landscape*
Edited by Emilio Ambasz

"Natural landscapes may exhibit the beauty of rhyme and contrast simply in their static structure. But to people who live in the landscape—as men live in cities—the dynamic structure, the diachronic rhymes, add a new dimension to aesthetic pleasure. They see the same landscape in a state of flux. But, through every change, the landscape retains its identity and each transformation gives them new insight into its essential character.

The dynamics of the natural landscape can be considered on at least three time scales:

1. Weather: the coming of storms, wind, rain, fog, sunshine, blue skies, silver clouds— every change in the weather gives the landscape new expression, new shades, new shapes . . .

2. Night and day: the daily cycle of the sun and the moon creates a rhythm of changing light—shadows advance and retreat, sweeping the ground like the hour-hand of a clock; the mountainside which was dark against the dawn sky catches the last rays of the evening sun . . .

3. Seasons: the cycle of summer and winter is reflected in the growth and decay of the earth's vegetation, transforming the landscape in colour and form—leaves appear on the trees, flourish, yellow and decay, cornfields ripen and are harvested . . .

The motions of weather and daylight themselves lie embedded within the motions of the seasons, giving the annual cycle an inner unity."

From "Natural Aesthetics" by Nicholas Humphrey
in Architecture for People, Holt Rinehart Winston, 1980

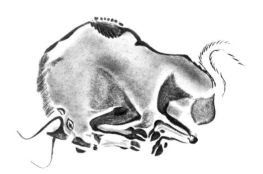

# THE MOTION OF THE EARTH AROUND THE SUN

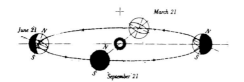

THE PATH OF THE EARTH AROUND THE SUN

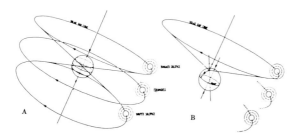

A. SOLAR RAY CONES FOR THE SOLSTICES AND THE EQUINOXES.
B. THE SOLAR RAY CONES ARE SIMILAR FOR EVERY POINT ON THE
EARTH (AFTER PLEIJEL).

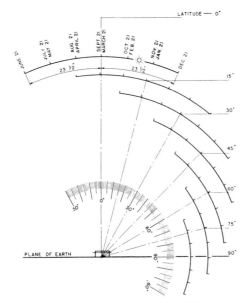

ANGLE OF THE SUNRAYS AT NOON AT DIFFERENT LATITUDES.

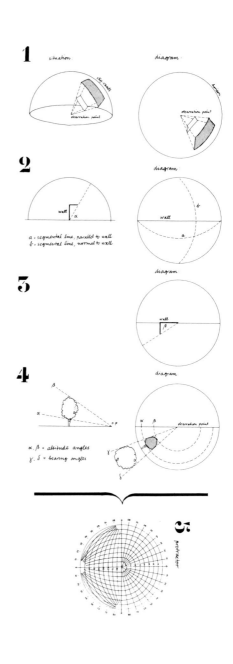

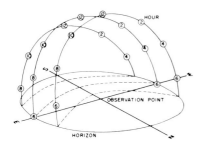

HALF SPHERE OF THE IMAGINARY SKY-VAULT WITH THE SUN-PATHS. THE PROJECTIONS OF THE SUN-PATHS ARE SHOWN IN DASHED LINES ON THE HORIZON PLANE.

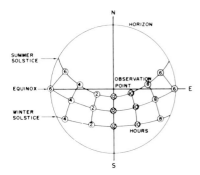

PROJECTED DIAGRAM OF THE SKY-VAULT, CALLED "SUN-PATH DIAGRAM."

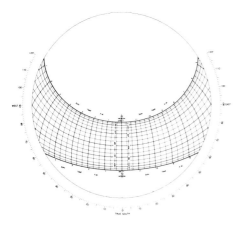

40 N. LATITUDE

## PROJECTING

The earth's rotational axis is tilted 23½° to the *ecliptic,* the plane of its almost circular orbit around the sun. When the axis is pointed toward the sun, the sun's rays are most vertical and concentrated, creating summer. Conversely, in winter, the more tangential rays cover more of the planet's surface and give less energy to each region. The moment when the sun appears to be highest overhead (most vertical) is called the *summer solstice.* It occurs around June 21 in the Northern Hemisphere, when its declination, or angular distance from the celestial equator, is +23½°. It is least overhead around December 21, at the *winter solstice,* when the declination is −23½°. Halfway between the solstices are the *vernal* and *autumnal equinoxes,* when declination is zero.

Since Copernicus we have known that the earth moves around the sun, but we still plot the sun's apparent motion across the celestial sphere to most easily visualize its changing positions in the sky during the year. The apparent daily motion of the sun around the earth's axis of rotation describes a *solar ray cone,* whose shape varies with the sun's declination. It is most acute at the solstices and a flat disc at the equinoxes. For an observer on earth, the intersection of the sky vault overhead with the solar ray cone will describe a *sun path* circle which measures the daily position of the sun on its annual migration from solstice to solstice. As the diameter of the sun is only about 1/1000 of its distance to the earth, we can assume that all solar rays reaching earth are parallel, so that the solar ray cone applies equally to every point on earth.

The sky vault and its sun paths can be geometrically projected onto a plane to make a *sun path diagram* to calculate sun angles for any position on earth. For each latitude sun path diagrams can be plotted which enable direct reading of altitude (height) and bearing (compass reading) of the sun's rays at every hour of every day of the year. These determine the angles for casting shadows in the projections described in previous Studies. See the Visual Glossary for more on this.

At the equator, the sun rises and sets during the whole year between 23½° north or south of due east and west. There are always about 12 hours of sunlight, and the noon sun is not far from overhead the year around, because the poles are on the horizon, due north and due south. At 40° North Latitude, the sun ranges between 73½° and 26½° at noon during the year; the sun paths describe longer and shorter circles on the sky vault. There are almost 15 hours of sun in the summer and only 9 hours at the winter solstice. At the Arctic Circle, 66½° North latitude, the sun's altitude is 47° at the summer solstice, when there is one full 24-hour day of sun, and 0° at the winter solstice, when the sun arrives at but never moves above the horizon. At the Poles, the sun sweeps around the compass day and night for six months, and then disappears, leaving the region in darkness for the next half year.

A sun path diagram can graphically show the position of the sun at any time and place on earth. Not only does this allow precise construction of shadow casts in projection drawings, but it also enables architects to calculate the effect of light, heat gain, and energy loss in the design of buildings. Computers models of such data now produce very sophisticated energy analyses. Yet a simple plan sketch showing north, sunrise and sunset at the solstices, and the path of prevailing winds will usually fulfill the architect's needs in developing a *parti* and overall sense of the energy and orientation needs of the design.

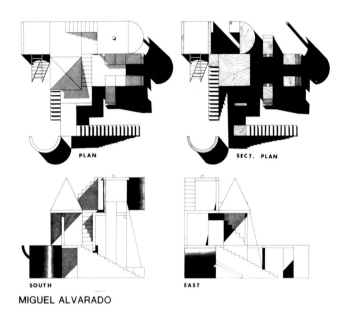

PLAN             SECT. PLAN

SOUTH             EAST

MIGUEL ALVARADO

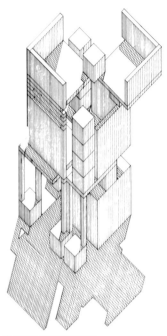

STEVEN GRINSTEAD

ADAM BIRNBAUM

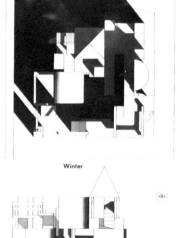

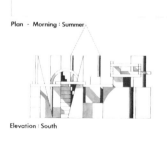

Plan - Morning : Summer           Winter

Elevation : South           East

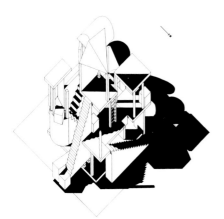

LINDA MANZ

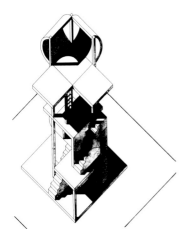

LARRY KRIZ

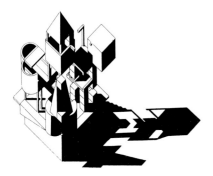

JAMES AUTY

## DOING

We live in the Space Age, and our point of view has extended beyond old horizons. Our home is a minor planet of a minor star in one of countless galaxies. The rhythmic pattern of light and shadow on earth is a function of planetary motion and orientation.

## ARCHITECTONICS

Make a place that measures the changes of time. Create a set of ordered *architectural* spaces in which people may observe, celebrate, and appreciate the cycles of time revealed by changes in the weather, night and day, the seasons, and memory. Express your feelings about the meaning and mystery of TIME through the plastic order of mass and void in light which you create.

*ELEMENTS:* Use the full STICKS AND STONES architectonic "Kit of Parts" including ramps, stairs, and ladders, as shown on page 143. In addition to these plastic elements, there are some new kinds of elements for you to manipulate.

*1. SITE:* Consider the field to be a portion of the earth composed of solid masses that can be cut at ¼", 1", or 3" intervals in each dimension (so the base can be composed of an assembly of such elements). This means that both thickness and extent of the "base" are not fixed, but should be no larger that what your scheme requires. The base is orthogonal to the cardinal points. The whole sits under the celestial dome of heaven. Up is north in all plan drawings.

*2. LIGHT:* The sun rises in the east, shines in the south, and sets in the west. The stars are brightest on the darkest nights. At 40 degrees North latitude the sun is 73½ degrees high at noon on June 21 and 26½ degrees low at noon on December 21. The sun rises and sets north of east in summer and south of west in winter. The atmosphere acts like a prism to bend sunlight into the full spectrum of visible color.

*3. SCALE:* The human body is roughly from 5 to 6 feet tall, and eyes are approximately 5'-6" off the ground. For this project assume that all the pieces in your kit are interchangeable architectural model parts at the same scale, which is 3" = 8'-0"; or 1" = 32"; or 1:32.

*4. MOVEMENT:* The dance of life through space includes places of arrival, passage, and repose (stillness). Vertical circulation is facilitated by using ramps, stairs, and ladders. The span of normal adult walking gait is from 2 to 3 feet. People can walk a mile in about 15 to 20 minutes.

*5. STRUCTURE:* Glue is your mortar. Sturdiness at model scale is a sufficient test of safety. All pieces must be used within the site of the white base and the contrasting field.

*6. INFORMATION:* The arrangement of symbols in a reference frame, which isolates form from context, can carry meaning in a compressed form. This is how language, television, and town squares work. Creating a meaningful sequence of elements, which can be perceived as one walks through a space, can stimulate the imagination powerfully, and may be considered a simple Theatre of Memory.

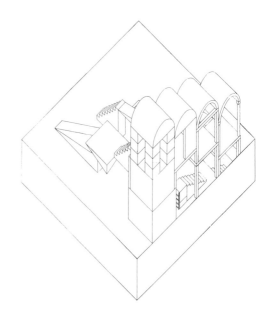

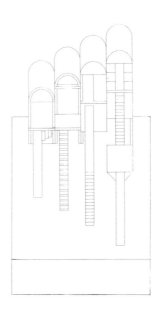

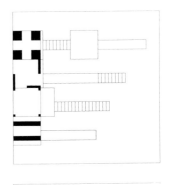

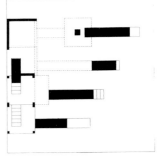

BARBRA HALLER

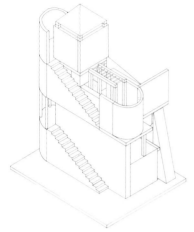

## GRAPHICS

On an 18″ square field, make an architect's calendar for the next New Year. Take advantage of everything you have learned during these Studies. Use found type, which may be cut out, retraced, and mechanically enlarged or reduced so long as all proportions of the letter forms remain constant. Work only in black and white. Organize your graphic design so that the spaces between the figures express your ideas about time, the seasons, etc. Consider the design's effect, location, use, and possible reproduction as a multiple. Are the layers of a book analogous to frames of time? Is there a single-surface equivalent to this idea?

## FREEHAND DRAWING

Working in your newprint pad, draw time changing a human figure in an interior.

## DOCUMENT

Document your TIMEPIECE as it changes through different time events. Document your design with a full set of architectural drawings including plans, sections, elevations, and axonometric and/or perspective projections as needed. Show shade and shadows as appropriate. Present all work in ink on paper. Final model to be presentation quality with rubber cement joints.

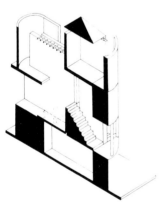

Suggestions: Note that the contrasting base presents a graphic presentation problem, since the convention used so far is that black in drawing represents a plan or sectional cut. You may wish to indicate the site some other way, for instance in outline, hatched in tones of gray, etc. As always, your full descriptive geometry drawings should maintain working drawing precision and presentation drawing clarity. These should document the spaces and forms you have created completely, and should be graphically elegant with careful placement of the figure on the page, comprising a full range of graphic weight, from crisp white to even gray to deepest black. Drawings may be 3/4 actual scale if full-scale drawings do not fit within your format. You may wish to label these drawings with clock and calendar to show time as well as space scale.

## PREPARE

Complete a portfolio of all previous projects.

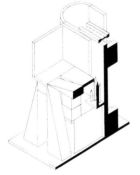

JOSEPH HUMMEL

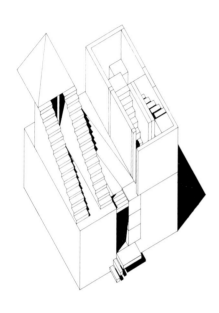

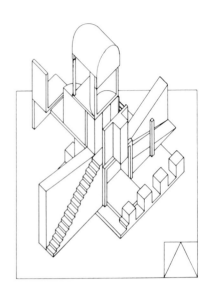

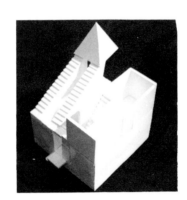

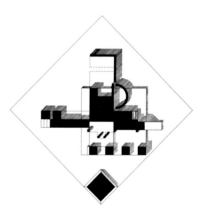

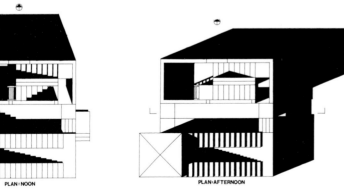

PLAN: NOON

PLAN: AFTERNOON

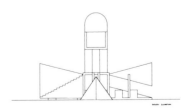

JOHN SCIARA

GEORGE GRENIER

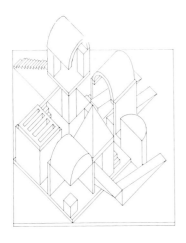

## REFLECTING

We cannot see time. We can see its effects in growth, rust, or wrinkles on a face, but the passage of an instant or a century remains invisible. Movies create the illusion of change by projecting frames of two-dimensional transparency, film, onto a luminous screen. The successive layering of still images in cinema make both time and space seem plastic. Slow motion, cutting from scene to scene, running the sequence backwards, matting, and closeups are all special effects which show how movies can play with our perceptions of both depth and duration. What then might layers of three-dimensional transparency produce?

The remarks by Empson, Ambasz, and Humphrey concerned the human consciousness of time as a basis for formulating an architectural program. The following article by Colin Rowe and Robert Slutzky considers the perception of movement through space and proposes a way of understanding how architecture may become multivalent, permitting numerous readings by an implied order of spacial intersections. If movies are a transparency of frames of time, what architecture might result from a transparency of frames of space?

## READINGS

Colin Rowe, *The Mathematics of the Ideal Villa and Other Essays*
Emilio Ambasz, *Italy the New Domestic Landscape*
John Hejduk, ''Out of Time and Into Space'' in *Mask of Medusa*
John Lobel, *Between Silence and Light*
Clark and Pause, *Precedents in Architecture*
William Poundstone, *The Recursive Universe*
Frances Yates, *The Art of Memory*
George Kubler, *The Shape of Time*

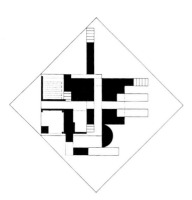

RON STALLONE

ARTHUR LOMBARDI

## TRANSPARENCY: Literal and Phenomenal
### by Colin Rowe and Robert Slutzky

'Transparency,' 'space-time,' 'simultaneity,' 'interpenetration,' 'superimposition,' 'ambivalence': in the literature of contemporary architecture these words, and others like them, are often used as synonyms. We are familiar with their use and rarely seek to analyze their application. To attempt to make efficient critical instruments of such approximate definitions is perhaps pedantic. Nevertheless, in this article pedantry will be risked in an attempt to expose the levels of meaning with which the concept of transparency has become endowed.

According to the dictionary definition, the quality, or state, of being transparent is both a material condition—that of being pervious to light and air—and the result of an intellectual imperative, of our inherent demand for that which should be easily detected, perfectly evident, and free of dissimulation. Thus the adjective transparent, by defining a purely physical significance, by functioning as a critical honorific, and in being dignified with far from disagreeable moral overtones, becomes a word which from the first is richly loaded with the possibilities of both meaning and misunderstanding.

A further level of interpretation—that of transparency as a condition to be discovered in a work of art—is admirabley defined by Gyorgy Kepes in his Language of Vision: 'If one sees two or more figures overlapping one another, and each of them claims for itself the common overlapped part, then one is confronted with a contradiction of spatial dimensions. To resolve this contradiction one must assume the presence of a new optical quality. The figures are endowed with transparency; that is they are able to interpenetrate without an optical destruction of each other. Transparency however implies more than an optical characteristic, it implies a broader spatial order. Transparency means a simultaneous perception of different spatial locations. Space not only recedes but fluctuates in a continuous activity. The position of the transparent figures has equivocal meaning as one sees each figure now as the closer now as the further one.'

By definition, the transparent ceases to be that which is perfectly clear and becomes instead that which is clearly ambiguous. Nor is this meaning an entirely esoteric one; when we read (as we so often do) of 'transparent overlapping planes,' we constantly sense that rather more than a simple physical transparency is involved.

For instance, while Moholy-Nagy in his *Vision in Motion* continually refers to 'transparent cellophane plastic,' 'transparency and moving light,' and 'Ruben's radiant transparent shadows' (2), a careful reading of the book might suggest that for him such literal transparency is often furnished with certain allegorical qualities. Some superimpositions of form, Moholy tells us, 'overcome space and time fixations. They transpose insignificant singularities into meaningful complexities. . . . The transparent quality of the superimpositions often suggest transparency of context as well, revealing unnoticed structural qualities in the object' (3). And again, in commenting on what he calls 'the manifold word agglutinations' of James Joyce, or the Joycean pun, Moholy finds that these are 'the approach to the practical task of building up a completeness from interlocked units by an ingenious transparency of relationships' (4). In other words, he seems to have felt that, by a process of distortion, recomposition, and double-entendre, a linguistic transparency—the literary equivalent of Kepes' 'interpenetration without optical destruction'—might be effected, and that whoever experiences one of these Joycean 'agglutinations' will enjoy the sensation of looking through a first plane of significance to others lying behind it.

Therefore, at the very beginning of any enquiry into transparency, a basic distinction must be established. Transparency may be an inherent quality of substance, as in a glass curtain wall; or it may be an inherent quality of organization. One can, for this reason, distinguish between a literal and a phenomenal transparency.

Our feeling for literal transparency seems to derive from two sources: from cubist painting and from what is usually designated as the machine aesthetic. Our feeling for phenomenal transparency probably derives from cubist painting alone; and a cubist canvas of around 1911 or 1912 would serve to illustrate the presence of both orders, or levels, of the transparent.

One may be skeptical of those too plausible explanations of cubism which involve the fusion of temporal and spatial factors. As Alfred Barr tells us, Apollinaire 'invoked the fourth dimension . . . in a metaphorical rather than a mathematical sense (5); and here, rather than attempt the relation of Minkowski to Picasso, it has been considered convenient to refer to somewhat less disputable sources of inspiration.

A late Cézanne such as the *Mont Sainte-Victoire* of 1904–06 (Fig 1) in the Philadelphia Museum of Art is characterized by certain extreme simplifications. There is a highly developed insistence on a frontal viewpoint of the whole scene, a suppression of the more obvious elements suggestive of depth, and a resultant contracting of foreground, middleground, and background into a distinctly compressed pictorial matrix. Sources of light are definite but various; and a further contemplation of the picture reveals a tipping forward of the objects in space, which is assisted by the painter's use of opaque and contrasted color. The center of the composition is occupied by a rather dense gridding both oblique and rectilinear; and this area, apparently, is buttressed and stabilized by a more insistent horizontal and vertical grid which introduces a certain peripheric interest.

Frontality, suppression of depth, contracting of space, definition of light sources, tipping forward of objects, restricted palette, oblique and rectilinear grids, and propensities toward peripheric development are all characteristics of analytical cubism. In these pictures, apart from the pulling to pieces and reassembly of objects, perhaps above all we are conscious of a further shrinkage of depth and an increased emphasis which is now awarded to the grid. We discover about this time a meshing together of two systems of coordinates. On the one hand, an arrangement of oblique and curved lines suggests a certain diagonal spatial recession. On the other, a series of horizontal and vertical lines implies a contradictory statement of frontality. Generally speaking, the oblique and curved lines possess a certain naturalistic significance, while the rectilinear ones show a geometrizing tendency which serves as a reassertion of the picture plane. Both systems of coordinates provide for the orientation of the figures simultaneously in an extended space an on a painted surface; while their intersection, their overlapping, their interlocking, and their building up into larger and fluctuating configurations permits the genesis of the typically ambiguous cubist motif.

As the observer distinguishes between all the resultant planes, he may become progressively conscious of an opposition between certain areas of luminous paint and others of a more dense coloration. He may distinguish between certain planes to which he is able to attribute a physical nature allied to that of celluloid, others whose essence is semiopaque, and further areas of a substance totally opposed to the transmission of light. And he may discover that all of these planes, translucent or otherwise, and regardless of their representational content, are implicated in the phenomenon which Kepes has defined as transparency.

The double nature of transparency may be illustrated by the comparison and analysis of a somewhat atypical Picasso, *The Clarinet Player*

1

2

3

4

5

(Fig 2), and a representative Braque, The *Portuguese* (Fig 3), in each of which a pyramidal form implies an image. Picasso defines his pyramid by means of a strong contour; Braque uses a more complicated inference. Thus Picasso's contour is so assertive and so independent of its background that the observer has some sense of a positively transparent figure standing in a relatively deep space, and only subsequently does he redefine this sensation to allow for the actual lack of depth. With Braque the reading of the picture follows a reverse order. A highly developed interlacing of horizontal and vertical gridding, created by gapped lines and intruding planes, establishes a primarily shallow space, and only gradually is the observer able to invest this space with a depth which permits the figure to assume substance. Braque offers the posibility of an independent reading of figure and grid: Picasso scarcly does so. Picasso's grid is rather subsumed within his figure or appears as a form of peripheral incident introduced to stabilize it.

In the first we may receive a pre-vision of literal transparency, and in the other, of phenomenal transparency; and the evidence of these two distinct attitudes will become much clearer if a comparison is attempted between the works of two slightly later painters, Robert Delaunay and Juan Gris.

Delaunay's *Simultaneous Windows* of 1911 and Gris' *Still Life* of 1912 (Figs 4, 5) both include objects that are presumably transparent, the one windows, the other bottles. While Gris suppresses the physical transparency of glass in favor of a transparency of gridding, Delaunay accepts with unrestricted enthusiasm the elusively reflective qualities of his superimposed 'glazed openings.' Gris weaves a system of oblique and perpendicular lines into some sort of corrugated shallow space; and in the architectonic tradition of Cézanne, in order to amplify both his objects and structure, he assumes varied but definite light sources. Delaunay's preoccupation with form presupposes an entirely different attitude. Forms to him—e.g. a low block of buildings and various naturalistic objects reminiscent of the Eiffel Tower—are nothing but reflections and refractions of light which he presents in terms analogous to cubist gridding. But despite this geometrizing of image, the generally ethereal nature of both Delaunay's forms and his space appears more characteristic of impressionisn, and this resemblance is further reinforced by the manner in which he uses his medium. In contrast to the flat, planar areas of opaque and almost monochromatic color which Gris invests with such high tactile value, Delaunay emphasizes a quasi-impressionistic calligraphy; and while Gris provides explicit definition of a rear plane, Delaunay dissolves the possibilities of so distinct a closure of his space. Gris' rear plane functions as a catalyst which localizes the ambiguities of his pictorial objects and engenders their fluctuating values. Delaunay's distaste for so specific a procedure leaves the latent ambiguities of his form exposed, without reference, unresolved. Both operations might be recognized as attempts to elucidate the intricacy of analytical cubism; but where Gris seems to have intensified some of the characteristics plastic principles with a new bravura, Delaunay has been led to explore the poetical overtones of cubism by divorcing them from their metrical syntax.

When something of the attitude of a Delaunay becomes fused with a machine-aesthetic emphasis upon physical substance and stiffened by a certain enthusiasm for simple planar structures, then literal transparency becomes complete; and it can perhaps be most appropriately illustrated by the work of Moholy-Nagy. In his *Abstract of an Artist* Moholy-Nagy tells us that around 1921 his 'transparent paintings', became completely freed from all elements reminiscent of nature, and to quote him directly: 'I see today that this was the logical result of the cubist paintings I had admiringly studied' (6).

Now whether a freedom from all elements reminiscent of nature may be considered a logical continuation of cubism is not relevant to this present discussion; but whether Moholy did indeed succeed in emptying his work of all naturalistic content is of some importance, and his seeming belief that cubism had pointed the way toward a freeing of forms may justify the analysis of one of his subsequent works and its comparison with another postcubist painting. Moholy's *La Sarraz* of 1930 (Fig 6) might reasonably be compared with a Fernand Léger of 1926: *The Three Faces* (Fig 7).

In *La Sarraz* five circles connected by an S-shaped band, two sets of trapezoidal planes of translucent color, a number of near horizontal and vertical bars, a liberal splattering of light and dark flecks, and a number of slightly convergent dashes are all imposed upon a black background. In *Three Faces* three major areas displaying organic forms, abstracted artifacts, and purely geometric shapes are tied together by horizontal banding and common contour. In contrast to Moholy, Léger aligns his pictorial objects at right angles to each other and to the edges of his picture plane; he provides these objects with a flat, opaque coloring; and he sets up a figure-ground reading through the compressed disposition of these highly contrasted surfaces. While Moholy seems to have flung open a window on to some private version of outer space, Léger, working within an almost two dimensional scheme, achieves a maximum clarity of both 'negative' and 'positive' forms. By means of restriction, Léger's picture becomes charged with an equivocal depth reading, with a value singularly reminiscent of that to which Moholy was so sensitive in the writings of Joyce, and which, in spite of the positive physical transparency of his paint, Moholy himself has been unable to achieve.

For in spite of its modernity of motif, Moholy's picture still shows the conventional precubist foreground, middleground, and background; and in spite of a rather casual interweaving of surface and the elements introduced to destroy the logic of this deep space, Moholy's picture can be submitted to only one reading.

On the other hand, through the refined virtuosity with which he assembles post-cubist constituents, Fernand Léger makes completely plain the multifunctioned behavior of clearly defined form. Through flat planes, through an absence of volume suggesting its presence, through the implication rather than the fact of a grid, through an interrupted checkerboard pattern stimulated by color, proximity, and discrete superimposition, Léger leads the eye to experience an inexhaustible series of larger and smaller organization within the whole. Léger's concern is with the structure of form, Moholy's with materials and light. Moholy has accepted the cubist figure but has lifted it out of its spatial matrix; Léger has preserved and even intensified the typically cubist tension between figure and space.

These three comparisons may clarify some of the basic differences between literal and phenomenal transparency in the painting of the last fifty years. Literal transparency, we notice, tends to be associated with the trompe l'oeil effect of a translucent object in a deep, naturalistic space; while phenomenal transparency seems to be found when a painter seeks the articulated presentation of frontally displayed objects in a shallow, abstracted space.

In considering architectural rather than pictorial transparencies, inevitable confusions arise; for while painting can only imply the third dimension, architecture cannot suppress it. Provided with the reality rather than the counterfeit of three dimensions, in architecture literal transparency can become a physical fact. However, phenomenal transparency will, for this reason, be more difficult to achieve; and it is indeed so difficult to discuss that generally critics have been willing to associate transparency in architecture exclusively with a transparency of materials. Thus Gyorgy Kepes, having provided an almost classical explanation of the manifestations we have noticed in Braque, Gris, and Léger, appears to consider that the architectural analogue of these must be found in the material qualities of glass and plastics, and that the equivalent of their carefully calculated composi-

tions will be discovered in the haphazard superimpositioins produced by the reflections and accidents of light playing upon a translucent or polished surface (7). And similarly, Siegfried Giedion seems to assume that the presence of an all glass wall at the Bauhaus, with 'its extensive transparent areas,' permits 'the hovering relations of planes and the kind of 'overlapping' which appears in contemporary painting': and he proceeds to reinforce this suggestion with a quotation from Alfred Barr on the characteristic 'transparency of overlapping planes' in analytical cubism (8).

In Picasso's *L'Arlesienne*, the picture that provides the visual support for these inferences, such a transparency of overlapping planes is very obviously to be found. There Picasso offers planes apparently of Celluloid, through which the observer has the sensation of looking; and in doing so, no doubt his sensations are somewhat similar to those of a hypothetical observer of the workshop wing at the Bauhaus. In each case a transparency of materials is discovered. But in the laterally constructed space of his picture, Picasso, through the compilation of larger and smaller forms, offers the limitless possibilities of alternative readings, while the glass wall at the Bauhaus, an unambiguous space, seems to be singularly free of this quality (Fig 8). Thus, for evidence of what we have designated phenomenal transparency, we shall be obliged to look elsewhere.

Le Corbusier's villa at Garches, almost contemporary with the Bauhaus, might fairly be juxtaposed with it. Superficially, the garden facade at this house (Fig 9) and the elevations of the workshop wing at the Bauhaus are not dissimilar. Both employ cantilevered floor slabs, and both display a recessed ground floor. Neither admits an interruption of the horizontal movement of the glazing, and both make a point of carrying the glazing around the corner. But now similarities cease. From here on, one might say that Le Corbusier is primarily occupied with the planar qualities of glass and Gropius with its translucent attributes. Le Corbusier, by the introduction of a wall surface almost equal in height to his glazing divisions, stiffens his glass plane and provides it with an over-all surface tension, while Gropius permits his translucent surface the appearance of hanging rather loosely from a fascia which protrudes somewhat in the fashion of a curtain box. At Garches we can enjoy the sensation that possibly the framing of the windows passes behind the wall surface: at the Bauhaus, since we are never for a moment unaware that the slab is pressing up behind the window, we are not enabled to indulge in such speculations.

At Garches the ground is conceived of as a vertical surface traversed by a horizontal range of windows; at the Bauhaus it is given the appearance of a solid wall extensively punctured by glazing. At Garches it offers an explicit indication of the frame which carries the cantilevers above; at the Bauhaus it shows somewhat stubby piers which one does not automatically connect with the idea of a skeleton structure. In this workshop wing of the Bauhaus one might say that Gropius is absorbed with the idea of establishing a plinth upon which to dispose an arrangement of horizontal planes, and that his principal concern appears to be the wish that two of these planes should be seen through a veil of glass. But glass would hardly seem to have held such fascination for Le Corbusier; and although one can obviously see through his windows, it is not precisely here that the transparency of his building is to be found.

At Garches the recessed surface of the ground floor is redefined on the roof by the two freestanding walls which terminate the terrace; and the same statement of depth is taken up in the side elevations by the glazed doors which act as conclusions to the fenestration. In these ways Le Corbusier proposes the idea that immediately behind his glazing there lies a narrow slot of space traveling parallel to it; and of course, in consequence of this, he implies a further idea—that bounding this slot of space, and behind it, there lies a plane of which the ground floor, the freestanding walls, and the inner reveals of the doors all form a part; and although this plane may

6

7

8

9

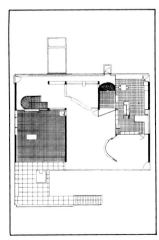

10

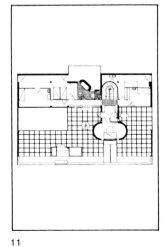

11

be dismissed as very obviously a conceptual convenience rather than a physical fact, its obtrusive presence is undeniable. Recognizing the physical plane of glass and concrete and this imaginary (though scarcely less real) plane that lies behind it, we become aware that here a transparency is effected not through the agency of a window but rather through our being made conscious of primary concepts which 'interpenetrate without optical destruction of each other.'

These two planes are not all; a third and equally distinct parallel surface is both introduced and implied. It defines the rear wall of the terrace and the penthouse, and is further reiterated by other parallel dimensions: the parapets of the garden stairs, the terrace, and the second-floor balcony. Each of these planes is incomplete in itself or perhaps even fragmentary; yet it is with these parallel planes as points of reference that the facade is organized, and the implication of all is of a vertical, layerlike stratification of the interior space of the building, a succession of laterally extended spaces traveling on behind the other.

This system of spatial stratification brings Le Corbusier's facade into the closest relationship with the Léger we have already examined. In *Three Faces* Léger conceives of his canvas as a field modeled in low relief. Of his three major panels (which overlap, dovetail, and alternatively comprise and exclude each other), two are closely implicated in an almost equivalent depth relationship, while the third constitutes a *coulisse* disclosing a location which both advances and recedes. At Garches, Le Corbusier replaces Léger's concern for the picture plane with a most highly developed regard for the frontal viewpoint (the preferred views include only the slightest deviations from parallel perspective); Leger's canvas becomes Le Corbusier's second plane; other planes are either imposed upon, or subtracted from, this basic datum. Deep space is contrived in similar *coulisse* fashion with the facade cut open and depth inserted in the ensuing slot.

One might infer that at Garches, Le Corbusier had indeed succeeded in alienating architecture from its necessary three-dimensional existence, and in order to qualify this analysis, some discussion of the building's internal space is necessary.

On first examination this space appears to be an almost flat contradiction of the facade; particularly on the principal floor, the volume revealed is almost directly opposite to that which we might have anticipated. Thus the glazing of the garden facade might have suggested the presence of a single large room behind and it might have inspired the belief that the direction of this room was parallel with that of the facade. But the internal divisions deny this statement and instead disclose a principal volume whose primary direction is at right angles to that which might have been presumed, while in both principal and subsidiary volumes the predominance of this direction is conspicuously emphasized by the flanking walls.

The spatial structure of this floor is obviously more complex than it appears at first, and ultimately it compels a revision of these initial assumptions. The nature of the cantilevered slots becomes evident; the apse of the dining room introduces a further lateral stress, while the positions of the principal staircase, the void, and the library all reaffirm the same dimension. In these ways the planes of the facade can be seen to effect a profound modification of the deep extension of space which is now seen to approach to the stratified succession of flattened spaces suggested by the external appearance.

So much might be said for a reading of the internal volumes in terms of the vertical planes; a further reading in terms of the horizontal planes, the floors, will reveal similar characteristics. Thus, after recognizing that a floor is not a wall and that plans are not paintings, we might examine these horizontal planes in very much the same manner as we have examined the facade, again selecting *Three Faces* as a point of departure. A complement of Léger's picture plane is now offered by the roofs of the penthouse and elliptical pavilion, by the summits of the freestanding walls, and by the top of the rather curious gazebo—all of which lie on the same surface. The second plane now becomes the major roof terrace and the *coulisse* space becomes the cut in this slab which leads the eye down to the terrace below. Similar parallels are very obvious in considering the organization of the principal floor. For here the vertical equivalent of deep space is introduced by the double height of the outer terrace and by the void connecting living room with entrance hall; and here, just as Leger enlarges spatial dimensions through the displacement of the inner edges of his outer panels, so Le Corbusier encroaches upon the space of his central area.

Thus throughout this house there is that contradiction of spatial dimensions which Kepes recognizes as a characteristic of transparency. There is a continuous dialectic between fact and implication. The reality of deep space is constantly opposed to the inference of shallow space; and by means of the resultant tension, reading after reading is enforced. The five layers of space which throughout each vertical dimension divide the building's volume and the four layers which cut it horizontally will all from time to time claim attention; and this gridding of space will then result in continuous fluctuations of interpretation.

These possibly cerebral refinements are scarcely so conspicuous at the Bauhaus; indeed, they are attributes of which an aesthetic of materials is apt to be impatient. In the workshop wing of the Bauhaus it is the literal transparency that Giedion has chiefly applauded, and at Garches it is the phenomenal transparency that has engaged our attention. If with some reason we have been able to relate the achievement of Le Corbusier to that of Fernand Léger, with equal justification we might notice a community of interest in the expression of Gropius and Moholy-Nagy.

Moholy was always preoccupied with the expression of glass, metal, reflecting substances, and light; and Gropius, at least in the 1920's, would seem to have been equally concerned with the idea of using materials for their intrinsic qualities. Both, it may be said without injustice, received a certain stimulus from the experiment of De Stijl and the Russian constructivists; but both were apparently unwilling to accept certain more Parisian conclusions.

For seemingly it was in Paris that the cubist 'discovery' of shallow space was most completely exploited, and it was there that the idea of the picture plane as a uniformly activated field was most entirely understood. With Picasso, Braque, Gris, Léger, and Ozenfant we are never conscious of the picture plane functioning in any passive role. Both it, as negative space, and the objects placed upon it, as positive space, are endowed with an equal capacity to stimulate. Outside the Ecole de Paris this condition is not typical, although Mondrian, a Parisian by adoption, constitutes one major exception and Klee another. But a glace at any representative work of Kandinsky, Malevich, El Lissitsky, or Van Doesburg will reveal that these painters, like Moholy, scarcely felt the necessity of providing any distinct spatial matrix for their principal objects. They are prone to adapt a simplification of the cubist image as a composition of geometrical planes, but are apt to reject the comparable cubist abstraction of space. For these reasons their pictures offer us compositions which float in an infinite, atmospheric naturalistic void, without any of the rich Parisian stratification of volume. And the Bauhaus may be accepted as their architectural equivalent.

Thus in the Bauhaus complex, although we are presented with a composition of slablike buildings whose forms suggest the possibility of a reading of space by layers, we are scarcely conscious of the presence of spatial stratification. Through the movements of the dormitory building, the administrative offices, and the workshop wing, the first floor may suggest a channeling of space in one direction. Through the countermovement of roadway, classrooms, and auditorium wing, the ground floor suggests a movement of space in the other. A preference for neither direction is stated, and the ensuing dilemma is resolved, as indeed it must be in this case, by giving priority to diagonal points of view.

Much as Van Doesburg and Moholy eschewed frontality, so did Gropius; and it is significant that, while the published photographs of Garches tend to minimize factors of diagonal recession, almost invariably the published photographs of the Bauhaus tend to play up just such factors. The importance of these diagonal views of the Bauhaus is constantly reasserted—by the translucent corner of the workshop wing and by such features as the balconies of the dormitory and the protruding slab over the entrance to the workshops, features which require for their understanding a renunciation of the principle of frontality.

The Bauhaus reveals a succession of spaces but scarcely 'a contradiction of spatial dimensions.' Relying on the diagonal viewpoint, Gropius has exteriorized the opposed movements of his space, has allowed them to flow away into infinity; and by being unwilling to attribute to either of them any significant difference of quality, he has prohibited the possibilities of a potential ambiguity. Thus only the contours of his blocks assume a layerlike character; but these layers of building scarcely act to suggest a layerlike structure of either internal or external space. Denied the possibility of penetrating a stratified space which is defined either by real planes of their imaginary projections, the observer is also denied the possibility of experiencing the conflict between a space which is explicit and another which is implied. He may enjoy the sensation of looking through a glass wall and thus perhaps be able to see the exterior and the interior of the building simultaneously; but in doing so he will be conscious of few of those equivocal sensations which derive from phenomenal transparency.

Le Corbusier's League of Nations project of 1927, like the Bauhaus, possesses heterogeneous elements and functions that lead to an extended organization, and to the appearance of a further feature which both buildings have in common: the narrow block. But here again similarities cease, for while the Bauhaus blocks pinwheel in a manner highly suggestive of constructivist compositions, in the League of Nations these same long blocks define a system of striations almost more rigid than that at Garches.

In the League of Nations project lateral extension characterizes the two principal wings of the Secretariat, qualifies the library and book-stack area, is re-emphasized by the entrance quay and the foyers of the General Assembly Building, and dominates even the auditorium itself. There, the introduction of glazing along the side walls, disturbing the normal focus of the hall upon the presidential box, introduces the same transverse direction. The contrary statement of deep space also becomes a highly assertive proposition. It is chiefly suggested by a lozenge shape whose main axis passes through the General Assembly Building and whose outline is comprised by a projection of the auditorium volume into the approach roads of the *cour d'honneur* (Fig 13). But again, as at Garches, the intimations of depth inherent in this form are consistently retracted. A cut, a displacement, and a sliding sideways occur along the line of its major axis; and as a space, it is repeatedly scored through and broken down into a series of lateral references—by trees, by circulations, by the momentum of the buildings themselves—so that finally, through a series of positive and negative implications, the whole scheme becomes a sort of monumental debate, an argument between a real and ideal space.

We will presume the Palace of the League of Nations as having been built and an observer following the axial approach to its auditorium. Necessarily, he is subjected to the polar attraction of its principal entrance. But the block of trees which intersects his vision introduces a lateral deflection of interest, so that he becomes successively aware, first, of a relation between the flanking office-building and the foreground parterre, and second, of a relation between the crosswalk and the courtyard of the Secretariat. And once within the trees, beneath the low umbrella they provide, a further tension is established: the space, which is inflected toward the auditorium, is defined by, and reads as, a projection of the book stack and library. While finally, with the trees as a volume behind him, the observer at last finds himself standing on a low terrace, confronting the entrance quay but sep-

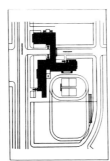

12

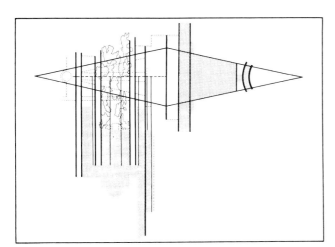

13

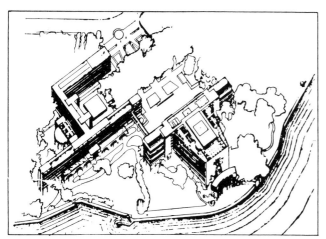

14

arated from it by a rift of space so complete that it is only by the propulsive power of the walk behind him that he can be enabled to cross it. With his arc of vision no longer restricted, he is now offered the General Assembly Building in its full extent; but since a newly revealed lack of focus compels his eye to slide along this facade, it is again irretrievably drawn sideways, to the view of the gardens and the lake beyond. And should the observer turn round from this rift between him and his obvious goal, and should he look at the trees which he has just left, the lateral sliding of the space will only become more determined, emphasized by the trees themselves and the cross alley leading into the slotted indenture alongside the book stack. If the observer is a man of moderate sophistication, and if the piercing of a screen or a volume of trees by a road might have come to suggest to him that the intrinsic function of this road is to penetrate similar volumes and screens, then by inference the terrace on which he is standing becomes not a prelude to the auditorium, as its axial relationship suggests, but a projection of the volumes and planes of the office building with which it is aligned.

These stratifications, devices by means of which space becomes constructed, substantial, and articulate, are the essence of that phenomenal transparencey which has been noticed as characteristic of the central postcubist tradition. They have never been noticed as characteristic of the Bauhaus, which obviously manifests a completely different conception of space. In the League of Nations project Le Corbusier provides the observer with a series of quite specific locations: in the Bauhaus he is without such points of reference. Although the League of Nations project is extensively glazed, such glazing, except in the auditorium, is scarcely of capital importance. At the Palace of the League of Nations, corners and angles are assertive and definite. At the Bauhaus, Giedion tells us, they are 'dematerialised.' At the Palace of the League of Nations space is crystalline; but at the Bauhaus it is glazing which gives the building a 'crystalline translucence.' At the Palace of the League of Nations glass provides a surface as definite and taut as the top of a drum; but at the Bauhaus, glass walls 'flow into one another', 'blend into each other,' 'wrap around the building,' and in other ways (acting as the absence of plane) 'contribute to that process of loosening up a building which now dominates the architectural scene' (9).

But we look in vain for 'loosening up' in the Palace of the League of Nations. It shows no evidence of any desire to obliterate sharp distinction. Le Corbusier's planes are like knives for the apportionate slicing of space. If we could attribute to space the qualities of water, then his building is like a dam by means of which space is contained, embanked, tunneled, sluiced, and finally spilled into the informal gardens alongside the lake. By contrast, the Bauhaus, insulated in a sea of amorphic outline, is like a reef gently washed by a placid tide.

The foregoing discussion has sought to clarify the spatial milieu in which phenomenal transparency becomes possible. It is not intended to suggest that phenomenal transparency (for all its cubist descent) is a necessary constituent of modern architecture, nor that its presence might be used like a piece of litmus paper for the test of architectural orthodoxy. It is intended simply to give a characterization of species and also to warn against the confusion of species.

1. Gyorgy Kepes: *Language of Vision*
2. Moholy-Nagy: *Vision in Motion,* Chicago 1947; pp 188, 194, 159, 157
3. Moholy-Nagy: *op cit* p 210
4. Moholy-Nagy: *op cit* p 350
5. Alfred Barr: Picasso: *Fifty Years of His Art*, New York 1946; p 68
6. Moholy-Nagy: *The New Vision* and *Abstract of an Artist*, New York 1947; p 75
7. Gyorgy Kepes: *op cit*
8. Siegfried Giedion: *Space, Time, and Architecture*, Cambridge, Mass 1954; p 491 and p 490
9. Siegfried Giedion: op cit p 489; and S. Giedion: *Walter Gropius*, New York 1954; pp 54–55

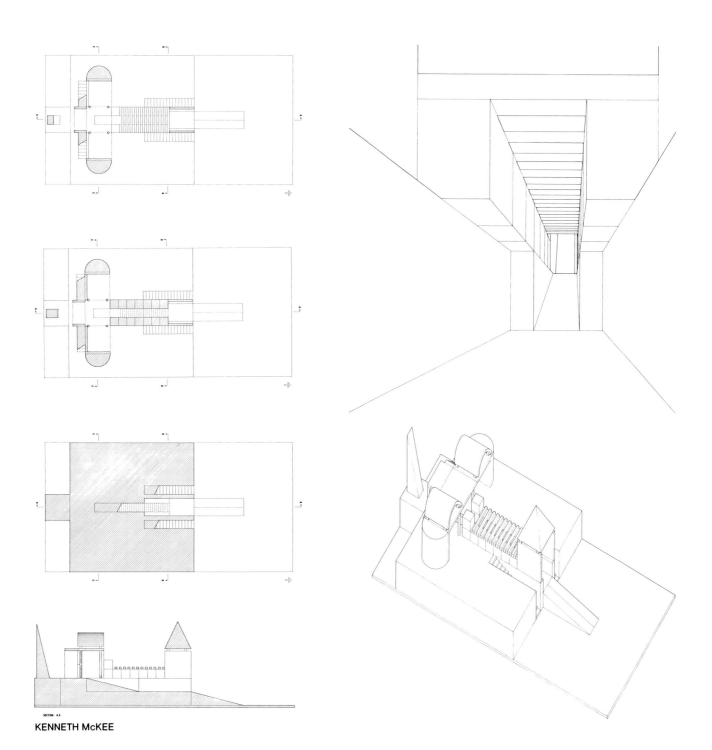

SECTION - A A

**KENNETH McKEE**

GORDON FINDLAY

## THINKING

By this time, if the progress through these *etudes* has become to some degree serious and passionate, it is likely that new branches of thought and form have sprouted with every turn and development in your plastic research experiments. When you find the free time, you may well want to pursue these openings into your own new world of creation in space. Surrounded by your instruments, insights, and new skills, you may wish to pursue your own *free exercises*, exploring the given medium to discover new avenues of investigation, new formal possibilities, new problem statements. This chapter presents some examples of spacial design projects and ideas which were suggested by implications found in the rules of the previous six studies and the medium itself, the Kit of Parts. The limitations provide the real challenge to invention and creativity. It is close to the architect's true lot and opportunity, found in actual practice— to achieve what Le Corbusier called the ability to "dance in one's fetters."

Of course, these expansions of design "fundamentals" turn out to be not simple at all. Each project in this book could become the basis for a graduate thesis or a lifetime of creative research. The impact of simple forms can be extremely powerful and vivid, and the implications found in simple shapes and elementary combinations can be complex indeed. In fact, many designers labor for a lifetime to reduce their aesthetic sensibilities and the work they make to communicate them to the barest essentials. Picasso has said, "I have spent my entire life learning to become a child again." When one compares the early and late works of such artists and architects as Rembrandt, Cézanne, Wright, Mondrian, Mies van der Rohe, Picasso, Jackson Pollock, and Henry Moore, one is often struck by how much more powerful the later and seemingly simpler work actually is.

Alexander Calder was perhaps the most prolific sculptor of the 20th Century. He was ring master of his own working model circus, transformer of coffee cans into children's toys, jewelry designer, and jet plane decorator, creator of delightful three-dimensional line drawings in wire, an early explorer of assemblage, and above all the inventor of the mobile, the embodiment of the radical idea that scupture could actually move. The photograph of Alexander Calder in his studio, late in life, surrounded by the chaos and junk from which he made such simple beauty and elegant forms, can be seen as a graphic description of the plastic creator's condition—working hands and sensitive eyes funneling the impulses of a mind filled with potential forms, shapes, projects, possibilities into unique, specific works.

If the mind is a room of possible resources, then the studio is the space in which to map the capacity of the mind. A studio is a place of study through work which creates a critical mass of form that reveals one's deepest concerns. The elaborations and interpretations of this particular sequence of *etudes* shown on the following pages suggest that just as the heart never stops beating the mind never stops planning. To complete a cycle of study, the mind seeks a means to rest without sleeping. To gain refreshment through the very activities that may exhaust, the lungs breathe in new air and we become inspired (from "*spirit in*"). We reconsider our progress and arrival, and perhaps in reverse order, reflect, project, do, and possibly even think, which is to say invent. At some magical moment one project will inspire the next. Then form follows form and idea suggests idea. . . .

"CALDER MOBILE, THE SEAL"

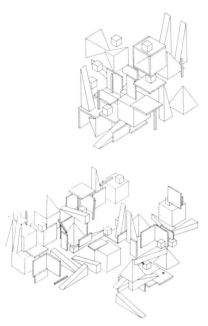

ALEC MARTUGE

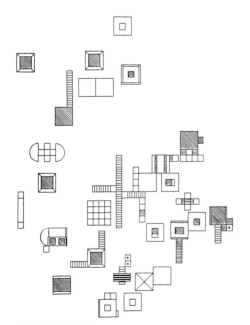

THOMAS MILLER

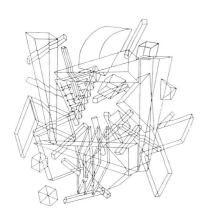

JAMES AINORIS

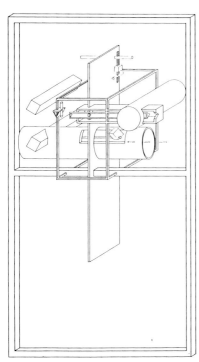

STEVE ZUKAITIS

## PROJECTING

The chaos of Calder's studio work space is a poignant, exhilharating inspiration. Some architectonic designers seek to cultivate a nostalgic recollection of this visionary sensibility in the kind of spacial orders they create. At least in part, these come from the desire to celebrate the re-opening of the libidinal faucet and the resulting concatenation of endless combinations and permutations. So many adults have lost the capacity to invent for the sheer joy of making, without second-guessing, that such a rediscovery of the infant's power to fabricate can be an important liberating experience in the progress toward full recovery of the mature capacity to create in space.

The elaboration of shapes beyond all known boundaries or necessity, based on the promises of chaos and confusion, can be invigorating in its energy. When executed in the medium of architectonics, the results can be elusive in projection, and sometimes downright impossible to build in three dimensions. Drawings of such projects can be full of spacial contradictions. The works illustrated here, done in Ron Petersen's class, present some of the robust outward extension and cryptic internal enigma to be found in explorations of these kinds.

Since architecture is such a demanding pursuit, there is a value in its practice known as "economy of means." Just as we expect to find beauty in a simple rather than an ornate bridge, where the purity of its lines are developed according to the implacable rules of engineering calculations, so too do many architects seek to communicate their plastic ideas through no more order or development than is absolutely required. There is a delicate balance between "too many notes, my dear Mozart," as Frederick the Great was suppposed to have said, and "Less is more", the famous dictum of the architect Ludwig Mies van der Rohe. But the balance is no more delicate than the performance of the the acrobat. Architecture is not easy! Its difficulty is what makes true architecture all too rare.

Jacob Bronowski has said, in the *Ascent of Man,*

"A dove experiences a hormone explosion . . . then she builds a perfect nest. . . . You couldn't get a human being to build anything, unless a child has learned with a set of bricks. That's the beginning of the Parthenon, of the Taj Mahal, of the Pentagon."

The children on page *xiv* of this book are arranging blocks not simply to fabricate complexity, but for a higher and subtler purpose. They seek to create spacial order, not spacial clutter, so as to express their needs and desires for living in an environment which fits them, both physically and mentally.

Forms which mirror Calder's clutter can remain provocative clutter to the eye and in the mind. Many architects today, having tired of the reductionist tendencies they find in too many contemporary works around them, are inspired by the possibilities of such spacial meta-complexity. Yet Calder himself made very pure forms of simple clean lines and curves. How different the profile of Calder's seal is from the photograph of Calder's studio!!

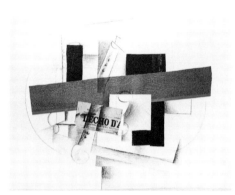

BRAQUE. *CLARINET*. (1913) PASTED PAPERS, CHARCOAL, CHALK, AND OIL ON CANVAS, 37½ × 47⅜". COLLECTION, THE MUSEUM OF MODERN ART, NEW YORK. NELSON A. ROCKEFELLER BEQUEST.

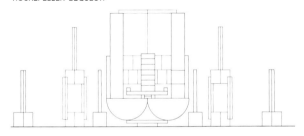

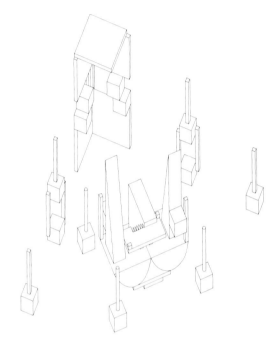

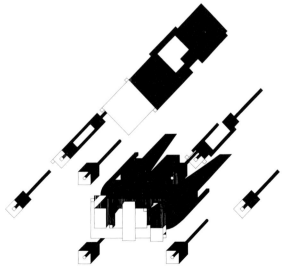

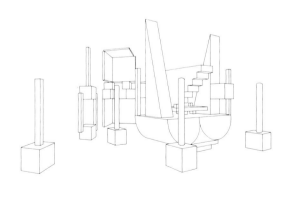

MANUEL ANDRADE

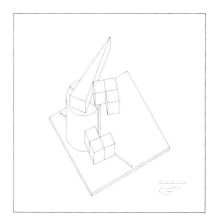

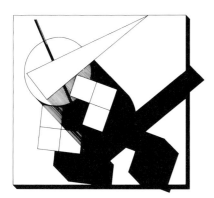

BILL MEANS

MOHOLY-NAGY. *YELLOW CIRCLE.* (1921) OIL ON
CANVAS, 18″ × 15¼″.

While some used the "Kit of Parts" to reflect and reveal the provocative clutter in the mind that inevitably precedes any plastic creation, others have used the "Kit of Parts" to explore artists' propositions of formal order in a more analytic re-creative manner. The works on this page encourage a more selective sensibility: one which not only generates but also evaluates and eliminates to *refine* a spacial idea. Although they refer to another's work at the outset, these interpretations are in fact highly original spacial creations. Many disciplines, from Chinese calligraphy to Western music, emphasize the importance of copying the works of known masters as a necessary early step, not only to understand the master's style, but also to gain mastery of the medium. Just as Picasso has reconsidered themes of Rembrandt, Velazquez, and Delacroix in some of his paintings, reworking a plastic theme in your own terms is a powerful way to discover the maturity of its philosophy and the profundity of its deepest feelings. In a sense, this is what a good builder does when reading an architect's plans. The construction is the builder's *re*-presentation of the spacial idea presented in the drawings. Re-presentation is a fundamental aspect of architecture.

The work of Victoria Meyer's students, illustrated here, is concerned with understanding the meaning and implication of the forms an artist creates, rather than the clutter surrounding the act of creation. The students sought to transform modern paintings and collages from two-dimensional propositions into the three-dimensional constructions and organizations which were implied or suggested by the painting's structure. There is, of course, no one "right answer" to any of these interpretaions, but there clearly can be wrong answers. The two models illustrated here reveal that the study of Moholy-Nagy's *Yellow Circle* responds to and parallels the order of the original far more directly than the study of Braque's paper collage *Clarinette* responds to its original, yet in no way could one be thought of as the closer interpretation of the original work.

In the Moholy-Nagy study, the clarity of the transformations is unmistakable. The circle becomes two half-cylinders separated by a thin plane; the other diagonal line becomes a ramp made into a wedge; and the sheared square in the painting becomes, by a very clever invention six small cubes whose shear in the third dimension expands the spacial implications of the painting. Here is what Bill Means, the designer of this project has to say:

"Moholy-Nagy's painting *Yellow Circle* was the basis for this investigation. After studying the painting, a three-dimensional representation was made depicting the main idea. Geometrical shapes floating freely in space, that are bisected continuously by other planes of space are a strong reading evident in the art piece. All pure shapes seem to cling to one another, but at the same time are independent. The power of the dark cutting lines illustrates that we are but viewing a small section of space and time and that its limitations are endless."

Geometric organizations in Manuel Andrade's study are based on formal interrelationships which parallel those in the original Braque collage. The rotation of elements, density of massing towards the center of the composition, volumetric intersections, and implied spacial overlappings occur in both model and the original. Yet the new three-dimensional construction also recognizes the formal properties and proportional rhythms of its own constituent elements. The result expands our understanding of both the possibilities of the Kit of Parts and the plastic implications of the artist's spacial intentions.

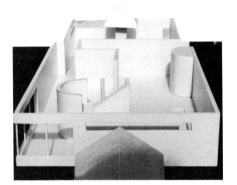

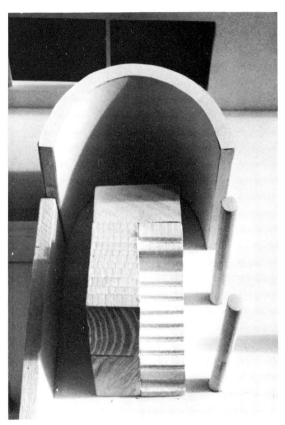

MICHAEL MESSINA

PLAN

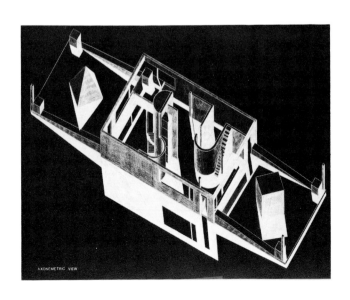

AXONEMETRIC VIEW

ERNEST STIGI

## DOING

How does one design beyond rules, from the inside out? What rules determine the success of a plastic design when no rules or precedents are given? Without external demands, internal constraints arise from the character of the project. The task is to discover the inevitable boundaries and constraints inherent in program, site, and means. Interestingly enough, when the limitations on a problem are severe, what often emerges is a stronger revelation of project objectives and properties of site and elements. Narrow constraints force confrontations between relationships. For the architect, the joy of limitations is that it can reveal the means of making space, that is, a *poetics* of space. The Kit of Parts can become a means to investigate both theoretical and actual design problems. Carl Karas has proposed two kinds of limitations: one project asked students to interpret a "loose" program on a severely restricted site; the other required solving specific program demands within a much more accommodating site.

JEFF MONGO

Shown on this page are designs for a Temple and a Labyrinth set on an extremely narrow site. These forms suggest poetic relationships. A temple is a center of sacred space, a focus of clarity and unity; whereas a labyrinth is a mystery, a maze of enclosures, a sequence that can only be understood as a sum of spacial experiences that cannot be visually unified. The narrow site amplifies the spacial and symbolic meaning of such possible relationships as temple in labyrinth, labyrinth through temple, temple above labyrinth, or labyrinth surrounded by temple. The cast plaster base permitted subtraction of masses equivalent to the solid pieces of the Kit of Parts, emphasizing the interaction between carving and assemblage. Section virtually becomes elevation. The space becomes both journey and arrival. Since the pieces nearly fill the width of the site, each form strongly affects its immediate region. Thus the stacked volumes and columns in Greg La Duca's project creates a dense and potent vertical space. This narrow world is a microcosm in which every space affects every other space in the realm. As in trains, planes, mobile homes, and other extrusions, which emphasize sequence along a major axis, the moves across and above or below, rather than along the line, are magnified in importance. (Although both roughly occupy the same volume, how different in detail is a locomotive from a caboose!)

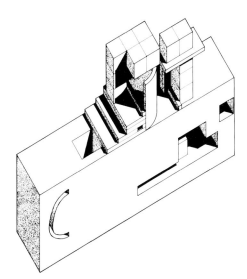

JOHN CILLA

It is but a short step from exploring a difficult site to designing "real space." The works on the facing page, illustrate Carl Karas' second project, which required the renovation of an existing cafeteria, using the elements of the Kit of Parts to articulate spacial organization. Existing structure, connection to exterior space, and transition from upper level parking to lower level classrooms were problems to be considered. Powerful architectural events emerge from the simple juxtaposition of stair, wall, and column. In Michael Messina's proposal, the stair, flanked by free-standing columns, terminates in a semi-circular niche to create an entry that is graceful, dramatic, and elegant in its simplicity of elements. Equally strong in its plastic effect is Ernest Stigi's study and use of these elements in a different configuration, in which the stair creates a smooth passage between levels by moving outside and around the curved wall of the apse.

These projects combine the instinctive generation of free form with the refinement of ideas through limited means. The Dionysian labyrinth of the uncontrolled, wild, unconscious human psyche needs the Apollonian temple of clear logic to attain its full measure of expressive capability. More than either of the two previous projects, this approach unifies both concerns.

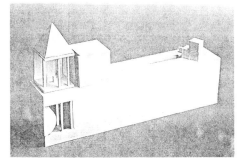

GREG LA DUCA

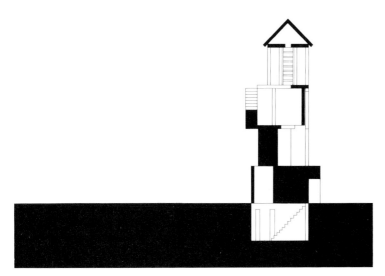

R. MORRISEY

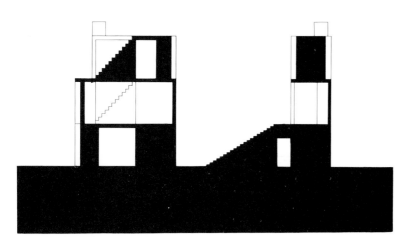

C. FELIX

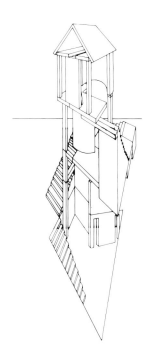

Some people have used the simple plastic elements of the Kit of Parts to open whole realms of deep emotional and philosophical speculation. Below are excerpts from two project statements, in which Michele Bertomen asked her class to explore two essential architectural events, the tower and the wall. The Kit of Parts is a medium of strong constraints but great freedom.

## TOWER

*". . . all building shares the daring sin of hubris or encroachment, committed by the sons of Adam when they built the Tower of Babel, 'whose top may reach unto heaven.' It represents the intrusion of the realm of matter into that of empty space, the raising of the basis of human action beyond the safety of common ground." Rudolf Arnheim,* The Dynamics of Architectural Form

Construct a tower at ¼" = 1'-0" scale on a 18" × 18" × 5" base. Use only the elements from the Kit of Parts, which can also appear (in negative form) in the base. The rich history of images associated with the idea of tower is matched by its specific formal presence. A tower presents a strong vertical against our ordinarily horizontal movement; its base and crest interact with ground and sky, while the connecting shaft mediates between them. The investigation is structured by the lightweight Kit of Parts and by the form of the base. Geometric properties of the predetermined forms are emphasized over their material necessities.

## W A L L

*"We find that artificial composition not only does not limit the spiritual but actually leads to it . . . the form is like a baited trap, to which the spiritual process responds spontaneously and against which it struggles." Jerzy Grotowski,* Towards a Poor Theater

In an extreme sense, the material products of our design explorations mirror our own physicality. The issues we explore with a Kit of Parts are paradigmatic of the issues we encounter in attempting to verify our corporeal existence. The materials from which we fabricate these products contain references to our scale within their form: the scale of our fingers, arms, and bodies. The complexity with which we fabricate refers implicitly to our own mental constructs; to the limits and nature of our ability to order our world. The idea of *datum,* or surface from which one proposes intrusion or extrusion, ascent or descent, and horizontal or vertical movement allows us to refer in the object to states of daily existence. Finally, with the making of an object, which then confronts us with a scale and presence alien to our own, but still of our own, comes self-knowledge.

Students were asked to design a portion of a wall from their Kit of Parts. Each student's portion of the wall could meander within a 12" square base but had to imply closure or at least mediation with adjacent portions. A scale of ¼" = 1'-0" was assumed. At issue were the character of each side of the wall, the passage from one side to the other, the journey along the wall, the experience of the dimension of the wall (its thickness, depth, and height), the integrity and the ability of each proposal to respond to its neighbor. When the wall was first assembled, it was observed that most projects could be identified as discrete proposals able to respond spatially to their neighbors, yet the project as a whole was not unified. The wall did not look like a wall but like a city.

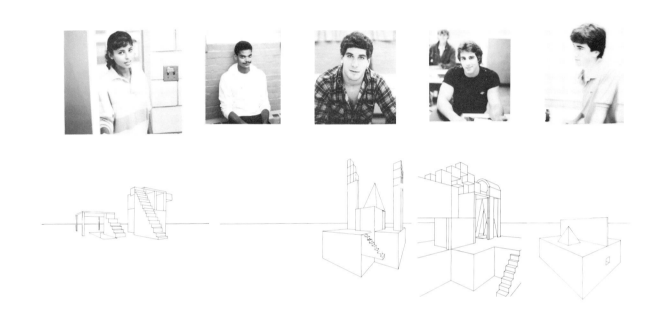

JAMES SHAUGHNESSY    MICHELINE GUIRGUIS    NESTOR ROBLES    PAUL LICATA    GLEN CRANDALL    PETE McEVOY

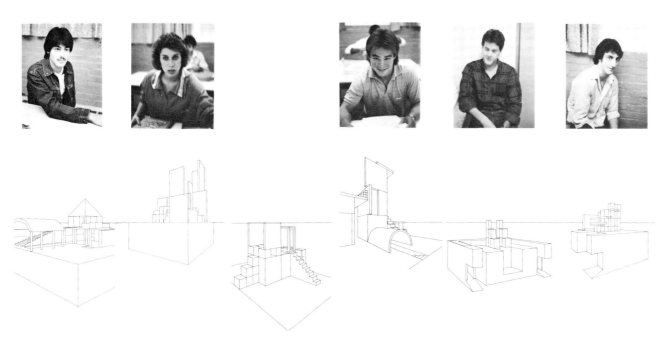

ALDO D'ADAMO    ELENA KRAVCHENCKO  LAWRENCE CARROLL JOSEPH DONNAN    JAMES COSTIGAN    DAVID NADOLNE

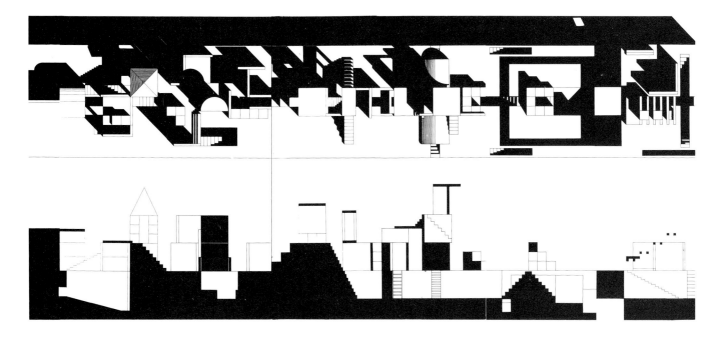

# REFLECTING

*"Through the placement of the stairs, half circles, vaults, and the overall positioning of the tower on the base, the ideas of rotation and spiral are demonstrated. These ideas start underneath the datum plane and continue up and around through the four levels of the tower until the very top. Each of the tower's levels are separate and have their own, individual open spaces to explore. All of the levels, however are tied together by one major space. As you experience the tower, you are constantly being directed inwards until finally, at the top, you are inside a very private and enclosed space."* Robert Morrisey, on the tower shown on page 130.

The top space of Robert Morrisey's tower does indeed create a sense of enclosure by presenting only certain views of the horizon, framing some while obscuring others. Yet this very spacial concentration also heightens a sense of outward expansion. The drawings indicate that the spiraling path to this pinnacle engages all 360 degrees of the surrounding field.

Any search for vision is a struggle, demanding real work to climb against the tug of gravity. A tower is a place for both seeing and being seen. Attaining height, placing distance between oneself and the commonplace of ordinary expectations gives the reward of being able to see clearly, to contemplate what is normally distant and hidden. However, such achievement also demands the responsibility that goes with eminence. These Studies present only the first steps in what can become a lifelong calling—to find order in the world and to reveal the human values in such order.

We began the companion readings for these *etudes* with remarks about the basic elements of plastic form and composition by the architect Le Corbusier. We conclude with another essay by him, produced some forty years later. They are the last recorded thoughts in his full and fruitful life. They are included here because they seem particularly sympathetic, and at the same time heroically inspiring, to the simple and honest, hence noble, calling of making things for human needs where none such existed before.

Being human, like humus, we are born of earth. We learn that Adam was shaped from clay by the Divine Hand. But we are not only born, we also give birth. We engender the next generation through the most human of acts. *Genius* was the Latin god presiding over birth, especially of potentially talented or otherwise remarkable people. *Genial* therefore describes someone possessed of unusual powers, dedicated to those powers, hence joyous. To practice a metier, to seek to master a realm of study, like architectonics, is to dedicate oneself to cultivating such inherent powers. We are plastic, clay, in the hands of the divine, but we are also divine when we form, reform, and transform the world with the best of our intentions, abilities, imagination and vision. We are participants in the evolution of the universe. To undertake creation in space is a most difficult venture. To achieve creation in space is to unify the earth-bound human element in our nature with the lofty realm of all that is generous, genuine, and perhaps even genius.

## READINGS

Le Corbusier, *Creation is A Patient Search*
Italo Calvino, *Six Memos for the Next Millenium*
Louise B. Young *The Unfinished Universe*

## NOTHING IS TRANSMISSIBLE BUT THOUGHT
### by Le Corbusier, from the *Complete Works*, volume 8.

*The following was written by Le Corbusier one month before his death. It is the last thing he ever wrote. It reads like an autobiographical monograph, like an intellectual testament, or like the dialogue of a man with himself in the act of summing up his life's work.*
*The following text is an excerpt.*

I am 77 years old, and my moral philosophy can be reduced to this: in life it is necessary above all to act, and by that I mean, to act in a spirit of modesty, with exactitude, with precision. The only possible atmosphere in which to carry on creative work is one in which these qualities prevail: regularity, modesty, continuity, perseverance.

I have already written somewhere that constancy is a definition of life, for constancy is natural and productive. In order to be constant, one must be modest, one must be perseverant. It is a mark of courage, of inner strength, a property of the nature of existence itself. Life comes into the world through the agency of human beings, or if you will, human beings come, are borne, by life. In this way all kinds of events come into being. Consider the surface of the waters. . . . Consider also the entire world rounded by the azure sky replete with the good that men will have achieved . . . for, after all, everything returns to the sea.

And, when you finally get down to it, the dialogue, the basic confrontation, can be formulated like this: man alone face to face with himself, the wrestling of Jacob and the angel within the human soul. There is only one judge. One's own conscience, that is, yourself. One may be a nobody or a somebody, but one can go from the repellent to the sublime. It depends on each individual, from the very beginning. One can choose the worthy direction, one can act from one's conscience, but one can also choose the opposite: interest, money. My entire life has been taken up with discoveries. It is a question of choice. One can drive wonderful Cadillacs or Jaguars, but one one can also be passionately devoted to one's work. The quest for truth is not easy. For truth is not to be found at the extremes. The truth flows between two banks, a tiny rivulet or a mighty torrent . . . and different every day. . . .

At the age of seventeen-and-a-half I built my first house. Already I had risked something against the advice of those who knew better. A shocking boldness: two corner windows. On the building site, when I started, I grasped a brick and I poised it in my hand. Its weight frightened me. I remain petrified. Well then, one brick . . . and then millions of bricks laid up one on top of the other.

The advice of those who knew better, of our functionaries? It matters little. I recall a conversation I had with Maurice Jardot around 1953. We were talking about Picasso. Picasso had asked Jardot: "it was a success, my show in Rome, wasn't it, etc.?" I replied to my friend Jardot: "If you had said, 'No, the exhibition was a flop', Picasso would have told you: 'I don't give a damn, I am right, what people think does not concern me.' "

I was 60 when I was given my first government contract, and that, no doubt, for the sake of a little laugh! Everyone was on the alert. The Spirit: a medieval period. The post-war: reconstruction, for Corbu: zero. All my buildings are due to private initiatives. A large number of excellent projects, let us admit in all modesty, were torpedoed by the bureaucrats. Once when praise was being showered on me, in order to get rid of me, I said that I had always missed the bus. This is true to the extent that my plans have not become realized, it is true to the extent that later when I shall have ascended to celestial realms, the horse-and-buggy age will go on. The gentlemen who always say No, you will ever be lying in wait, always against. The mediocrities will go on, idiocies will go on being written, said or proclaimed . . . the dams will go on being built . . . my dear colleagues . . . the authorities, the assignments, the executive committees. . . . Do you remember the jibes at the time of the *Unité d'habitation* of Marseilles, for example: "Hovels where people can bang their heads against the walls. . . ." And that psychiatrist: "A hatchery for mental disease. . . ." And again: "Against the laws of hygiene. . . ." (from the Executive Council of the Public Health Department).

At the age of 32, I was with the "Esprit Nouveau", out of fervent conviction, loyalty, temerity, but also courage, accepting all risks. At 32 I wrote *Towards an Architecture,* a clear affirmation of a vision of reality (risks included), when the roots were being put down. Youth means toughness, intransigeance, purity. Then the spring loses its tension, has lost its tension. This is man's fate. From infancy to the age of 30, what intense uproar, what schemes, what acquisitions! He never knew what was happening, the little fellow. He just went straight ahead.

In Bogota, in 1950, I had had the feeling that a page in life was being turned over: the end of a world, both immanent and imminent. There remains nothing more to know except duration in human hours, seconds or minutes of this . . . catastrophe? What delivered me? A perfectly matter-of-fact circumstance: a business trip to Bogota put into my hands within five days only a veritable harvest of facts and general findings capable of proving to me that the page is going to turn over, a great page in human history, the history of the life of men before the machine, the life that the latter has

shattered, ground up, pulverized. Example in the USA. In New York 15 million inhabitants, the horror of an affluent society without aim or reason. On Long Island, my friend Nivola, son of a mason, cultivates vegetables between blank space-determining walls. USA: the women, psychoanalysis everywhere, the act without resonance, goal. Days passed without sequel, except to get through them. People work for twenty-four hours, without forecasts of the future, without wisdom, without any plans, without meaningful stages. New York! This city is atrocious, towering up into the sky, hairy, lacking courtesy, every man for himself. Real estate is sold on a plan basis, a block at a time, by the square metre. You have the right to do whatever you like! A city of trade, where things ard sold, where everyone gets through the day! There is excavating in all directions . . . without pity, without playfulness. . . .

In Chandigarh, one evening, I said to Pierre Jeanneret: "Only those who play are serious types!" Pierre having objected to this, I replied: "The mountain climbers, the rugby players and the card players, and the gamblers, are all frauds, for they do not play. . . ."

Conformism and non-conformism. Everything that one learns in the schools, in the political clubs, at the dancing lesson, amounts to a constellation of fixed points for each individual, an unalterable design, a defensive barrier between free judgement and the free and proper use of the things given us by God Almighty, or the arrangements thereof offered by other men. Montaigne is right: "A man sitting on the most exalted throne in the world is still sitting merely on his behind." Yes, the general rule commanding life is play. There was money to serve us, then it enslaved us, and men have forgotten how to play. When a client of mine stuffs my head with such and such little requirements, I accept, yes, up to to the point where I say no, impossible!

For then the thing gets outside the rules of my game, of the game in question, the game of this given house, of this combination whose rules have emerged at the moment of creation, have developed, affirmed themselves, become commanding. Everything within the rules—that's my motto! Nothing outside the rules! If not, then I no longer have reason for existing. There we have the key to the situation. A reason for existing: to play the game. To participate, but as a human being, that is to say, within a system of order, within a pure order. But first, it is necesary to have watched, seen, observed.

Now then, one can isolate sensations, perceptions and ideas. Metaphysics is only the foam blowing over the surface of a conquest, the down-sloping side of the wave, where the muscles have ceased functioning. It is not an act, not a fact, it is an echo, a reflex. And this has a bearing on and influences particular human types: the speakers in discussions. I have been endowed with occult powers, higher mathematics, wisdom of numbers, etc.

I am a stupid ass, but one which has an eye that sees. What I mean here is the eye of an ass which is capable of sensations. I am an ass with an instinct for proportions. I am and I remain an impenitent visionary. It is beautiful when, it is beautiful. . . . But it's the Modulor! Actually I don't give a damn about the Modulor, what do you want me to do with the Modulor? And yet, again, the Modulor is always right, but you are the ones who feel nothing. The Modulor elongates the ears of the ass. But here I mean another ass from the one mentioned above.)

At the end of 1951, in Chandigarh; possible contact with the essential delights of the Hindu philosophy: fraternity between cosmos and living beings: stars, all of nature, sacred animals, birds, monkeys and cows, and in the village, the children, the adults and the still active old people, the pond and the mangroves, everything has an absolute presence and smiles; everything is miserably poor but well proportioned.

Within me, I have one consolation, I bring consolation to others, like an honest donkey that has done its work, finished its task! I know that the horizon is free and that the sun is going to rise there. . . . Consider this little story: one day, a century ago, gas was installed in all the kitchens of Paris. . . . The next morning the population "woke up alive". There were no dead bodies on every floor; there were no ambulances in the street to carry away the corpses. The firemen remained at home. What had happened? To warm up the evening soup, people had opened the gas jet, and had turned it off again until it was time for morning coffee. . . . And since then, the following admonition has been given to children: "Don't touch the gas jet!"

Far from the madding crowds in my lair (for I am a contemplative soul, I have even compared myself to an ass, out of conviction), I have for 50 years been studying the chap known as "Man" and his wife and kids. I have been inspired by one single preoccupation, imperatively so: to introduce into the home the sense of the sacred; to make the home the temple of the family. From this moment on, everything became different. A cubic centimetre of housing was worth gold, represented possible happiness. Starting with such an idea of dimensions and of ultimate purpose you can in our times fashion a temple on the scale of the family, outside the cathedrals which were built . . . in another age. You can do this because you will put a bit of yourself into it.

Now then, the 19th and the 20th centuries have instituted degrees in architecture, have defined the concept of architecture, have entrusted control to the Institute of Fine Arts, which is to keep watch over the matter. . . . Down to the defeat in 1940, France was the only country which did not require any official diploma of its builders, leaving it to free spirits to invent and to build. France had its pioneers, France, a country of inventors. . . . The first law enacted by Vichy was that covering the obligatory diploma, which the legislators had up to that time always rejected. Training was given in the schools how to create palaces for all useful purposes and not "family containers", "work containers", "leisure containers", etc., that is to say, premises. There were built the "town halls" of France, churches in various styles, railway stations like that of Orsay, where trains serving one fourth of France converge in a basement, beneath a ceiling 3.50 metres high; above, a titanic nave surpassing in size the Baths of Caracalla in Rome serves as a haunt for sparrows. There was also constructed the "Grand Palais", not far away, likewise titanic in scale, for exhibitions. What was exhibited? Objects produced by men and women. Men average 1.70 metres in height; the hall of the "Grand Palais" was 50 metres high!

For sixty-one years, the lipsticks, the benches 43 cm high, the tables 70 cm high get lost beneath august vaults! This palace was the mortal enemy of all exhibitions: pictures displayed in it were without scale, the statues ditto. For sixty-one years, it was necessary to effect costly renovations (and several times a year at that) every time an exhibition was held in order to put the objects displayed at their ease. Fortunes were spent here—millions and millions! Lifetime concessions were granted for these annual remodelings. Despite this ill-success, despite this drastic lesson administered over a period of sixty years, they did not hesitate to repeat the mistake, they did not hesitate, at the Defense Ministry, to construct the largest vaulting in the world, "which can in one span sweep the Place de la Concorde". But the Place de la Concorde is staying in Paris! The Defense Ministry is twenty kilometres away.

Beneath the dome of the Defense building there will be lipsticks, chairs 43 cm high and tables 70 cm high. "The greatest in the world"—that's what this vault was called. A magical word! But the cars and the pedestrians do not go to and fro here. They are making underground railway lines, are enlarging the Pont de Neuilly, redoing the "Avenue Triomphale" as it has been styled by the real estate agents. It (the Avenue) will lead into the Arc de Triomphe, now already choked with traffic, and go on to the Obélisque de la Concord; it will come up against the walls of the Tuileries. . . . There is already talk of running it underneath the Louvre, underneath Saint-Germain l'Auxerrois: they will fall upon the Hotel de Ville and they will pass beneath it. Never has the word "grrrrand" been employed so tragically. And that's how "modern" architecture was created in Paris. As for me, I have devoted fifty years of my life to the study of the problem of housing. I have brought the temple to the family, to the domestic hearth. I have re-established the conditions of nature in the life of man. I never could have achieved what I have without the wonderful assistance of the young people in my atelier, at 35, rue de Sevres: passion, faith, integrity. I thank them all. It will remain there, everything we have done, a useful sowing. Perhaps in years to come, they will think a little of Père Corbu, who now tells them: "We work in terms of our own conscience. . . . The human drama unfolds within this closed circle. . . ."

The monument of the Open Hand, for example, is not a political emblem, a politician's creation. It is an architect's creation; this creation is a specific case of human neutrality: whoever creates something does so by virtue of the laws of physics, chemistry, biology, ethics, aesthetics, all unified together in one single sheaf: a house, a city. The difference from politics is that the architect's equation comprises physics, chemistry, resistance of materials, the law of gravity, biology, failing which everything collapses, everything breaks, everything crumbles. It is like the airplane: either it flies or it doesn't fly, and we get our answer very soon. Well, in the man-material complex (complexity of building programmes) we realize that everything is possible and that all conflicts can be reduced. It is necessary only to be convinced of this and to study the problem, to open one's hands to all materials, techniques and ideas, to find the solution. To be content, to be happy. And not to reach for the cash. Who follows me?

This Open Hand, symbol of peace and reconciliation, is to be erected in Chandigarh. This emblem which has haunted my thoughts for many years ought to exist to bear witness that harmony is possible among men. We must cease preparing for war, the cold war should cease providing a livelihood for men. We must invent, decree the projects of peace. Money is nothing but a means. There is God and the Devil—the forces confronting us. The Devil is simply in the way: the world of 1965 is capable of living in peace. There is still time to choose, to equip ourselves rather than to arm. This emblem of the Open Hand, open to receive the wealth that has been created, to distribute it to the peoples of the world, ought to be the symbol of our age. Before joining the stars (some day), I shall be happy to see, in Chandigarh, in front of the Himalaya soaring up on the horizon, this Open Hand, which marks for Père Corbu an accomplished fact, a stage of life. I beseech you, Andre Malraux, you, my associates, you, my friends, to help me to realize this sign of the Open Hand in the skies of Chandigarh, city desired by Nehru,

the disciple of Gandhi. Just recently I had to correct the manuscript of a work written in 1911: "*Le voyage d'Orient.*" Tobito, an old-timer of the atelier, 35, rue de Sevres, had come to visit me from Venezuela at my home in the rue Nungesser. Jean Petit then came in with the text of "Le voyage d'Orient". Together we sipped *pastis* and had a long talk. I remember telling them both that the comportment of the young Charles-Edouard Jeanneret at the time of the journey to the East was the same as that of Père Corbu. Everything is a question of perseverance, of work, of courage. There are no glorious signs in the heavens. But courage is an internal force, which alone can qualify existence or not. I was glad to see Tobito again, to see that he was persevering, that he was one of the faithful band. When we all parted I said to Tobito, who was considering revisiting me the following year: "Yes, in Paris or on another planet . . .", and I said to myself: "Well, no doubt, from time to time they will have a kind thought for old Père Corbu." When I was alone once more, I recalled that admirable line from the Apocalypse: "And in the heavens all was still for a time. . . ."

Yes, nothing is transmissible except thought, the crown of our labour. This thought may or may not become a victory over fate in the hereafter and perhaps assume a different, unforeseeable dimension. To be sure, political men fashion their missiles out of any material available and aim at the weak spots in order to attract recruits: they have to reassure the weak and the undecided, the timid souls. But life can be reborn in our plans, potential life in the pastures and the flocks, in these plots of waste land, in these sprawling cities which it will be necessary to dismantle, in places where people work, the factories which must be made beautiful out of enthusiasm . . . with no thought for routines and the objections of jaded functionaries.

We must rediscover man. We must rediscover the straight line wedding the axis of fundamental laws: biology, nature, cosmos. Inflexible straight line like the horizon of the sea.

The trained man, too, inflexible like the horizon of the sea, ought to be an instrument for measuring things, capable of serving as a level, as a datum line in the midst of flux and mobility. That's his social role. This role means that he must see clearly. His disciples have installed the orthogonal in his mind. Morality: do not give a damn for worldly honours to count on oneself to act only in accord with one's own conscience. It is not by playing the hero that one can act, tackle jobs and realize projects.

All this happens within a brain, gets formulated and grows little by little in the course of a life that flits by like a vertigo, the end of which comes before we realize it.

Paris, July 1965

## APPENDIX

1. Kit of Parts: Sticks and Stones
   a. inventory
   b. diagram

2. Documentation:
   a. reprographics
   b. portfolio
   c. photography
   d. notes on design and production of this book

3. Tools and Equipment/Setting Up a Studio

4. Visual Glossary
   1. geometry of projection systems
   2. geometry of fabrication
   3. geometry of organizing principles

## STICKS AND STONES

The Kit of Parts used throughout this book is only one of many possible sets that would serve the purpose. Children's blocks, from Wright's famous "Froebel gifts" to Lego™ are truly kits of parts. The Sticks and Stones set shown here was especially designed to encourage an architectural sensibility, with dimensions carefully chosen to yield unlimited combinations of archtectonic form, reveal clear proportional relationships, and perhaps create a range of plastic emotions from bold to graceful. At the appropriate scale these elements begin to suggest places of inhabitation.

The Kit was in part inspired by the "Nine-Square Problem", developed by Robert Slutzky, Lee Hirsche, and John Hejduk at the University of Texas in the 1950's and later elaborated at The Cooper Union in New York City. Our Kit differs from the Cooper set in its emphasis on the use of rubber cement, which permits many unforeseen positions for the pieces and rapid rearrangement of any or all elements. Its deeper architectural roots include Durand's Ecole Polytechnique courses, Brunelleschi's order of arcades at San Lorenzo, and even the columns and entablature of the Parthenon.

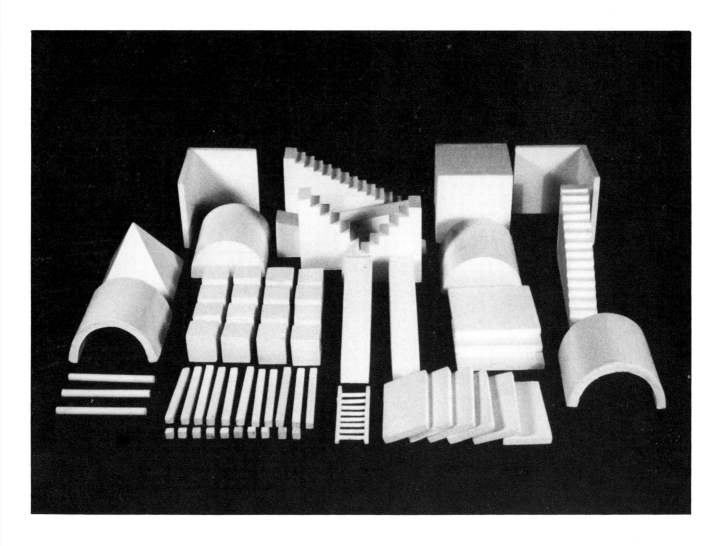

STICKS
+
STONES

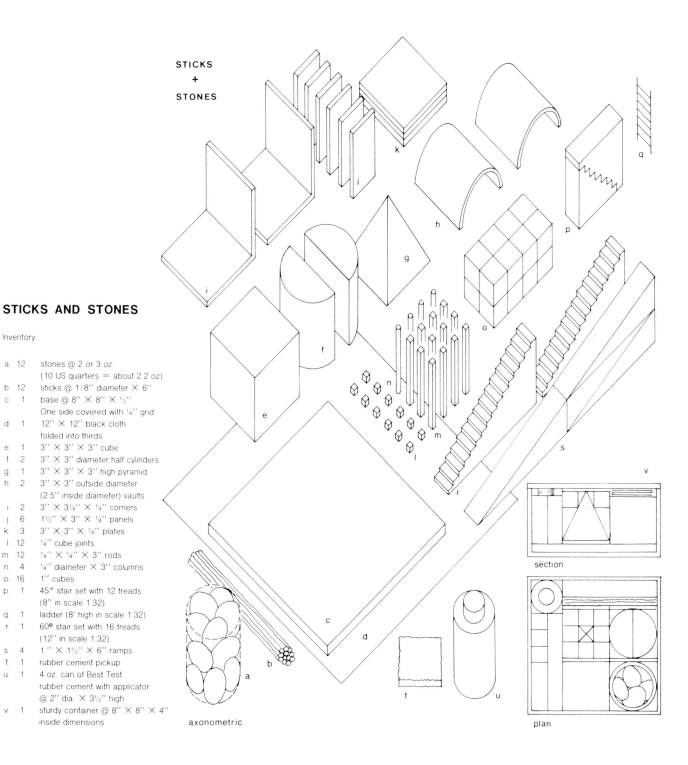

# STICKS AND STONES

Inventory:

a. 12  stones @ 2 or 3 oz.
       (10 US quarters = about 2.2 oz)
b. 12  sticks @ 1/8″ diameter × 6″
c. 1   base @ 8″ × 8″ × 1/2″.
       One side covered with 1/4″ grid
d. 1   12″ × 12″ black cloth
       folded into thirds
e. 1   3″ × 3″ × 3″ cube
f. 2   3″ × 3″ diameter half cylinders
g. 1   3″ × 3″ × 3″ high pyramid
h. 2   3″ × 3″ outside diameter
       (2.5″ inside diameter) vaults
i. 2   3″ × 3¼″ × 1/4″ corners
j. 6   1½″ × 3″ × 1/4″ panels
k. 3   3″ × 3″ × 1/4″ plates
l. 12  1/4″ cube joints
m. 12  1/4″ × 1/4″ × 3″ rods
n. 4   1/4″ diameter × 3″ columns
o. 16  1″ cubes
p. 1   45° stair set with 12 treads
       (8″ in scale 1:32)
q. 1   ladder (8′ high in scale 1:32)
r. 1   60° stair set with 16 treads
       (12″ in scale 1:32)
s. 4   1″ × 1½″ × 6″ ramps
t. 1   rubber cement pickup
u. 1   4 oz. can of Best Test
       rubber cement with applicator
       @ 2″ dia. × 3½″ high
v. 1   sturdy container @ 8″ × 8″ × 4″
       inside dimensions

axonometric

section

plan

## TOOLS AND EQUIPMENT

All you really need to design are pencil and paper to use with the instruments of eye, hand, mind, and heart. A studio expands the notebook into drawing table, good lighting, and storage. Tools help to mark space with precision: triangles and T-squares or paralllel rules control lines; compasses and templates create shapes. As in specifications:

("or equal") is implied, but until you know what you are doing, beware of cheap substitutes that make the task miserable or impossible. Optional additions are always welcome (getting new equipment is half the fun). The following list is a relatively inexpensive and complete set that has been used by many for the studies in this book.

### Making and Removing Lines
1. clutch pencil with HB, F, and 2H pencil leads
3. lead pointer and/or pocket sharpener
4. Rapidograph set of technical pens (# 00, 0, 1, 2 and ink)
5. paintbrush for ink
6. eraser (ink): white vinyl or imbibed yellow plastic
   eraser (pencil): small kneaded, pink pearl, and art-gum
7. erasing shield
8. Liquid paper white out

### Shaping Lines
9. T-square (24" + acrylic edge) or parallel rule (36" +)
10. 30–60° triangle: 10" clear
11. 45° triangle: 8" clear
12. adjustable triangle: clear 8"
13. large bow compass (and parts)
14. Universal compass adaptor for rapidograph pens
15. circle template; (ellipse template(s) optional)

### Scale Measuring
16. dividers
17. 12" architect's scale
18. 12" engineer's scale
19. graph paper for underlaying tracing paper

### Drawing Paper
20. 12" roll white tracing paper
21. 12" roll yellow tracing paper
22. 18" roll vellum
23. canson paper (optional)
24. mylar drafting film (optional)

### Sketching
25. black 5½" X 8½" sketch bk
26. 18" X 24" newsprint pad
27. 6B art pencil
28. Berol soft charcoal pencil

### Workspace—Table, Board, Chair and Light
29. work table: hollow core door on saw-horse trestles
30. drawing surface: part of work table covered with vinyl or cardboard or carrying drawing board; or drafting table
31. "Spiroll" oversize drawing protector (optional)
32. adjustable counterpoise "architect's light, vented
33. comfortable chair or stool, fixed or on casters
34. 100 aluminum ½" push pins + 4' X 8' homosote tack up wall, white
35. book shelf
36. Artbin toolbox #8399 (or fishing tackle box)
37. "Boby" rolling storage cart (optional)

### Board Maintenance
38. ¾" 60 yd. drafting tape
39. trace-clean in can or powder filled bag
40. 14" drafting brush
41. pen cleaning fluid/Fantastik/paper towels

### Model Materials
42. basswood rods: ¼" X ¼" X 24" (3)
43. birch dowels: ¼" round X 24" (1)
44. balsa or basswood as needed
45. foamcore: 20" X 30" (¼")
46. strathmore board: 23 X 29" 3-ply high surface

### Cutting and Gluing
47. self-healing cutting board, 18 x 24", green or grey
48. Stanley #99 Mat Knife
49. X-acto knife with 5 # 11 blades
50. X-acto razor saw mitre box set with 1¼" deep fine toothed saw
51. 15" cork backed metal rule
52. white Sobo or Elmers glue 4 oz.
53. rubber cement: Best Test 4 oz. can includes brush
    (refill with quart size, add quart of thinner as needed)
54. rubber cement pick up 2 X 2"
55. Magic Plus tape (3M ½" roll)
56. Fiskars 8" scissors (they come right or left handed)

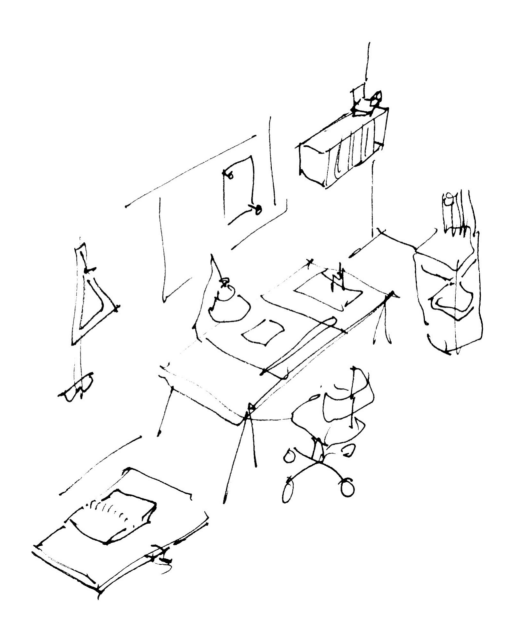

## DOCUMENTATION

*Traditional Eskimos create ephemeral art, for example carving the head of a polar bear from a small seal bone, and passing the result around to be admired by others in the igloo. The last person to enjoy the carving discards it. This makes sense for a nomadic people who must survive in a harsh environment, where extra baggage costs vital calories. Drawings and models are also ephemeral, but a portfolio preserves ideas. At this early point in your design career, it is important to preserve drawings and models (through photographs) of your projects while they are still fresh. As Frank Lloyd Wright said, for an architect "all that matters is a body of work."*

**REPROGRAPHICS:** Most shops that make prints for architects also make photostats, which are prints made from camera film images of the original drawing. Ink on paper drawings reproduce beautifully when made into photostats. Reducing the size of the original in the photocopy makes the reproduction cheaper. As a side effect, the reduction tends to minimalize mistakes and emphasize a precision of line and form which can seem at times almost magical. Xerographic reductions are also available, and will accomplish the same purpose, although usually without the same high quality of line, contrast, and fidelity of tone as a photostat.

**PORTFOLIO:** A good portfolio size for the projects just completed is a binding that can carry 8½" × 11" sheets. Multiple ring binders are better than three-hole loose-leaf ones because they allow the entire art work to be held without having to punch holes in the photostat or print. They also keep the plates flat when the pages are being turned. The East Coast architectural supply firm *Charrette* makes its own inexpensive portfolio binder with fillers that serves the purpose very well. The suggested model is the Charrette "Mult-O-Ring" Binder (Item 38–0011, manufacturers # 11B; 11" × 13" overall dimension; black color; under $20) Special fillers for photo prints or slides (of the Kit and models) are available for use with this type of binder. When the layout of images and text is done carefully, this portfolio of course work should be extremely attractive to any architect seeking accomplished beginners as prospective employees.

Save all original work. The large newsprint pad for freehand sketches becomes its own portfolio. You can make a large portable flat file to store original architectonic drawings and graphics by joining two 20" × 30" foam core boards with duct tape along an edge both inside and out to make a hinge. Fold the two boards together, insert the original drawings, and hold the boards together with large "bulldog" clips along the other edges. Store this file horizontally if possible. Store thicker mounted work in a separate plastic bag.

**PHOTOGRAPHY:** With patience and an intelligent eye, you can make photographs which beautifully document your models. Do not make the mistake of shooting outdoors, where blades of grass can seem enormous and destroy the scale of your model. Set up a simple, temporary studio to control the background, lighting, and framing of the image. Tack a cloth or roll of paper to a back wall and drape it, without creasing, underneath the model, to eliminate the line where the table meets the wall. (Blue, gray, white or black are generally best for background colors.) Cover the windows to control the light in the room. Use two light sources to be able to adjust the lighting on the model to best effect. To produce even illumination across the surface, for example when making your own photocopies of drawings, set the lights at 45° to the wall, moving them in and out along these lines to vary intensity. Use 3200° K Tungsten bulbs in photoflood reflectors with Ektachrome Tungsten ASA 160 film for the truest slide color. Use Pan-x or Tri-x film for fine grain and high resolution of detail in black and white. If possible, use a 35mm single-lens-reflex camera which permits through-the-lens viewfinding and control over exposure and shutter speed settings. A (macro-)zoom lens is handy for properly framing the image. Use close-up filters to enlarge details. Find proper exposure settings with a light meter set to the ASA film speed. Use a gray card, available at camera stores, to fool the camera into averaging light levels for the overall image. A closed shutter (near f16 rather than f2.8) gives greater depth of field so that more of the model from front to back remains in focus, but requires a long exposure of several seconds. To avoid blurred images, steady the camera on a tripod or book and use a cable release for the shutter. Make the most of each set-up by bracketing the picture, setting exposure and speed to the ideal light meter reading, then deliberately over- and under-exposing the next two shots so that at least one of the three comes out right.

**BOOK PRODUCTION:** This book was created as a collage of several kinds of material. The design study mock-ups were produced using text created on a word processor and dot-matrix printer, images were transferred from books and student work using a copying machine with image enlargement and reduction capability. Some of the author's drawings were created on a computer with automated drafting capability driving a profesional ink plotter, while others were drawn by hand with technical pens or felt tip pens on vellum or plain bond paper. The pieces were assembled over a master format page which indicated margins and heading positions, using a light table. Scotch™ Magic Plus tape and Liquid Paper™ permitted easy relocation of images and correction of drawings. The most time-consuming aspect of the whole process was the design/editing effort made to match text with images for consistent double-page layouts throughout the book.

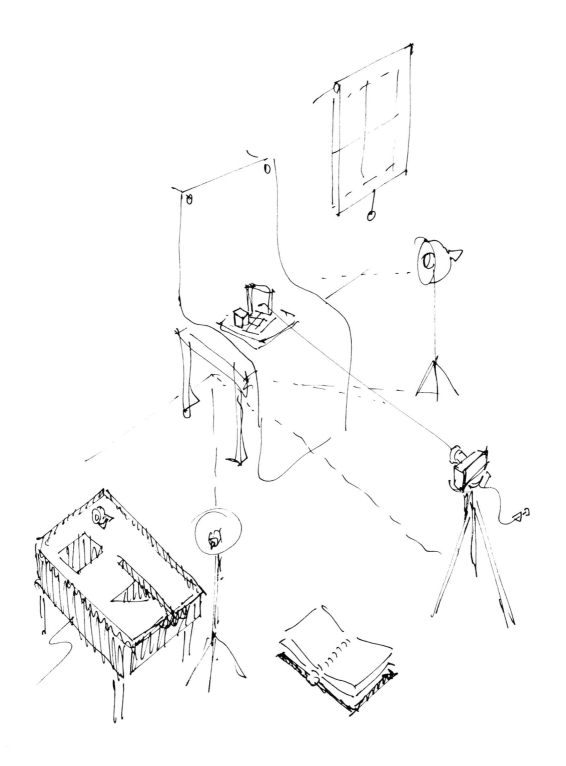

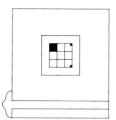

## Part 1: Geometry of Projection Systems

1. Planimetrics
2. Axonometric
3. Shade and Shadow in Planimetrics
4. Shade and Shadow in Axonometric
5. Perspective; Shade and Shadow in Perspective
6. Sun Angles

*Projection systems in descriptive geometry depict three-dimensional information in two-dimensional drawings. Each entry includes general notes followed by a step-by step description of how to make the projection, set in italics (like this paragraph). These projections may be mechanically constructed or sketched freehand to study spacial ideas. Mastering how to visualize spaces simultaneously from many views allows both drawings and model constructions to become informed means for composing directly in the medium of space.*

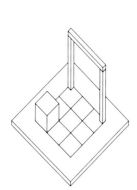

## Part 2: Geometry of Fabrication

1. Cubes and Rods
2. Stairs and Ramps
3. Pyramid, Cylinder, Vault and Platonic Solids

*Constructive geometry enables precise fabrication of model elements. Making things directly in three dimensions is a powerful stimulus to inventing solutions to complex spacial design problems.*

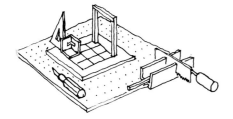

## Part 3: Geometry of Organizing Principles

1. Element and Field: Parti and Properties of the Square
2. Proportion: Ratios and Relationships
3. Contrast and Ambiguity: Figure-ground and Solid-void
4. Transformation and Hierarchy
5. Expression: Shape and Form
6. Scale: Path, Landscape, and Time

*Geometry facilitates the analysis and synthesis of form. It is the key to studying the arrangement of elements and field, proportional relationships, the play of oppositions, the manipulation of patterns, the means for expression through form, and the relationship of human to building size.*

## A Visual Glossary

Words cannot explain the essential vocabulary of architecture as well as diagrams. This glossary is a *visual* compendium of crucial terms and ideas. The entries for its three sections are arranged not alphabetically but in the order that techniques or concepts are introduced in the main text. They show how to draw, build, or analyze existing or proposed elements in space. These diagrams are simple outlines and reminders; more detailed instructions are beyond the scope of this book but can be found in many texts, some of which are indicated in the bibliography. A trained teacher in these areas is invaluable. The Kit of Parts is the model for illustrations in the Visual Glossary. The basic form for all entries is a cube and three rods on a ruled base. These simple elements are easy to draw, and the 9-square on the base represents part of the Cartesian grid which locates every point in space along three axes with (x,y,z) coordinates, where (0,0,0) is the origin. This is a common reference framework often used by architects. More complex figures with additional cubes, a cylinder, pyramid, vault, or stair are shown as illustrations when needed. The format here differs from the main body of the text. Relationships between word and image have been reversed, to facilitate quick identification and ease in associating written instructions with how-to diagrams.

**Orthogonal** *means "at right angles to each other."*
**Diagonal** *means "at 45°," but may also mean "at any angle which is not orthogonal."*
**Model** *refers to the thing in real space which is to be drawn.*

Architecture requires a profound understanding of geometry. The original sense of geometry means "earth-measure." The first geometers may have been ancient Egyptian surveyors, who re-established the bounds of each farmer's fields after Nile River floods obliterated all landmarks every spring. With simple triangulation, the surveryors could locate sticks in the mud in relation to a distant fixed point (perhaps the Great Pyramid of Gizeh!) and annually remeasure the earth and reconstruct their world through geometry. The Greek world was different. The violent landscape of Greece was rugged and folded, not at all like the horizontal flood plane of Egypt. Here geometry found a different function. The Greeks needed to describe and understand, not merely reconstruct, their world through measurement. For followers of Pythagoras and Euclid, geometry became a means of analysis, classifying spacial patterns and relationships to speculate about the content of form. Geometry, in attempting to explain and explore formal relationships, is now as philosophical as it is technical.

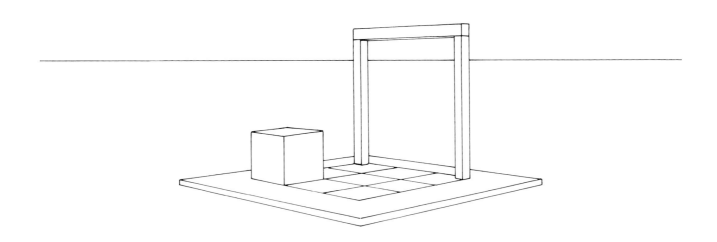

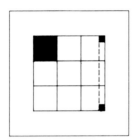

## 1. PLANIMETRICS: PLAN, SECTION, AND ELEVATION

A **PLAN** is a horizontal projection taken by passing a reference plane through elements in space parallel and near to the base or ground plane. Since gravity compels us to walk with our feet on the ground and eyes on the horizon, the plan is primary for understanding architecture.

*1. Imagine a reference plane passed through elements very close to where they meet their ground base. On a plan sheet record the intersections of elements with the reference plane, indicating where cuts are taken through solid mass by shading that part of the drawing. Use parallel rule or T-square and triangle on the drawing board to locate precisely every element in the plan. Note: when using the Kit of Parts, the gridded side of the base may help locate projected plan positions. Tracing over graph paper may facilitate drawing the plan.*

*2. Indicate the "uncut" forms below the reference plane as solid lines, and forms above as dotted lines. Note: This conforms to standard architect's conventions which differ from conventions for the orthographic projections used in mechanical drawings. For architects, hidden lines (below) are not usually shown in plan; dotted lines indicate all elements above the reference plane, marking areas where an ant could stay dry in the rain.*

*3. Develop subsequent plans by passing the imagined reference plane through the structure at higher levels. Architects often pass these planes just above each upper floor level of a building to cut through the walls and doors that define the space and circulation. Note: Once you have drawn the first plan, you have located many significant points in space. Put another piece of tracing paper on top of the first for the next level, retrace what still shows from below, and indicate the cuts taken at this new level. Use your eye to choose plan levels to show significant spacial information. Continue for each needed level until the roof or bird's eye view level is reached, where no cuts are shown.*

A **SECTION,** like a plan, is a slice through three-dimensional space. But it is taken perpendicular, not parallel, to the ground plane. To mark a reference datum, show the ground as a cut through a mass or as an edge line between empty air and solid earth. You may indicate discretely the section plane's location on plan (A-A, B-B, etc.) *but you don't always have to.*

*To draw a section, put tracing paper directly over the plan drawing(s). Then you will not have to remeasure the horizontal (X and Y) locations of each element. Rather, just project lines lightly up from the key plan locations and mark important vertical (Z) points, then "connect the dots." As in plan, show section cuts as solid.*

An **ELEVATION** is a section taken completely outside the elements that create the structure. Although for surveyors "elevation" means altitude, the architect's ELEVATION, is a particular kind of architectural drawing. Elevations show what the outside of things look like. Many people mistakenly think that architects' primary task is the composition of elevations. Many architects think their primary task is the ordering of space through plan and section.

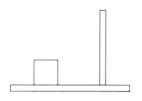

*Elevations can be made by putting tracing paper directly over the section. If you wish to communicate even more information about your spacial ideas, you may have to develop additional elevations, which can be created from the plan just like sections. In an elevation, only the ground plane outside the structure will be shown as a solid cut.*

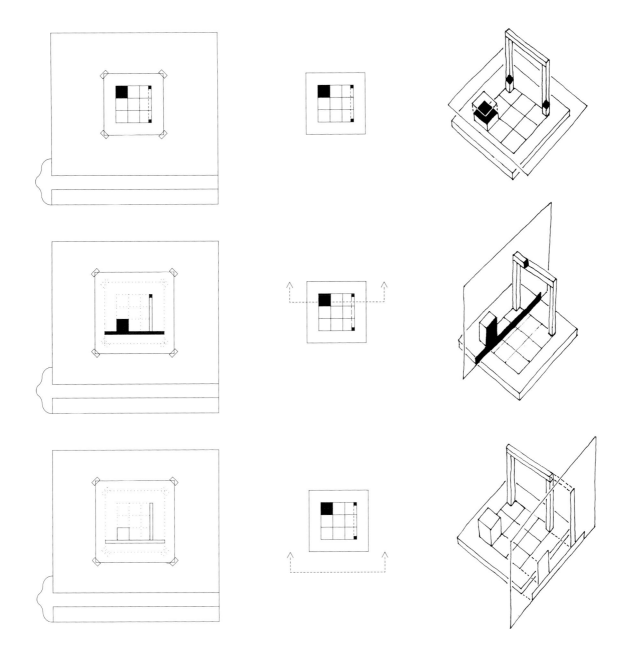

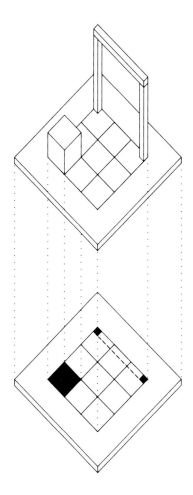

## 2. AXONOMETRIC

An **AXONOMETRIC** projection is a drawing which projects a third dimension over a two-dimensional figure to create the illusion of depth within the page. For example, verticals can be projected over a plan, showing true sizes along axes corresponding to all three dimensions of volumetric space. Oblique axonometrics keep the verticals oblique to the right angles in plan, while frontal axonometics (see the "diamond thesis" page 50) project the verticals directly over and along the orthogonals of the plan, so that both plan and elevation are true views, although at the cost of information about the section. In axonometrics, *all* spacial relationships remain true in plan, although not in elevation. Thus circles remain circles in projected plan, but become ellipses in projected elevation. Axonometrics differ from *isometric* projections, which also show true dimensions along the three spacial axes set at equal angles of 120° to each other on the page. Circles become ellipses in all three planes of an isometric projection, which simplifies drawing for engineers but makes the results generally unsuitable for architects. Architects now often prefer to draw their designs in axonometric projection because there is no distortion to size or shape in plan.

*1. Set the plan orthogonal to the drafting board leaving enough room for the projected third dimension to come.*

*2. On a tracing paper overlay, cast the verticals obliquely using a triangle at a convenient angle (30, 45, and 60 degrees are common), and measuring vertical dimensions at the same scale as plan dimensions. Be smart. Start with the base or foundation and work upward. Start the projection in the lower left so you won't have to draw what becomes obscured. Do not look through solids to see other solids. If needed, construct hidden edges to help locate things in space (but don't darken them in the final drawing.) Drawing an imagined reference volume may help locate elements in space.*

*3. When drawing elements "floating" above the ground plane, project their position on the ground, and measure the vertical distance to both the top and bottom planes of the element along the vertical projection. All lines which are parallel in the model will be parallel in the axonometric, including all true verticals. Important: all right angle corners in a plan view remain right angles in the axonometric projection!*

*4. To draw a pyramid in axonometric, find the center of the base at the intersection of the diagonals and project a vertical from it. Measure the true height directly along this vertical, and connect the apex to the visible corners with straight lines.*

*5. To draw an axonometric cylinder whose circle is in plan, project the center of the circular base to the desired height and redraw the circle with the compass located at this new center point; then extend vertical tangents to connect the two circles and define the figure.*

*6. Drawing a cylinder whose circle is in elevation requires a bit more care. First draw a circle and tangent square of the required size in plan in the axonometric. Then project a square in elevation from the edge of the plan square. Draw the quadrants and diagonals across both circles to obtain eight circle points derived from the square. These and additional points may be plotted from the plan tangent square onto the elevation tangent square. Connect the points in a smooth arc with an ellipse template or French curve.*

*7. An alternative method for oblique axonometrics is to rotate the plan to a convenient angle (30, 45, and 60 degrees are common) with respect to the orthogonals of the board.*

*8. Cast the verticals directly up on the page so that they remain true verticals to the eye.*

*9. Add elements as indicated in step 3 above.*

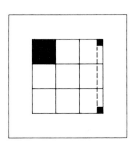

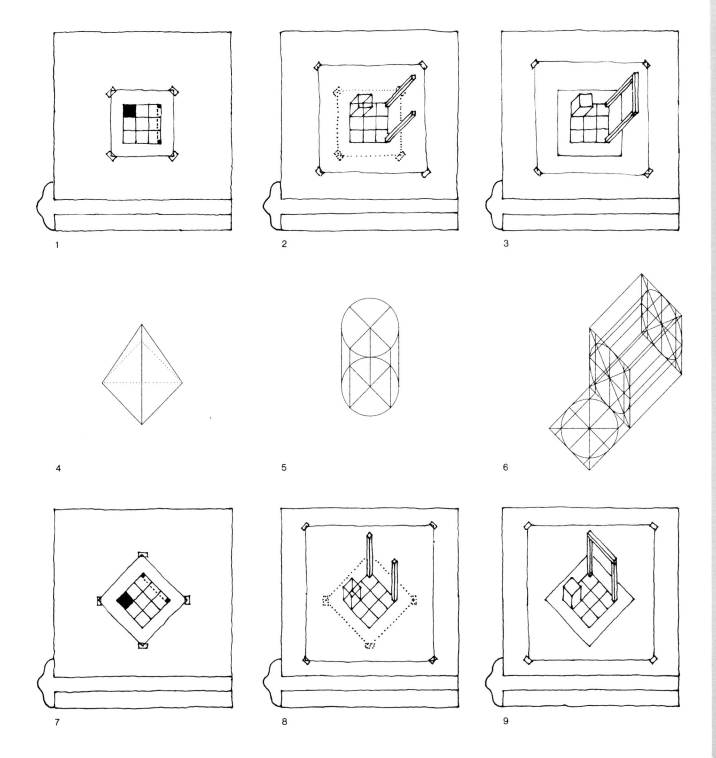

1

2

3

4

5

6

7

8

9

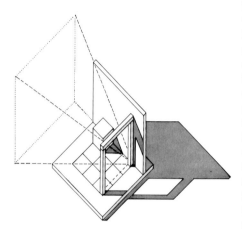

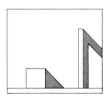

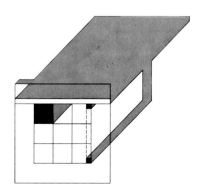

### 3. SHADE AND SHADOW IN PLAN / SECTION / ELEVATION

A space is in **SHADE** when an opaque object cuts off rays of light. When a shaded volume intersects a surface, that surface is in **SHADOW.** Thus the side of an opaque object away from the sun is in shade but not shadow. A shaded surface is lighter than a shadowed one, because it can pick up reflected light from neighboring surfaces, while a shadowed surface cannot. Shades and shadows enhance the three-dimensional sense of a drawing on a two-dimensional surface. Without them, even an axonometric projection seems flat. With them, it is easy to read parallel planes in three dimensions, to understand which masses are behind or below others, and to see how light and space are interrelated. Since the sun is so far away, its rays are virtually parallel. So we can construct shades and shadows geometrically as they would appear in space. The shape of shades and shadows can get very complex. But there is no reason to panic when drawing them. Just remember that complicated forms can be understood as the sum of many simple elements, and that the shadow projection of each simple element is easy to draw. You can set up a light to see how shadows are cast on your architectonic compostion, but this "rule of thumb" method of is not accurate because the light bulb is far closer to the object than the sun. As a result, shadows will be diffuse, fuzzy, and not parallel. Determine shade by finding which surfaces visible in the drawings are away from the sun. In general no surface on the ground will be in shade, but the underside of an overhang will. Indicate shaded surfaces lighter than the shadowed areas, but darker than those in direct sunlight. Commercial press-on films are available for this, but you can also render medium dark regions with stippling or hatching.

*1. Shown is the original plan on the drawing board, with wall added for this demonstration.*
*2. Put the elevation above the plan on the drafting board and lay a sheet of tracing paper over both. Select the* bearing, *the compass direction that the sun will come from, and draw that angle on the plan.*
*3. Select the* altitude, *the overhead direction the sunlight will come from, and draw that angle on the elevation. It makes life simple to choose these angles according to standard drawing instruments, so 45° for both altitude and bearing is common.*
*4. Now on the plan, project from all corners construction lines along the bearing angle, and on the elevation, project construction lines along the altitude angle from all the sunlit edges. Project a vertical line from where the altitude angle intersects the ground (or any horizontal plane) in elevation to the corresponding position in the plan. This will determine the extent of the shadow on the plan. (This shadow will not be seen in the elevation.)*
*5. If instead the plan shadow line intersects a vertical surface like a wall, project this intersection up to the elevation to determine the extent of the shadow on the wall.*
*6. Render all shadows on both plan and elevation. Some rules of thumb can speed completion of shadow construction: for example, parallel edges cast parallel shadows; vertical edges cast shadows along bearing lines on flat planes, etc.*
*7. When niches or multiple overhangs are not clearly indicated in plan and elevation, a section must be used as well. Casting shadows for stairways is not difficult when you understand that a set of steps is just a pile of cubes or rectanglular solids.*
*8. Casting shadows on or from curved surfaces like a cylinder, column, tube, vault, or niche require more care but can be accomplished by the same geometric construction method.*
*9. To cast shadows from or on inclined surfaces like a pyramid or a sloped roof, just remember to cast each critical point separately, using the section to plot the intersection of the angled plane with the shadow. Shown is a shadowed roof plan, from above the whole project.*

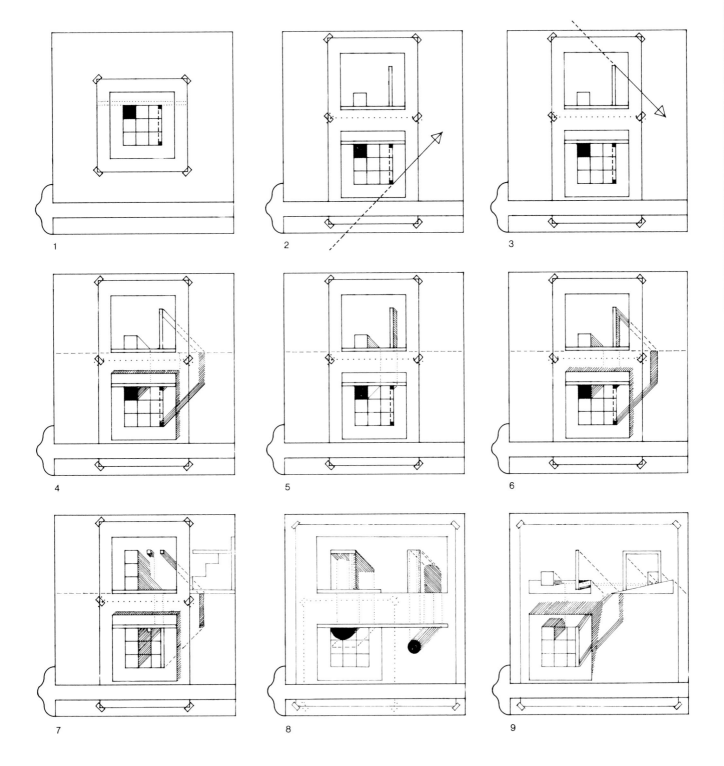

1

2

3

4

5

6

7

8

9

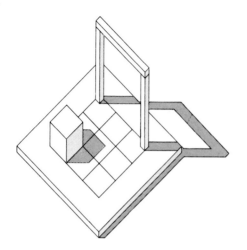

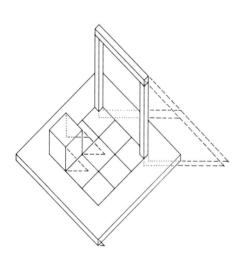

### 4. SHADE AND SHADOW IN AXONOMETRIC

*All material in nature, the mountains and the streams and the air that we breathe, are made of Light which has been spent, and this crumpled mass called material casts a shadow, and the shadow belongs to Light. . . . The sun does not realize how wonderful it is until after a room is made. A man's creation, the making of a room, is nothing short of a miracle. Just think, that a man can claim a slice of the sun.* —Louis I. Kahn

For **SHADE AND SHADOW IN AXONOMETRIC** projection, the "triangle method" is a simple way to directly visualize how light falls on surfaces in space. For some people, visualizing shadows in a three-dimensional projection is actually easier than seeing them in planimetric space. The relationship between light and space is central to architecture. What is nice about this technique is that the construction of the shadows can tell you directly whether or not a shadow will intersect a wall before it hits the ground, and so on.

The triangle method for axonometric shade and shadows is described below.

*1. Shown is the original orientation of the plan on the drawing board.*
*2. Shown is the plan (with wall added) rotated for purposes of illustrating an axonometric view which will show shade as well as shadows. Select a bearing so that the light rays appear to be coming directly from the side ("due west") of the rotated plan.*
*3. In the axonometric projection note the bearing. Choose an altitude for the sun elevation to match the angle of your drafting triangle, generally 30, 60 or 45° if you are not using an adjustable triangle.*
*4. Apply the vertical edge of the drafting triangle to all vertical surfaces and determine the altitude line of all shadows. Use your parallel rule or T-square to draw the bearing line of the shadow. The intersection of bearing and altitude marks the edge of the shadow. Proceed as you did with planimetric shade and shadows. Note that the* projected altitude, *which determines shadows cast on walls, is the angle that the true altitude vector projects in the vertical plane, just as the bearing is the angle the true altitude vector projects onto horizontal surfaces. Remember, parallel edges cast parallel shadows and vertical edges cast shadows along bearing lines on flat planes, etc.*
*5. Shade surfaces away from the light source not in shadow, and render shadows in a darker tone than shades.*
*6. For complex spaces the shadow construction can get complicated, but don't panic! You can always break down an irregular form into simple geometric elements to cast a series of partial shadows. Thus the shadow from a stairway onto a surface is still the sum of the shadows of a set of increasingly high offset cubes. And the shadow of a wall onto a staircase is just the sum of the shadows of a plane onto a set of layered base planes. When a mass hovers in space, project its position onto the ground plane, just as you did when constructing simple axonometric projections.*
*7. Shadows on or from inclined planes (like a chimney on a roof) can be constructed as the intersection of the shadow volume with the volume of the wedge prism.*
*8. Casting shadows on curved surfaces is similar, but again care must be taken to plot enough points to be able to generate and draw a smooth curve.*

Sometimes drawings are clearer *without* shadows, especially when they describe organizations as well as spaces. This is true in part 3 of the Visual Glossary below.

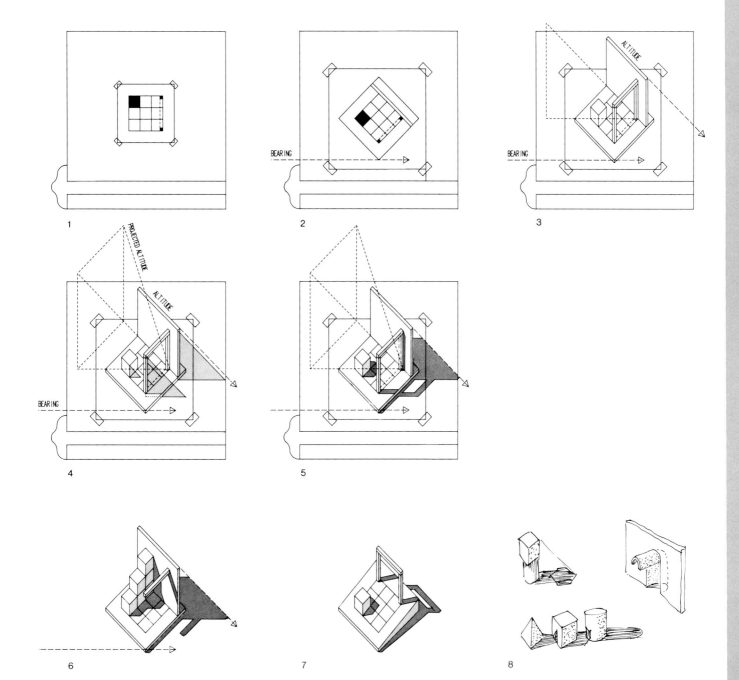

1

2

BEARING

3

BEARING

PROJECTED ALTITUDE

ALTITUDE

BEARING

4

ALTITUDE

5

6

7

8

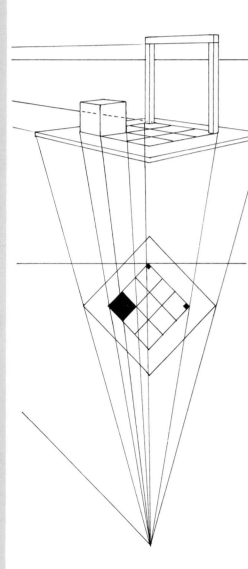

## 5. PERSPECTIVE

**PERSPECTIVE** is a projection which diminishes the size of objects to indicate spacial depth on a picture plane. The Romans knew how to construct optically correct perspectives. Their lost art was rediscovered by the Florentine architect Brunelleschi in 1425. Many methods have been developed to simplify the fairly tedious task of constructing a perspective projection by hand. You can find detailed instructions in handbooks from Alberti's *Della Pittura* (1436) and Durer's *Underweysung der messung* (1525) to many modern texts including *Architectural Graphic Standards*. The steps indicated below outline one simple method of developing a two-point perspective from plan and section information.

*1. Shown is the original orientation of the plan on the drawing board.*
*2. Position the subject plan obliquely on the drawing board so that the nearest point in the final view will be closest to you as you sit. On a tracing paper overlay, mark the point on the plan from which you wish to see the perspective view. This is called the* station point *and locates the viewer's eye. Be sure it is at least twice as far from the subject as the subject is wide to minimize distortion at the sides of the perspective. (Da Vinci solved this problem by using a curved picture plane.)*
*3. Project* vanishing points *parallel to the perpendicular faces of the subject, or of a rectangular solid circumscribed about a curved or irregular subject.*
*4. Establish the* picture plane, *the spacial intersection of the subject volume with an imaginary plane that represents the surface of the perspective drawing. The picture plane is represented by a line drawn at any convenient point across the plan perpendicular to a vertical line through the station point and the subject.*
*5. Project all rays from the station point to the picture plane that pass through significant points in the plan such as corners, overhangs, openings, etc.*
*6. Set a new tracing paper overlay to represent the picture plane and draw the* horizon line *across the sheet directly over the picture plane line on the sheet below. Mark the vanishing points on the horizon line, and project the intersection of the rays with the picture plane (from the sheet below) as verticals that cross the horizon. Where picture plane intersects the plan, establish a true vertical in the same scale as the base plan drawing, and locate this vertical above, below, or across the horizon to indicate the height of the viewer's eye in relation to the subject.*
*7. From the top and bottom of this "real" vertical, draw oblique lines to the vanishing points. Where these obliques intersect the verticals projected from the corners of the plan, they will define the boundaries of the vertical plane faces in the perspective.*
*8. Continue to project lines and surfaces as needed. Measure horizontal intervals from plan and vertical intervals from the true vertical. Retrace or erase to remove hidden lines (or leave them as construction lines).*
*9. To draw a cylinder or pyramid in perspective, proceed as above establishing the cubical/ rectangular volumes in which these occur. Locate their non-cubical points as you did when drawing a cylinder and pyramid in axonometric. Steps, inclined planes, and even domes (as parts of spheres inscribed in cubes with intersecting diagonals and subdiagonals) can be located in the same way. Vaults are drawn as two nesting cylinders. Be smart and set up all the repetitive points at once; for example, tick off marks for stair treads and risers.*

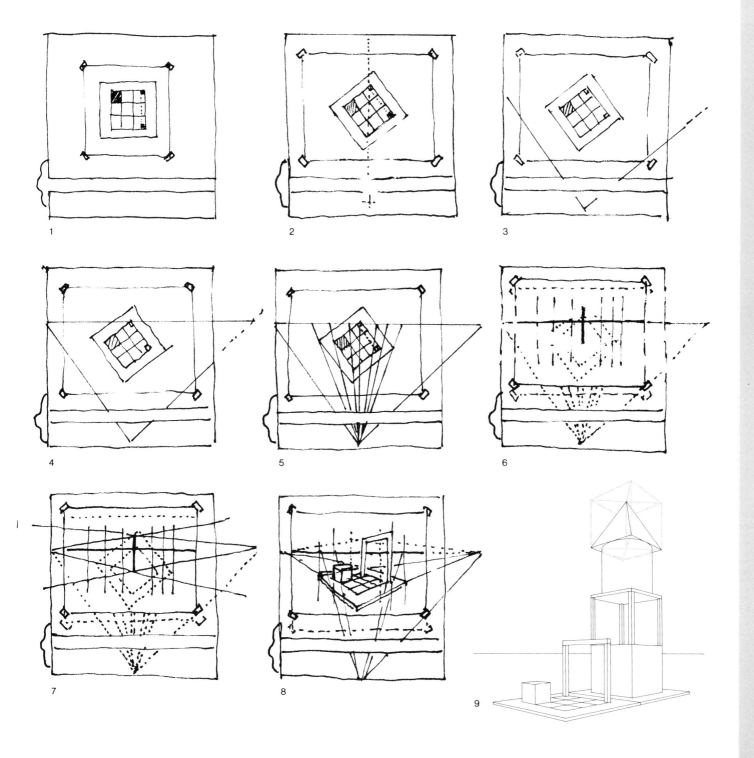

1

2

3

4

5

6

7

8

9

## SHADE AND SHADOW IN PERSPECTIVE

**SHADES AND SHADOWS** can be directly constructed **IN PERSPECTIVE** by overlaying vanishing points for the sun's rays on the basic projection.

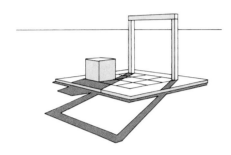

*1. Select a point on the horizon for the compass direction of the sun. Call this VB, for the vanishing point of the bearing.*

*2. Select a height for the sun in the sky, perpendicular to the horizon at VB. Call this VA, for the vanishing point of the altitude. When VA is above VB, the sun is behind the picture plane in relation to the viewer; when it is below , the sun is behind the viewer, that is the viewer is between the sun and the picture plane.*

*3. Determine shadow directions by projecting shadow edges from VB. Determine shadow lengths by projecting shadow edges from VA to intersect the lines from VB.*

## ONE POINT PERSPECTIVE

**ONE POINT PERSPECTIVE** is a special case of two point perspective. When one major face of the subject is parallel rather than oblique to the picture plane, the only visible vanishing point is straight back into the picture plane (the other would meet the horizon at infinity). There are also three point perspectives, in which verticals also converge to vanishing points. Alberti's technique is still the basis for the quick method of making one-point perspectives decribed below.

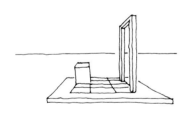

*1. Establish a frame for the picture plane, and mark off equal intervals along its edges.*

*2. Place a horizon line within the frame to establish the eye level of the viewer. Mark a single vanishing point along the horizon within the frame. From this vanishing point project radiating lines to the intervals along the base edge.*

*3. Locate a diagonal point outside the frame on the horizon line. Its distance from the vanishing point is equivalent to the distance of the observer to the picture plane. Project a line from this diagonal point to the opposite corner of the frame. It measures equal depth intervals where it crosses the radiating lines, creating a floor of unit tiles. A diagonal to the near corner extends the depth grid in front of the picture frame.*

*4. Using the floor grid as guide, project grids from the other three edges of the frame, onto the "walls" and "ceiling" of the projected space.*

The geometry of visual perspective forms the basis for the powerfully convincing computer animations of today's TV logos and films such as *Tron*. It is important to understand these principles not only to be able to construct mechanically precise renderings, but also to use as a freehand tool for quickly visualizing the spaces, forms, and sequences of architectural experiences you design. Perspectives are easy to sketch freehand. Methods which closely approximate constructed perspectives count on the eye to help proportion design elements. Such direct layout methods permit rapid adjustment of views without requiring the tedious repositioning and reconstruction of the plan projection. Frank Lloyd Wright was a master of constructed perspective renderings, which remain unsurpassed for their evocative quality and uncanny ability to accurately project the finished building. Le Corbusier was a master of the rough persective sketch. In a very few lines he was able to not only delineate the masses of a building, but indicate the play of light over their surfaces.

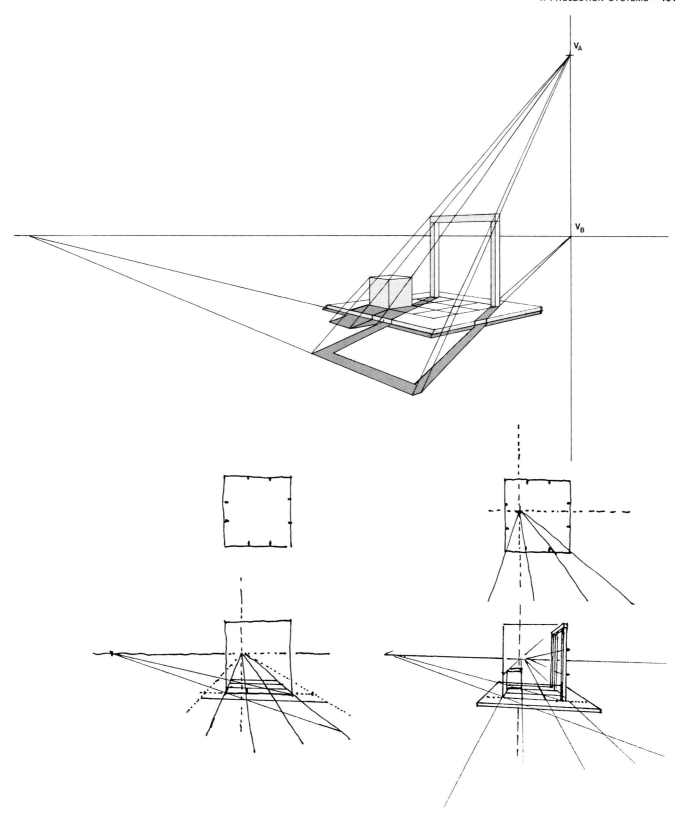

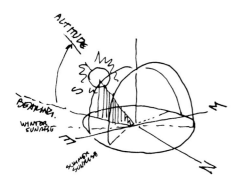

## 6. SUN ANGLES

For any point on earth, the position of the sun in the sky is unique for every moment of the year. That means that an accurately constructed shadowed projection can communicate not only shapes and relationships of spaces, but also the time of day and day of the year on which the view is taken. Computer programs for energy analysis are based on insolation data calculated through the geometric location of sunlight and position. Architects must design according to how much sunlight will come into a room and how much heat is generated. They need to know how to take advantage of natural sunlight and heat to make a room cool in the summer and warm in the winter. Paolo Soleri has rediscovered the efficacy of south facing apsidal niches in hot dry climates to give large shaded spaces in the summer and to bring warm light deep into a structure in the winter. Frank Lloyd Wright used deep horizontal overhangs to temper the residential climate. Le Corbusier studied how to control direct sunlight while providing maximum view from interiors, and developed apartments with full glass exterior walls protected by deep balcony-and-fin room-sized "venetian blinds" he called *brise soleils*, which means "sun-breakers" in French. The chapter "Tonal Interest and Light" in William Kirby Lockard's book *Design Drawing* is especially good on the relationship between light, shadow, and space. Its clear diagrams show shadowed spaces and the effects of changing light on interior space.

What follows is based on the information in the late A. and V. Olgyay's seminal work *Solar Control and Shading Devices*. For a given latitude, sun paths are plotted across the sky and projected onto a horizontal plane to create a *sun-path diagram*. The circle at the outside of the diagram represents the horizon, and the inner curves project the sun paths on the ground. The book provides sun path diagrams which chart sun position for every hour of the year at latitudes from 24° to 52°. The steps below describe how to determine **SUN ANGLES** for the 40° North Latitude, which is roughly the parallel for New York City, Madrid, and Peking, among other places. Note that except for the solstices, each point on the chart represents the two dates when the sun occupies the same position in the sky, in both spring and fall.

*1. Determine the latitude of the site in question. select the appropriate sun angle chart. For our example of New York City, although the actual latitude is at 40° 45', we can select the 40° N chart, which will be close enough for our purposes.*
*2. On this chart, read up or down around the noon vertical to find the day of the month, and across the graph to find the hour of the day for the time in question. The accompanying cursor is marked in degrees of the sun's altitude in the sky.*
*3. Place the cursor over the center point of the chart and rotate it to cover the time and date in question. At this point the cursor will indicated in degrees the sun's altitude in the sky. The angle of the cursor read along the horizon circle will give the sun's bearing at that moment.*
*4. Use this altitude and bearing for casting accurate shadows in plan, section, elevation or shadowed roof plan.*
*5. Use this altitude and bearing to determine the shape of the triangle for an axonometric "triangle method" shadow construction.*
*6. Use this altitude and bearing to establish the location of VPrays in a perspective.*

*Repeat the process for as many points as you need to describe the annual natural heating and sunlight cycle.*

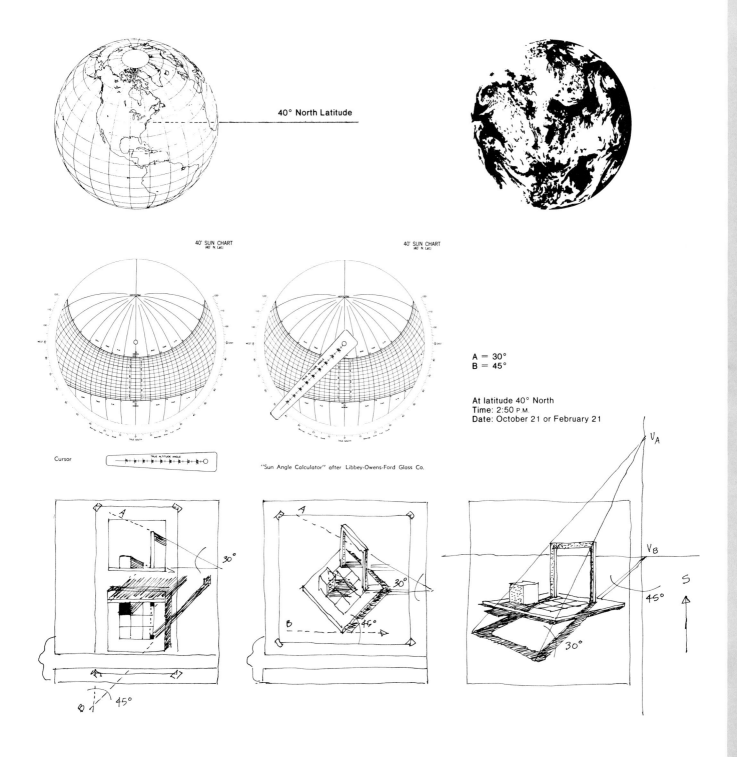

40° North Latitude

40° SUN CHART
(40° N. Lat.)

40° SUN CHART
(40° N. Lat.)

A = 30°
B = 45°

At latitude 40° North
Time: 2:50 P.M.
Date: October 21 or February 21

Cursor

"Sun Angle Calculator" after Libbey-Owens-Ford Glass Co.

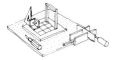

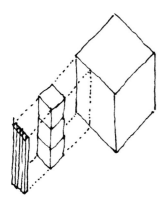

## CUBES AND RODS

There is an art to making something seemingly so simple as a cube. It is difficult to make a *true* **CUBE,** one in which all edges are equal, all corners are right angles, all faces are parallel and true squares, and all volumetric dimensions the same. You can tell when your rods and cubes are accurate, by placing three 1″ cubes together against four 3″ rods. They should all be flush, no matter which way any of the rods or cubes are rotated. A cube is a special kind of geometric solid. All its faces are parallel and all its corners are at right angles. In addition, in a cube all faces and edges are of equal dimensions. The general class of such solids whose sides are not equal—the typical "shoe-box" form is properly called a right rectangular parallelipiped. The **RODS** in the Kit of Parts are right rectangluar parallelipipeds.

When making the cubes and rods, take care in using the right tools and materials in the right sequence. Inspect the grain of the basswood you use; be sure it is firm and dense. Be sure that the board you use for making the cubes is white all the way through, not just on the outer plies. Hold the wood tight against the miter box, and hold the whole assembly tight against an edge to keep a firm base when you cut the lengths of rod with the razor saw. Do not forget to account for the kerf, the thickness of wood that the blade turns into sawdust. For the cubes, be sure to draft the correct dimensions for the cube pieces in pencil on the board you will use. Remember to account for the thickness of the board itself when calculating the dimensions of the six sides of a cube. When you cut the pieces for the cubes, be sure to use the cork-backed rule so the knife will not slip. Use fresh sharp blades and hold the knife vertically. Glue two pieces together, using an old triangle to be sure the pieces meet at a 90° or right angle. After they set add the third plane, and make sure all three are at right angles to each other. After all six are glued, sand the excess glue, being careful not to round the corners of the cube. If you follow these procedures with care, you will be rewarded with having three cubes which are exactly as long as one rod, and with four rods which are exactly as wide, when laid next to each other, as one cube (no matter how the elements are rotated or oriented!) Only then can you use these elements to make spaces with precision. With this kind of attention to detail comes a healthy respect for the qualities of all forms. An artist makes UNITY by organizing all the elements with the highest level of care and attention is an order of arrangements and perceptions.

## RAMPS AND STAIRS

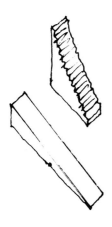

The ramps needed for the kit of Parts are solid prisms, wedges which have five surfaces, one less than a cube or rectangular solid. To make them you need to cut rectangles for the base, back, and top inclined surface, and triangles for the sides. Join the parts as you did for the large cube. Stairs may be thought of as stacks of rectangular solid or cube-like elements. Build the stairs by drawing 2 sides for each first on Strathmore board, then cutting back and base, and the risers and treads, and gluing the whole set with white glue. Or, take ¼″ foamcore and stack layers of decreasing size on top of each other. Then cover the sides with pre-measured and cut Strathmore thin paper sheathing. Or do the same with layers of wood, gluing them as they are stacked, and sanding them to a smooth finish. Note: Only the overall dimensions of the ladder are given, not those of its parts. They are left for you to determine. Be sure that the ladder, both in thickness, size of rungs, and spacing, is in scale with the stairs.

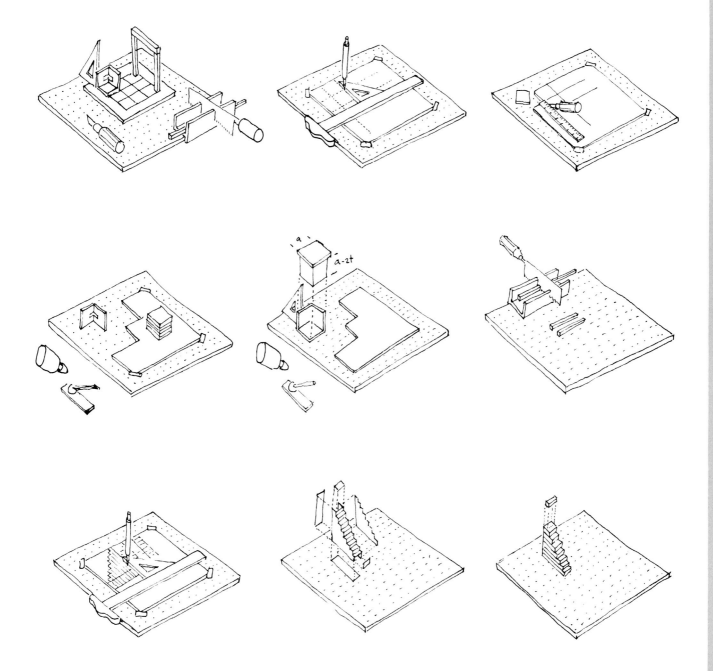

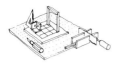

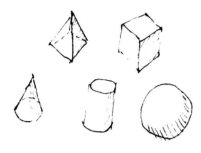

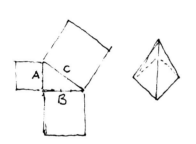

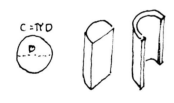

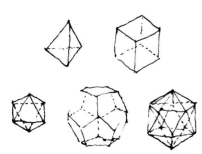

## CONSTRUCTING SOLIDS

*Euclidean Solids:* Building basic non-cubic Euclidean solids like pyramids and cylinders is easy, using no more high school geometry than the Pythagorean Theorem and an understanding of Pi to construct the shapes to cut from paper or the locations and angles of saw blades and cutting beds to machine them from solid blocks of wood or other material.

*PYRAMID* (with square base):

1. On the plan, by the Pythagorean Theorem, find the length of the base's diagonal (AC) as $\sqrt{(a^2 + a^2)} = a\sqrt{2}$. Then on section through AC find edge length (PC) directly, showing triangle PAC. Since PO is the altitude, and meets the base at a right angle, then AO = OC, so solve PC by the Pythagorean theorem. That is: $(PC^2) = \sqrt{(PO^2) + (OC^2)} = \sqrt{a^2 + \left(\dfrac{a\sqrt{2}}{2}\right)^2}$. So PC = 1.2247a. If **a** = 3'', then PC = 3.734''.

2. By (geometric) construction, directly draw the needed triangle PBC. Draw a base line with a straightedge, and from a central point mark **a**/2 in each direction. From these points set a compass to length PC = 1.2247a (= 3.734'') and swing arcs to intersect at point P.

3. Plot triangle PAC and three more just like it on 2 or 3 ply Strathmore board. Note, you cannot simply trace the elevation to get these triangles, because the sloped sides will not yield true dimensions in elevation!

4. On a self-healing cutting surface, cut out the four pyramid face triangles and the base, using sharp blades and a non-slip corked back rule.

5. Set the four against the square base you have also made and cut, bring them together at apex P, and glue all edges. Don't forget to allow for the thickness of the modelling material. To make a truly beautiful pyramid, bevel the edges when you cut the four triangles.

*CYLINDERS* (for the Kit of Parts, only half-cylinders are needed):

1. Since the circumference of a circle = $\pi$ times the diameter, $c = \pi D$, make the drum of the half-cylinder from a single rectangle of thin-ply Strathmore paper that has the dimensions **a** and $\pi a/2$, or 1.57a. If **a** = 3'' then the dimensions are 3'' and 4.71''. Score this piece to make a controlled arc bend.

2. The face of the half cylinder is a square of **a** sides, 3'' × 3''. The ends are two half circles of diameter **a**, drawn with compass set to radius **a**/2 or 1.5''. Allow for the thickness of the modelling material. You can strengthen the cylinder by inserting ribs of half circles at the third or quarter points of the prism.

3. Vaults are built like the half-cylinders. Remove an interior half circle from the half-circles for the ends and ribs, to leave the required thickness for the vault. Instead of a square face, the inside of the vault will also be a curved plate whose dimensions are determined as $c = \pi d$, where $d = a - \frac{1}{2}''$, if the thickness of the vault is $\frac{1}{4}''$. Thus the rectangle for the inside curved plate will have the dimensions $c = \pi(2.5'')/2 = 3.925'' \times 3''$. Again, allow for the thickness of the modelling material.

*Platonic Solids:* There are only only 5 regular polyhedrons, that is, those whose sides are identical regular polygons. These are the only regular solids with this property and such a high degree of symmetry. They are the tetrahedron, cube, octahedron, dodecahedron, and icosahedron, with 4, 6, 8, 12, and 20 regular polygon sides respectively. They are also easy to build using the patterns of their unfolded sides, as indicated. Cut along the solid lines, and fold along the dotted lines. The implications of their forms is beyond the scope of this book, but are important in the studies in Volume 2.

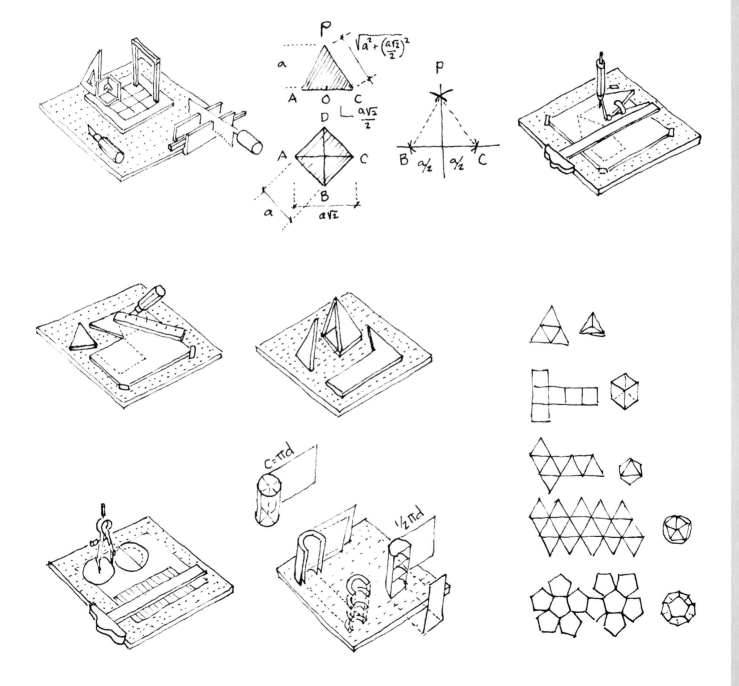

$$\sqrt{a^2 + \left(\frac{a\sqrt{2}}{2}\right)^2}$$

$C = \pi d$

$\frac{1}{2}\pi d$

## 1. ELEMENT AND FIELD: PARTI AND PROPERTIES OF THE SQUARE

*A work of architecture may be significant, organic, dramatic, but it will fail to be a work of art unless it is also schematic. This means a systemmatic disposition of parts according to some co-ordinating principle.* —Claude Bradgon

The geometry of elements in a field carries meaning in several ways. When the elements are arranged into a recognizable form they create a distinct *PARTI*. When the essential qualities of the field (as a given context) suggests or implies strategies for formal organization, we can study the unique *PROPERTIES OF THE FIELD*. When relationships between sets of elements, and between field and parti are clear, then a UNITY in design may occur.

### PARTI: INTERNAL GEOMETRIC ORDER

Architects use the French term **PARTI** to describe the pattern of arrangement of given elements in two or three dimensional space. A group of pieces can be arranged in many different configurations within the same field. For example the six pips on one face of a die can be placed in a number of ways within a square. Each of these ways will not only be a different pattern of six marks, but may also organize the square field into different areas of two-dimensional spaces. The same set of elements configured in different ways can develop different kinds of geometric order. The same *parti* can be expressed through different sets of elements. And one *parti* can yield many possible arrangements of the same elements. In the design of buildings, the *parti* is especially descriptive of the internal relationships between rooms and other functional areas. But each *parti* will of course also organize the spaces around and between functional areas.

### PROPERTIES OF THE FIELD: EXTERNAL GEOMETRIC ORDER

A **FIELD** in space exerts forces that organize the elements within and outside it. The geometry of the field determines the character of these forces. As a generalization of all two-dimensional space, the square is unique in that it measures equal extension along the two perpendicular dimensions of planar space. As a frame it encloses a microcosm of the infinitely larger general surface of two-dimensional space. The formal properties of the square can imply preferred configurations of compositional elements. Its high degree of symmetry makes it kin to the circle. They can be tangent to each other, and both imply rotation. When *parti* and the properties of the field reinforce each other, the design result can be especially strong.

The *parti* of a scheme describes the order of the arrangement of the elements. Although a *parti* can be derived from the internal possibilities of arrangement alone, it is more usual to consider *parti* as the union of the order of the given elements with the special geometric properties of the field in which the elements occur. Thus the characteristics of a site will often determine which of many possibilities is a preferred *parti*. In graphic design, the "site" is a surface of plane geometry. The square is an important simple case which has many implications for design in general. You must use your eye to find what the formal properties of this geometric figure may be, perhaps invent new ones, and discover how they may influence the organization and articulation of space.

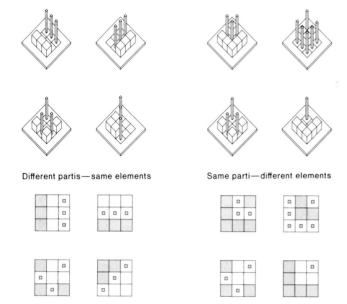

Different partis—same elements

Same parti—different elements

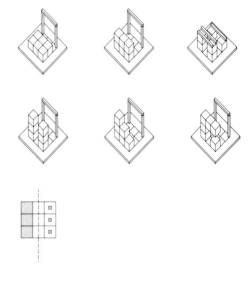

One parti—same elements—many configurations

## PROPERTIES OF THE SQUARE

1. square: four equal sides
2. right angles/perpendiculars
3. quadrant: midpoints of sides create four squares.
4. horizontal/vertical
5. diagonals: cross at right angles
6. diamond
7. $\sqrt{2}$ isosceles triangles
8. half-diagonals
9. circle round/tangent square
10. arc
11. diameter
12. rotation: clock- and counter-clock-wise
13. frame: center and edge
14. nine-square
15. phi/golden section
16. mandala

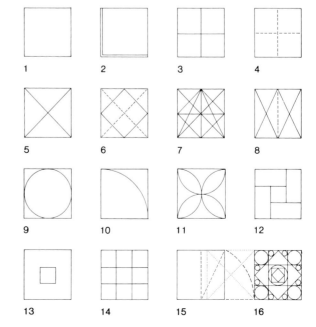

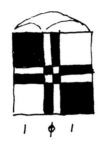

$$1 \quad \phi \quad 1$$

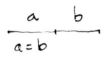

$$a = b$$

$$a : b = b : a + b$$

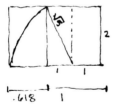

$$.618 \qquad 1$$

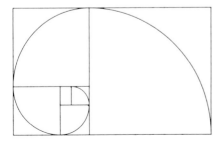

## 2. PROPORTION

**PROPORTION** is the study of the relationship of the size and shape of parts to the size and shape of the whole. Euclid calls proportion "the equality of two ratios". Proportion creates beauty by relating eye and intellect. The elegant rooms in Andrea Palladio's villas often related height, width, and length with simple proportions like 3:4:5. The important proportion between human size and built form is called *scale,* and is further discussed on pages 000. Proportional systems based on simple numerical operators (doubling each term) or geometric operators (the diagonal of one square forming the side of the next—1:$\sqrt{2}$ can generate many mathematical series. The most consistently fascinating one for architects throughout history is based on The Golden Section, also called the Divine Proportion.

A (one-dimensional) line presents the simplest instance of proportion. The Pythagoreans sought "interesting" ways to divide a line segment. One obvious way they found is to cut the line in the middle, making the two parts equal, creating *symmetry,* (which means "measuring with"). The eye can enjoy the evident and strong equivalence between elements, which is perhaps one reason symmetry is so satisfying. Symmetrical parts have the proportion of 1:1 and establish identity by repetition of exact or mirror-image forms. Then the Greeks asked if a line segment could be cut so that the parts relate to each other and to the whole in the same proportion. This can occur if the smaller part is proportional to the larger in the same ratio that the larger is to the sum of both. This can be expressed as **a:b = b:a + b**, or **a/b = b/a + b.** Solving this by the Binomial theorem, if **b** = 1, then the positive root of **a** is the irrational term 1 + $\sqrt{5}/2$, or 1.61803 . . . denoted by the Greek letter $\Phi$ (Phi). For well over 2000 years we have learned the beauty and power of this unique proportion, which has come to be called the Golden Section. Like $\pi$ (Pi), which relates diameter to circumference for all circles, $\Phi$ is a proportional constant which relates, among other things, the sides of a Golden Rectangle whose dimensions are .618 . . . and 1.

Since .618/1 = 1/1.618, $\Phi$ is its own reciprocal. This curious property has important implications for architects. The diagonal of a half-square projected onto the square's base produces a Golden Rectangle, making a constructed version of 1 + $\sqrt{5}/2$. Adding square and Golden Rectangle produces another Golden Rectangle, as does subtracting a square from a Golden Rectangle. So smaller parts with this proportion can easily be related to the whole form, where each element is measured in multiples of unit (1:1) or $\Phi$ (1:1.618) proportions.

Leonardo Da Pisa, nicknamed Fibonnaci "son of good nature", discovered in 1202 while breeding rabbits a number series which was neither arithmetic (1 2 3 4 5 6 . . .) nor exponential (1 4 9 16 25 . . .) but still described an orderly form of growth of whole numbers. The terms in the Fibonacci Series 0 1 1 2 3 5 8 13 21 34 55 89 144 . . . are made from the sum of the two previous terms. Thus the next term is 233 (89+144) and the following is 377 (144+233). The proportions of successive terms in this series, i.e. 0/1=0 1/1=1 1/2=.5 2/3=.66 3/5=.60 5/8=.6125 8/13=.6153846 . . . 13/21=.6190476 . . . 21/34=.617647 . . . 34/55=.6181818 . . . converge to the Golden Section! Squares with these proportions build a rectangle that more and more closely approaches a Golden Rectangle. Arcs inscribed in these squares generate a close approximation of the beautiful curve of the logarithmic spiral, which can be more exactly generated within a set of growing Golden Rectangles.

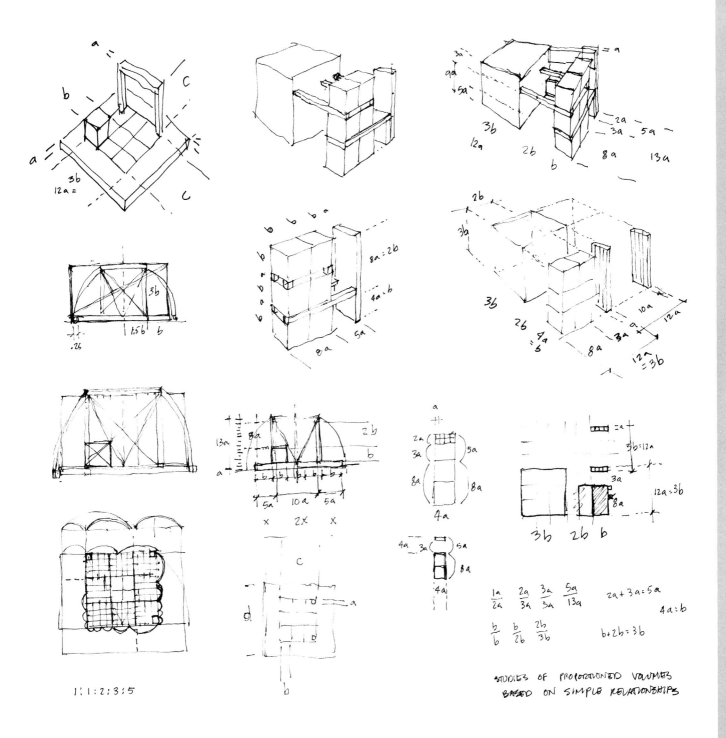

STUDIES OF PROPORTIONED VOLUMES
BASED ON SIMPLE RELATIONSHIPS

## 3. IDENTITY AND CONTRAST; FIGURE/GROUND and SOLID/VOID AMBIGUITY

### Identity and Contrast

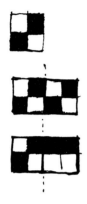

Identical things are the same in all essential qualities. An exact copy of a set of black and white squares in a checkerboard pattern is an **IDENTITY** to the original. But if the order of black and white is changed in the second pattern, so for example the black squares are not diagonally across but next to each other, then the copy is not identical, although the amount of black to white in the two patterns make them graphically equivalent. Graphic *equivalence* occurs when there are equal values of elements in two fields, even though their arrangements may not be exact identitites. An array of four by four identical copies will make a checkerboard, an array of equivalent copies will not. A similar architectonic study can be made in three dimensions, using solid cubes alternating with cubical voids.

To truly see an identity one must employ contrast. A white square is most visible against a black field. **CONTRAST** is the opposition of pairs that differ and complement each other. After the repetition of identical elements, contrast is the second most basic means of developing meaning through form. Simple contrasts like black to white as well as large to small, many to few, horizontal to vertical, closed to open, orthogonal to diagonal, inside to outside are all important carriers of architectonic as well as graphic design intentions. Composites of these contrasts can increase the range of expression.

### Figure-Ground and Solid-Void Ambiguities

The *parti* and field geometry of any whole form determine the overall recognizable configuration known as the *gestalt*. Our visual perception recognizes certain wholes even when only part of the form is present—for example a square with a "bite" taken out of it. Some figures, however, elude a single clear interpretation of the *gestalt*—for example Yin-Yang symbol, or the famous optical illusion which can be seen as either a pair of faces or a single chalice. These images exhibit graphic *ambiguity*.

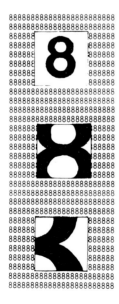

A fundamental graphic contrast exists between figure and ground. A figure like the letter A or the number 8 is normally distinguished from its (back-)ground through the contrast of black ink on white paper. But the proportion of figure to field can be adjusted so that it is not clear which area is figure and which is ground. It will not be clear whether white ink has been printed on black paper, or the reverse, to make the form. Then a most fascinating phenomenon, the **FIGURE-GROUND AMBIGUITY,** can be achieved. Architectural plans can often reveal figure-ground ambiguities, not only in the distinction between walls and the space between them, but also between interior and exterior space, between public and private zones, etc.

For expression through architectonics, the most basic contrast is perhaps also the most powerful: solid to void. The area filled by architectonic masses is solid while the areas between and around them is void. A reference datum like a base is not vital, but can help to define a zone in which spaces can be relatively solid or void depending on the sense of density between the pieces that is achieved. It is possible to arrive at a moment when even the void feels solid, perhaps as solid if not more solid than the blocks of mass themselves. This is a **SOLID-VOID AMBIGUITY.**

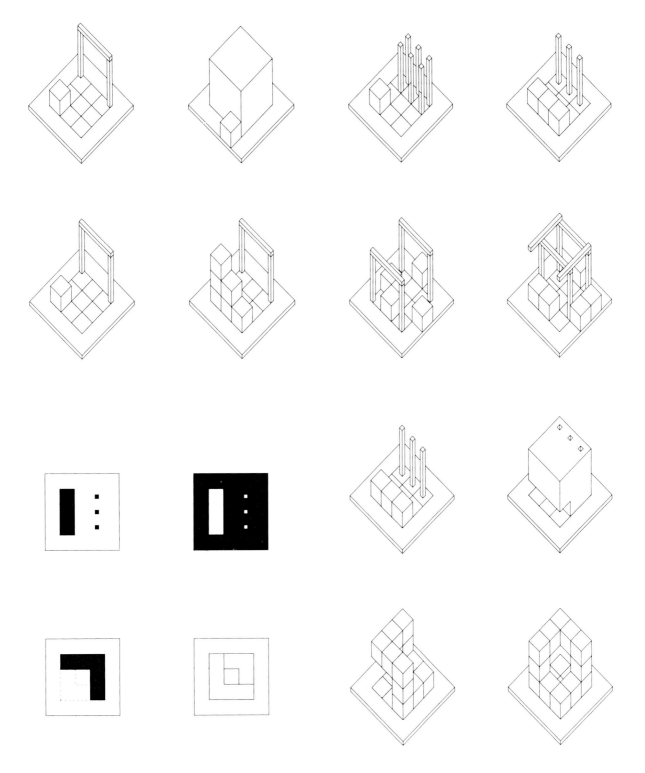

## 4. TRANSFORMATION

*I advance the whole canvas at the same time*—Cézanne

**TRANSFORMATION** manipulates a form everywhere at once to produce a new configuration. A few of the elements or whole patterns can be changed. For example shearing a field slips all elements in the two parts past each other. Some formal transformations which enlarge design options are those made by similarity, position, sequence, and layering. Whole forms can interact through addition, subtraction, union, and intersection. The transforming operations may be cumulative even though the number of elements do not change. The figure-ground ambiguity alone creates a subtle, but basically simple graphic order. A series of geometric operations, used in any order, can transform a simple organization into a more complex formal order. Thus the designer need not seek the "perfect" parti at the outset, but rather simply embark on the plastic research, transforming any first proposal with one operation after another until the scheme starts to "move".

*Hierarchy* is the ranking of things in order of importance. A *hierarchy of forms* distinguishes significant spaces from others through exceptional size (bigger or smaller), unique shape, or strategic location (center vs. periphery, node vs. grid, etc). In addition there can be a *hierarchy of organization,* in which the form reveals primary and secondary transformations. A *hierarchy of decisions* determines a sequence of operations. An "algebra" of geometric operations is not necessarily commutative: it may matter whether a rotation occurs before or after a shear. The final form reveals all patterns simultaneously, but not necessarily the order of the operations. For example, rotating 4 corner squares in a 25-square checkerboard field, then rotating a second diagonally opposite set, and finally rotating the central section of the new pattern within the larger field creates a new and complex organization without changing the number of black or white squares. When each square carries its own graphic pattern, and many of these are combined through transformation, they may create additional layers of graphic order counter to the geometric order of the tiles themselves. Thus the whole field can carry many levels of hierarchic information. If the tiles can create an illusion of depth, then at each apparent layer of space, different hierarchies of organization may occur. (See pages 63 and 79 for examples.)

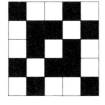

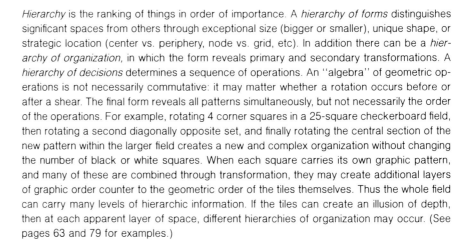

Transformation can also create a similar hierarchy of order in three dimensions. The facing page shows: an identity, replicating similar elements, shearing the position of the elements, rotating the cube set 90°, splitting the cubes to articulate the slot of space defined by the rods, translating some rods to define a cube of volume between the rods, translating two small cubes to engage rods, and shifting small cubes to define a small square in plan.

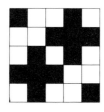

Most architectural design problems require a whole set of transformations to work out the details of elements and spaces in a manner consistent with the original design intentions. The result will show these "moves" simultaneously, but may also reveal which were most important and which were subordinate—ranking the concerns from most to least important. The discovery of the double helix structure of DNA revealed a marvel: life's unity and variety is transmitted through the genetic code by replication of the instructions that the nucleus gives the rest of the cell. Evolution occurs when these instructions are altered. Not just one part is altered, but the character of the whole organism is *transformed*.

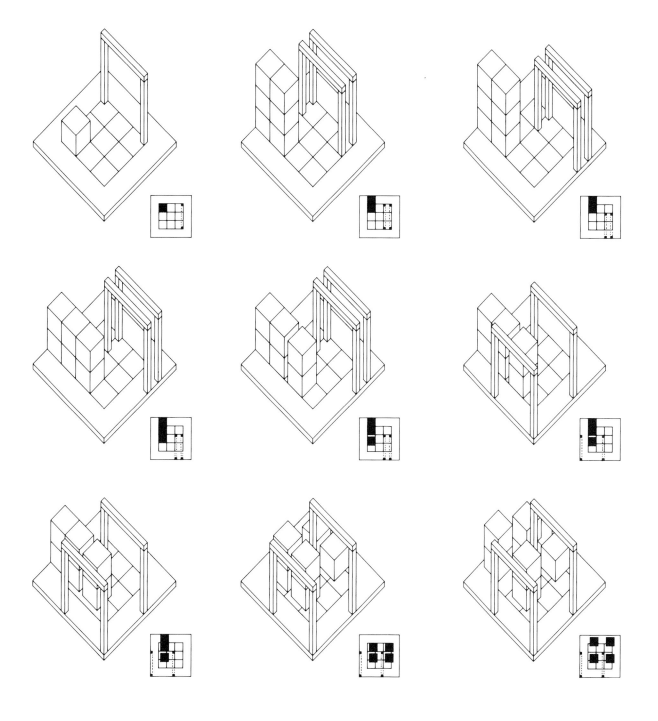

## 5. EXPRESSION: SHAPE AND FORM/EUCLIDEAN SOLIDS

Architects sometimes distinguish shape from form. **SHAPE** may refer to the contour, outline, and idiosyncratic character of a composition, while **FORM** usually refers to the deeper structure of spacial unity of the whole ensemble. Thus, while the *shapes* of mouse, giraffe and elephant differ, their *forms* are similar, since they each have four legs, a tail, and a head.

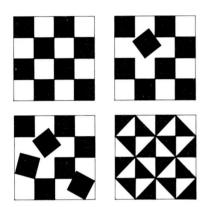

A rotated square in a checkerboard seems out of place, or at least out of order. It is a distinct shape, separate from the formal order that governs the rest of the field. A series of diamonds, all rotated at different angles, will not coalesce into an organized pattern. They remain shapes, distinct in outline and position. But they do not necessarily create a new order of form. Whereas a set of diamonds, all oriented alike, will imply a structure to the whole field that may be read in addition to the original, underlaying orthogonal geometry of the checkerboard. These diamonds create new form, as well as new shapes.

A simple set of cube and frame on a grid base creates a strongly directional space. Repeating the set will enhance this spacial directionality. If the orientation of one of these sets is changed, it will break the original order of the larger assembly of the four sets, like one rotated square in a checkerboard. Yet additional rotations of two more sets will eventually create the unique *form* of a rotating pinwheel of spaces. **EXPRESSION** in architecture comes when an order of spaces is so clear that breaking the order becomes vivid enough to create not just new shapes, but complex form and a higher level of order, a kind of logical and emotional counterpoint between expectation and surprise. The subtle distinction between shape and form is a question of limitless ramifications.

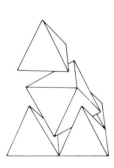

New solids not only expand the possibilities of shape in line, curve, and contour, but can also extend the ways of making expressive form. A pyramid suggests rotation, generating both diagonal and orthogonal order in its field. Circles are found in squares, but imply concentric as well as orthogonal fields. Cylindrical niches and vaulted or domed ceilings so powerfully carry our spirit beyond the realm of everyday boxy rooms that they often create poetic, public or religious spaces. Pyramid, cylinder, and cube (plus cone and sphere) comprise the *Euclidean Solids*. It is possible to use all the Euclidean solids to generate forms of spacial order, rather than simply to arrange a variety of shapes. Frank Lloyd Wright used geometries based on the hexagon, triangle, and circle, as well as the square, for planning modules. Buckminster Fuller's geodesic domes are composed of triangles meshed over spherical surfaces. There can be fields of cylindrical or pyramidal space, and in fact, they can be composed of cubes as easily as cylinders. The plastic "algebra" of addition, subtraction, union, and intersection of forms, suggests relations between masses that foster comparisons of spaces. (Algebra comes from the Arabic root *jbr,* meaning *to bind together,* and describes a mathematics of reduction and comparison by equations.) Thus one combination of vaults and half-cylinders permits a reading of plastic subtraction, as if mass were carved from a middle zone in a long half-cylinder.

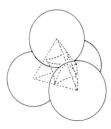

Beyond the Euclidean Solids, the Greeks and subsequent geometers have discovered many classes of spacial figures. The *Platonic Solids* are the 5 regular polyhedrons called tetrahedron, cube, octahedron, dodecahedron, and icosahedron. Other systems of form include close-packing spheres, warped surfaces like hyperbolic paraboloids, pneumatic structures, stellated (pointed star-like) solids, coils and branches. Each have their own formal implications and rules. What architecture might occur beyond the flattening distortion of gravity?

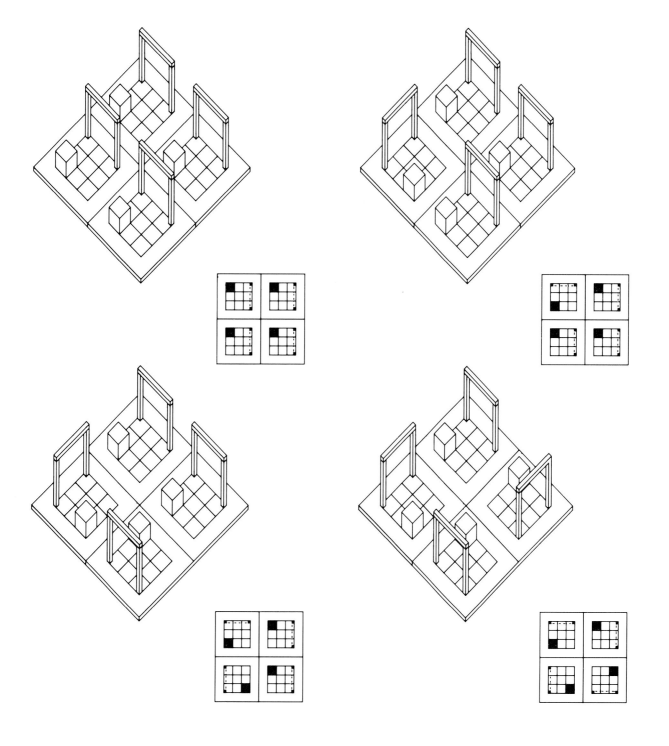

## 6. SCALE

**SCALE** in architecture is the measure of built form in relation to human form. The Latin term *scala,* meaning ladder or staircase, and the Sanskrit *skan,* "he leapt" suggest that the human body is the origin for our system of measuring. We still measure things in fractions and multiples of "feet". "Mile" comes from the Latin *milia passuum,* meaning a thousand paces. Mt. Everest's 29,000 foot elevation still suggests a climb of at least 29,000 steps. If the standard interval of the scaling unit is a human dimension, like a heartbeat or a footstep, then the rhythm of the whole order is measured in human scale. It is not simply the addition of stair elements that insure human scale in your "Timepiece" composition, but rather the spacial rhythm for the whole scheme that they imply. When stairs, ramps, and ladders are added to the Kit of Parts they transform pure geometries of simple elements into propositions for human habitation. Architectonics becomes architecture when scale enables imagination to place human experience within ordered spaces.

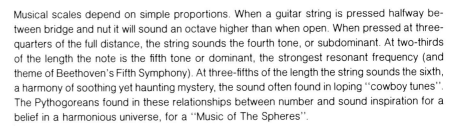

Artists have long studied the human body to find proportional relationships between the sizes of its parts and the sizes of spaces people inhabit. Da Vinci knew that a person's span equals his or her height. For almost everyone, the proportion of one's height to the distance from the navel to floor is very close to the Golden Section. Architects have developed proportional systems based on human scale. The Parthenon, Gothic Cathedrals, Palladio's villas and Japanese temples are all in part based on Golden Section multiples of the size of a person. Le Corbusier developed a Fibonacci series in which the primary unit was the height of a man set to 6'-0" and derived a useful set of dimensions, called Le Modulor, for everything from furniture and room heights to city plans. He claimed to find evidence of its use throughout the world in railway cars, steamships, and ancient architecture. Many architects now apply Le Modulor to their designs. A small but well-proportioned building in human scale can seem monumental, and a large one can seem intimate. People fit comfortably in them while the spirit soars because the body remains the measure of the smallest detail and the greatest spans. A building in human scale is like an orchestra in tune.

Musical scales depend on simple proportions. When a guitar string is pressed halfway between bridge and nut it will sound an octave higher than when open. When pressed at three-quarters of the full distance, the string sounds the fourth tone, or subdominant. At two-thirds of the length the note is the fifth tone or dominant, the strongest resonant frequency (and theme of Beethoven's Fifth Symphony). At three-fifths of the length the string sounds the sixth, a harmony of soothing yet haunting mystery, the sound often found in loping "cowboy tunes". The Pythogoreans found in these relationships between number and sound inspiration for a belief in a harmonious universe, for a "Music of The Spheres".

We "scale" heights and emulate Daedalus, seeing clearly from above what seems obscure from below, to attain a realm of higher consciousness. At each scale form reveals new order. Magnify the human hand 10,000 time and discover a structure of independent blood cells. Does the miracle of life depend somehow on mathematical patterns? Studies of tesselations, fractals, and cellular automata make provocative hints in this direction. Proportions based on the Golden Section are found frequently in life. Sunflower seeds grow on the flower's head along opposing spirals. The number of these spirals will be Fibonacci numbers, such as 34 in one direction and 55 in the other, or 55 and 89, etc. Numbers like 53 or 87 do *not appear!*

# BIBLIOGRAPHY

## INTRODUCTION: FOUNDATION

Duncan, David Douglas. *Goodbye Picasso*. Grosset and Dunlap, New York, 1974
Gerster, Georg. *Flights of Discovery: The Earth from Above*. Grosset and Dunlap, New York, 1978.
Goldscheider, Ludwig. *Michelangelo: Paintings, Sculptures, Architecture*. Greenwich CT, (Phaidon) New York Graphic Society, 1964.
Hemming, John. *Machu Picchu*. Newsweek Book Division, New York, 1981.
Kellogg, Rhoda. *Analyzing Children's Art*. Mayfield Publishing Co, Palo Alto, 1970.
Klee, Paul. *The Thinking Eye*. George Wittenborn, New York, 1964.
Lipman, Jean. *Calder's Universe*. Viking Press, New York, 1976.
Matisse, Henri. *Jazz*. Braziller, New York, 1983 (reprint of 1947 edition).
Meier, Richard. *Richard Meier Architect*. Rizzoli, New York, 1984.
Mili, Gjon. *Picasso's Third Dimension*. Triton Press, New York, 1970.
Piaget, Jean. *A Child's Conception of Space*. Norton, New York, 1967.
Steirlin, Henri. *Encyclopedia of World Architecture*. Van Nostrand Reinhold, New York, 1983.
The Cooper Union School of Art and Architecture. *Education of An Architect: A Point of View*. Museum of Modern Art, New York, 1971.

## Study 1: UNITY

Ardalan, Nader. *The Sense of Unity: The Sufi Tradition in Persian Architecture*. University of Chicago Press, Chicago, 1973.
Carl, Peter. *Thematic Organization, in mimeo*.
Kepes, Gyorgy. *Language of Vision*. Paul Theobald, Chicago, 1974
Le Corbusier. *Towards a New Architecture*. Dover, New York, 1986 (reprint of 1922 edition)
————*Notebooks (Voyage to the Orient)*
Lotti, Giorgio. *Luce Mare*. Edizione Fotoselex, Como, 1982.
Mainstone, Rowland. *Developments in Structural Form*. MIT Press, Cambridge, 1975.
Millon, Henry. *Key Monuments in the History of Architecture*. Prentice Hall, Englewood Cliffs, 1964.
Norberg-Schulz, Christian. *Meaning in Western Architecture*. Rizzoli, New York, 1980.
Ozenfant, Amedee. *Foundations of Modern Art*. Dover, New York, 1952.
Schwarz, Rudolf. *The Church Incarnate,* H. Regnery Co., Chicago, 1958.
Schwenk, Theodor. *Sensitive Chaos*. Schocken, New York, 1976.
Vitruvius. *Ten Books on Architecture*. Dover, New York, 1960.
Wright, Frank Lloyd. *Writings and Buildings*. Horizon Press, New York.
————"To the Young Man in Architecture" in *An American Architecture*. Horizon Press, New York, 1955.

## Study 2: DIALOG

Doremus, Thomas. *Frank Lloyd Wright and Le Corbusier: The Great Dialogue*. Van Nostrand Reinhold, New York, 1985.
Mircea Eliade. *The Two and the One*. University of Chicago Press, Chicago, 1979.
————*Sacred and Profane: The Nature of Religion*. Harcourt Brace Janovich, San Diego, 1968

————*Cosmos and History: The Myth of the Eternal Return*. Garland, New York, 1985
Tange, Kenzo, and Kawazoe, Noboru. *Ise: Prototype of Japanese Architecture*. MIT Press, Cambridge, 1965.

AD Profiles #14, 7/78 "Hand Built Hornby"
Blaser, Werner. *Japanese Temples and Tea-Houses*. F. W. Dodge, New York, 1965.
Frisch, Karl von. *Animal Architecture*. Van Nostrand Reinhold, New York, 1983.
Heidegger, Martin. "Building Dwelling Thinking", *Poetry Language Thought*. Harper, New York, 1971.
Hejduk, John. *The Mask of Medusa*. Rizzoli, New York, 1985.
————Hejduk. special issue of *A+U* July 1986.
Ryckwert, Joseph. *On Adam's House in Paradise*. MIT Press, Cambridge, 1981.

Brown, G. Spencer. *The Laws of Form*. Allen and Unwin, London, 1969.
Ching, Francis. *Architecture: Form Space and Order,* Van Nostrand Reinhold, New York, 1979.
Dewdney, A. K., *The Planiverse: Computer Contact with a Two Dimensional World*. Poseidon Press, New York, 1984.
Mâle, Emil. *The Gothic Image*. Harper and Row, New York, 1972.
Rowe, Colin. *The Mathematics of the Ideal Villa and Other Essays*. MIT Press, Cambridge, 1982.
Temko, Alan. *Notre Dame of Paris*. The Viking Press, New York, 1955.

## Study 3: VOLUME

Aalto, Alvar. *Synopsis: Painting, Sculpture, Architecture*. Birkhauser, Cambridge, 1980.
Arnheim, Rudolf. *Dynamics of Architectural Form*. University of California Press, Berkeley, 1977.
Chillida. *Chillida*, Carnegie Institute, Pittsburg, 1980.
de Sausmarez, Maurice. *Basic Design*. Van Nostrand Reinhold, New York, 1983.
Gerster, Georg. *Churches in Rock*. Phaidon, London, 1970.
Le Corbusier, *Complete Works*. L'Editions D'Architecture, Artemis, Zurich 1970.
Neumann, Erich. *The Archetypal World of Henry Moore*. Pantheon, New York, 1959.
Van den Ven, Cornelis. *Space in Architecture*. Van Gorcum, Amsterdam, 1978.
Van der Laer, *Architectonic Space*. Amsterdam.
Wingler, Hans. *The Bauhaus*. MIT Press, Cambridge, 1969.
Wright, Frank Lloyd. *Buildings, Plans, and Designs*. Horizon Press, New York, 1968.
————*The Early Work*. Horizon Press, New York, 1968. Together these two reprint the 1910 "Wasmuth" Edition.
Wright, Frank Lloyd. *The Wendigen Edition*. Horizon Press, New York, 1965. Reprint of 1925 edition.
Zevi, Bruno. *Architecture as Space*. Horizon, New York, 1974.

## Study 4: TRANSFORMATION

Arnheim, Rudolf. *The Genesis of a Painting: Picasso's Guernica*. University of California Press, Berkeley, 1962.
Davies, Paul. *The Cosmic Blueprint*. Simon and Schuster, New York, 1988.
Eisenman, Peter, et. al. *Five Architects*. Oxford University Press, New York, 1975
Eisenman, Peter. *HOUSE X*. Rizzoli, New York, 1982.
Hitchcock, Henry-Russell. *In the Nature of Materials: The Buildings of Frank Lloyd Wright. 1887-1941*. New York: Da Capo Press, 1973.

Hofstetter, Douglas. "Metamagical Themas: The Music of Frederic Chopin", *Scientific American*, April 1982.

Kaufmann, Edgar Jr. *Falling Water: A Frank Lloyd Wright Country House*. Abbeville, New York, 1986

Mandelbrot, Benoit. *The Fractal Geometry of Nature*. W. H. Freeman, New York, 1983.

Michener, James. *The Source*. Random House, New York, 1965.

Nilsson, Lennart. *Behold Man*, Little Brown, Boston, 1973.

Rowe, Colin and Koetter, Fred. *Collage City*. MIT Press, Cambridge,

Rowe, Colin and Slutzky, Robert. "Transparency: Literal and Phenomenal", *Perpsecta 8*. Yale University Press, New Haven. 1965

————"Transparency 2." *Perpsecta 13–14*. Yale University Press, New Haven. 1974.

Sargent, John. *The Usonian Houses of Frank Lloyd Wright*.

Thompson, D'Arcy. *On Growth and Form*, Cambridge University Press, New York, 1961.

Wright, Frank Lloyd. *The Natural House*. Horizon, New York, 1954.

## Study 5: EXPRESSION

Bachelard, Gaston. *The Poetics of Space*. Beacon, Boston, 1969.

Chiang Yee, *Chinese Calligraphy*. Harvard University Press, Cambridge, 1973.

Edgerton, Jr. Samuel. *The Renaissance Rediscovery of Linear Perspective*. Harper and Row, New York, 1979.

Ely, John Wilton. *The Mind and Art of Piranesi*. Thames and Hudson, London, 1978.

Everitt, Anthony. *Abstract Expressionism*. Thames and Hudson, London, 1975.

Kandinsky, Wassily. *On the Spiritual in Art*. Dover, New York. 1977.

Le Corbusier. *Ronchamp*. Verlag Gerd Hatje, Zurich, 1957.

Leger, Fernand. *Functions of Painting*. Viking, New York, 1965.

Oubrerie, Jose et.al. *Le Corbusier's Church at Firminy*. Rizzoli, New York, 1981.

Snow, Edward. *A Study of Vermeer*. University of California Press, Berkeley, 1979.

Spicker, Stuart. *The Philosophy of the Body*. Quadrangle, New York, 1970.

Stravinsky, Igor. *The Poetics of Music*. Harvard University Press, Cambridge, 1975.

White, John. *The Birth and Rebirth of Pictorial Space*. Harper and Row, New York, 1972.

Wittkower, Rudolf. *Architecture in the Age of Humanism*. Norton, New York, 1971.

## Study 6: TIMEPIECE

Ambasz, Emilio. *Italy the New Domestic Landscape*, Museum of Modern Art, New York, 1972.

Calvino, Italo. *Mr. Palomar*. Harcourt Brace Janovich, San Diego, 1983.

Ferris, Timothy. *Coming of Age in the Milky Way*. Morrow, New York, 1988.

Giedion, Siegfried. *Space, Time, and Architecture*. Harvard University Press, Cambridge, MA 1982.

Hawkins, Gerald S. *Stonehenge Decoded*. Doubleday, Garden City, 1965

Henderson, L. D. *The Fourth Dimension and Non-Euclidean Geometry in Modern Art*, Princeton University Press, Princeton, 1983

Kubler George. *The Shape of Time*. Yale University Press, New Haven, 1962

Lobel, John. *Between Silence and Light*, Shambala, Boulder, 1979

Louise B. Young, *The Unfinished Universe*, Simon and Schuster, New York, 1986.

Rose, Kenneth. *The Body in Time*, New York, 1988

Yates, Frances. *The Art Of Memory*. University of Chicago Press, Chicago, 1966

## Study 7: FREE EXERCISE

Arendt, Hannah. *The Human Condition*. University of Chicago Press, Chicago, 1958.

Bertomen, Michele. *Tower Project*, New York, 1984.

Calvino, Italo. *Six Memos for the Next Millenium*. Harvard University Press, Cambridge, 1988.

Eardley, Anthony and de la Fuente, Jullian. *35 Rue de Sevres*. University of Kentucky Press, 1975.

Feynman, Richard. *Surely You're Joking Mr. Feynman: Adventures of a Curious Character*. Norton, New York, 1984.

Gabo, Naum. *Of Diverse Arts*, Princeton, 1962.

Le Corbusier, *Creation is a Patient Search*. Praeger, New York, 1960.

Libeskind, Daniel. *Between Zero and Infinity*, Rizzoli, New York, 1981.

Lipman, Jean. *Calder's Universe*. Viking, New York, 1976.

Poundstone, William. *The Recursive Universe*. Morrow, New York, 1984.

## VISUAL GLOSSARY

### General

Ching, Francis. *Architectural Graphics*. Van Nostrand Reinhold, New York 1985.

Duberry, Fred and Willats John. *Perspective and other drawing systems*. Van Nostrand Reinhold, New York 1983.

Kline, Morris. *Mathematics in Western Culture*, Oxford University Press, London, 1953

Pedoe, Dan. *Geometry and the Liberal Arts*, Penguin, Baltimore, 1976.

Porter, Tom and Goodman, Sue. *Manual of Graphic Techniques*, Volumes 1–4. Scribners, New York, 1982

Ramsey and Sleeper, *Architectural Graphic Standards*, 8th edition. John Wiley, New York, 1988. (1956 5th edition still very useful!)

### Part 1. Geometry of Projection Systems

#### 1. Planimetrics

Abbott, Edwin. *Flatland,* New York, 1952.

Dewdney, A. K., *The Planiverse: Computer Contact with a Two Dimensional World*, New York, 1984

Blaser, Werner. *Drawings of Great Buildings*. Basel, 1983.

Burger, Dionys. *Sphereland*. Crowell, New York, 1965.

Cook, Peter. *Architecture: Action and Plan*, Reinhold, New York, 1967

Gerster, Karl. *Below From Above: Aerial Photography*. Abbeville, New York, 1985.

Le Corbusier, *Towards a New Architecture*. Dover, New York, 1931/1986.

Steirlin, Henri. *Encyclopedia of World Architecture*, Van Nostrand Reinhold, New York, 1983.

Le Tarouilly, Paul. *Edifices de Rome Moderne*. Princeton, Architectural Press, 1982. (Reprint of 1840 original.)

Wayne Copper, "The Figure/Grounds" *Cornell Journal of Architecture #2*. Rizzoli, New York, 1982.

Wurman, Richard Saul. *Cities: Comparisons of Form and Scale*. Philadelphia, Joshua Press, 1974.

#### 2. Axonometrics

Choisy, Auguste. *Histoire de l'Architecture*. Vincent Fréal, Paris, 1954. (Reprint of 1899 original.)

Eisenman, Peter. *HOUSE X*. Rizzoli, New York, 1982.

#### 3 and 4. Shades and Shadows

Lockard, William Kirby. *Design Drawing*, Tucson, 1982

### 5. Perspective

Alberti, Leon Battista. *On Painting,* Yale, New Haven, 1956.

Da Vinci, Leonardo. *Notebooks.* Dover, New York. 1970

Descargues, Pierre. *Perspective: History, Evolution, Techniques.* Van Nostrand Reinhold, New York, 1982.

Durer, Albrecht. Underweysung der messung, Nürnberg, 1536.

Edgerton, S.Y. *The Renaissance Rediscovery of Perspective.* Harper and Row, New York, 1975.

Forseth, Kevin. *Graphics for Architects.* Van Nostrand Reinhold, New York, 1980.

King, Robert and Pisani, Francis. *Architectural Drawing Manual,* New York, 1973.

### 6. sun calculations

Olgyay and Olgyay, *Solar Control and Shading Devices,* Princeton University Press, Princeton, 1957.

Hanses, John Gregory. *Our Solar Calendar.* Box 30005, Winona, Minnesota. A cardboard orrery, with poster and pins, showing a plan view of the planets and their positions throughout the year.

### Part 2. Geometry of Fabrication

Cundy, H. M. and Rollett, A. P. *Mathematical Models,* Oxford, 1961.

Frampton, Kenneth, ed. *Idea As Model.* Rizzoli, New York, 1981.

Lines, L. *Solid Geometry,* New York: Dover, 1965.

Lodder, Christina. *Russian Constructivism.* New Haven: Yale University Press, 1983.

Pugh, Anthony. *Polyhedra: A Visual Approach,* Berkeley, 1976.

Current architectural supply catalogs (Charrette, etc.)

### Part 3. Geometry of Organizing Principles

#### 1. *a. Parti*

Arnheim, Rudolf. *The Genesis of a Painting: Picasso's Guernica,* Berkeley, 1962.

Bannister Fletcher, Sir. *A History of Architecture on The Comparative Method.* 19th Ed. New York, Scribner, 1987.

Ching, Francis. *Architecture: Form Space & Order.* Van Nostrand Reinhold, New York. 1979.

Clark and Pause. *Precedents in Architecture.* Van Nostrand Reinhold, New York, 1975.

de la Fuente, Guillermo Jullian. *H VEN LC: The Venice Hospital Project of Le Corbusier.* Architecture at Rice #23, Houston, 1968.

Durand, J.N.L. *Lecons d'Architecture: Partie Graphique des Cours d'Architecture.* Verlag Dr. Alfons Uhl, Nordlingen, 1981. (reprint of 1819 edition)

Ehrenzweig, Anton. *The Hidden Order of Art.* University of California Press, Berkeley, 1971.

Frankl, Paul. *Principles of Archtectural History.* MIT Press, Cambridge, 1968.

Grillo, Paul Jacques. *What Is Design?* Theobald, Chicago, 1960.

Lincoln, Louise, ed. *Leger's Le Grand Dejeuner.* Minneapolis Institute of the Arts, 1980.

Loran, Erle. *Cezanne's Compositions,* University of California Press, Berkeley, 1963.

Pevsner, Nickolaus. *A History of Building Types.* Princeton University Pres, 1976.

#### b. Properties of the field

Jaffe, H. L. C. *Mondrian.* Abrams, New York, 1970

Lawlor, Robert. *Sacred Geometry: Philosophy and Practice,* New York, 1982.

Le Corbusier. *Poeme de l'Angle Droit (The Poem of the Right Angle).* Teriade, Paris. 1955.

Martin, Sir Leslie. *Circle.* Praeger, New York, 1971.

Munari, Bruno. *Discovery of the Square.* Wittenborn, New York, 1960.

———*Discovery of the Circle.* Wittenborn, New York, 1965.

Weiger, S. L. *Chinese Characters.* Dover, New York, 1965.

Weyl, Hermann. *Symmetry,* Princeton, 1952.

### 2. Proportion

Doczi, Gyorgy. *The Power of Limits: Proportional Harmonies in Art, Nature, and Architecture,* Shambhala, Boulder, 1981.

Ghyka, Matila. *The Geometry of Art and Life,* Dover, New York, 1977.

Hambridge, Jay. *Dynamic Symmetry,* Yale University Press. New Haven, 1920.

Hersey, G. L. *Pythagorean Palaces.* Cornell University Press, Ithaca, 1976.

### 3. Figure/ground and Solid/void

Allen, Joseph. *Entering Space: An Astronaut's Odyssey,* Stewart Tabori and Chang, New York, 1984.

Arnheim, Rudolf. *Art and Visual Perception.* University of California Press, Berkeley, 1974.

Berger, John. *Ways of Seeing.* Penguin, New York, 1972.

Crichtlow, Keith. *Order in Space.* Viking Press, New York, 1970.

Kim, Scott. *Inversions.* McGraw Hill, New York. 1981.

Vignelli, Massimo. *Design: Vignelli.* Rizzoli, New York, 1981

### 4. Transformation

Coomoraswary. *Transformation of Nature Into Art.* Dover, New York, 1937.

Hofstetter, D. R. *Godel Escher Bach: The Eternal Golden Braid.* Basic Books, New York, 1979.

Nilsson, Lennart. *A Child is Born.* Dell, New York, 1986.

Perez-Gomez, Alberto. *Architecture and the Crisis of Modern Science.* Cambridge MA: MIT Press, 1983.

Poundstone, William. *The Recursive Universe.* Morrow, New York, 1984.

Smith, E. Baldwin. *The Dome, a study in The History of Ideas.* Princeton, 1971.

### 5. Expression: Shape and Form

Bentley, W. A. Humphreys, W. J. *Snow Crystals.* Dover, New York, 1931.

Boys, C. V. *Soap Bubbles,* Dover, New York, 1959.

Descharnes, Robert. *Gaudi: The Visionary.* Viking, New York. 1971.

Fuller, Buckminster. *Synergetics,* MacMillan, New York, 1979.

Greene, Herb. *Mind and Image.* University of Kentucky Press. Lexington, 1976.

Hildebrandt, Stefan and Tromba, Anthony. *Mathematics and Optimal Form.* Scientific American Library, New York, 1985.

Mainstone, Rowland. *Developments in Structural Form.* MIT Press, Cambridge, 1975.

Marks, Robert. *The Dymaxion World of Buckminster Fuller.* Southern Illinois University Press, Carbondale, 1960.

Otto, Frei. *Tensile Structures.* MIT Press, Cambridge, 1969.

Roland, Conrad. *Frei Otto: Tension Structures,* New York, 1970.

Snelson, Kenneth. *Kenneth Snelson.* Kunstverein, Hannover, 1971.

Wachsmann, Konrad. *The Turning Point of Building.* Reinhold, New York, 1967.

### 6. Scale

Bodanis, David. *The Secret House.* Simon and Schuster, New York, 1986.

Le Corbusier. *Le Modulor,* Cambridge MA, 1968.

Licklider, Heath. *Architectural Scale.* Braziller, New York, 1966.

Moore, Charles. *Dimensions.* Architectural Record Books, New York, 1976.

Morrison, Phillip and Phyllis, and the Office of Charles and Rae Eames. *Powers of Ten,* Scientific American Library, New York, 1982.

Scharf, David. *Magnifications.* Schocken Books, New York, 1977.

Thoreau, Henry David. *Walden,* Doubleday, Garden City, 1963 (1854).

### Periodicals

*A+U, Daidalos, Global Architecture, Lotus, Oppositions, Perspecta, Process, Via, Zodiac*

## STUDENT ILLUSTRATIONS

James Ainoris, 125
Miguel Alvarado, 108
Paul Anderson, 9
Manuel Andrade, 126
Dana Andrysiak, 100, 101
Joseph Auty, 51, 80, 109
Louis Baldino, 78
John Baron, 104
Sangita Bhayan, 40
Adam Birnbaum, 108
Don Brennan, 62
Lawrence Carroll, 26, 133
Kathy Chesnovitz, 62
Nicole Chung, 64
John Cilla, 129
James Costigan, 133
Glen Crandall, 132
Aldo D'Adamo, 26, 133
Robert De Rico, 67
Joseph Donnan, 133
Robert Dructor, 90
C. Felix, 130
Chris Fernandez, 29
Gordon Findlay, 66, 122
Harriet Gettleman, 52, 79, 90, 99
George Grenier, 52, 78, 112
Steven Grinstead, 108
Micheline Guirguis, 132
Barbara Haller, 53, 110
Debbie Halpern, 27
George Hobel, 85
Debra Hopke, 40
Joseph Hummel, 66, 111
Jeff Jahnke, 73
Peter Johannes, 65, 79
Terry Kelly, 27
Mike Kennedy, 66
Tom Kispert, 64
Elena Kravchenko, 133
Larry Kriz, 109
Greg La Duca, 129
Vincent Laino, 67
Susanna Leung, 40
Paul Licata, 132
Arthur Lombardi, 93, 113

Gino Longo, 78
Susan Lorentzen, 43
Linda Manz, 63, 66, 93, 109
Alec Martuge, 124
Theresa McCarty, 66
Pete McEvoy, 132
Kenneth McKee, 90, 120
Bill Means, 127
Greg Meindl, 29
Michael Messina, 128
Jan Miller, 63
Thomas Miller, 124
Jeff Mongo, 129
James Moore, 53
Diane Morano, 79
R. Morrisey, 130
Michael Motta, 53
David Nadolne, 133
Tom Nejezchleba, 65
Michael Pandolfi, 90
Carey Press, 98
Ted Pupilla, 67
Domenico Rauccio, 27, 63, 90
William Recce, 93
Jonathan Reo, 93
Nestor Robles, 132
Mike Romani, 41, 80, 81
Greg Sanzari, 28, 33, 54
Tom Scavo, 42
Michael Schettino, 41
John Sciara, 112
James Shaughnessy, 132
Martin Somers, 64
Ron Stallone, 113
Sarma Steinger, 92, 93
Kim Stemmler, 28, 29
Ernest Stigi, 128
Andrew Tychaz, 91
Steve Wallstedt, 54
Karin Wettels, 90
Douglas Wilken, 59
Greg Willey, 81
Trevor Wisdom, 91
Anthony Zara, 52
Steve Zukaitis, 125

# FIGURE CREDITS

## NYIT Design Fundamentals Staff 1983–88

Reino Aarnio
Ralph Albanese
Donald Alberto
Paul Amatuzzo
Peter Anders
Mojdeh Baratloo
Craig Barton
Robert Beattie
Salvador Behar
Michael Berthold
Michele Bertomen
Phyllis Birkby
Robert Braun
Kaung Chen
Christopher Chimera
Brad Cloepfil
James Coady
Livio Dimitriu
Jonathan Friedman
Arlene Gamza
William Gati
Bruce Gemmell
Judy Gordon
Frederick Gorree
Laurence Green
Martin Hero
David Hingston
Beyhan Karahan
Carl Karas
John Keenen
Alyce Knight
Dennis Kuhn
Bret Lafving
Stephen Leet
Iver Lofving
Wilbur Lupo
Robert Madey
Robert Magaw

David McAlpin
Errol McIntosh
Michael McNerney
Victoria Meyers
Phillip Monastero
Vladimir Morosov
Quentin Munier
Diane Neff
Jose Oubrerie
Ron Peterson
Ludmilla Pavlova
Karin Payson
Vincent Polsinelli
Joseph Porcelli
Peter Pran
Pascal Quintard-Hofstein
Barbara Resnicow
Terence Riley
Mark Robbins
Alan Sayles
Joseph Scarpulla
Robert Schwartz
Raymond Scott
Lindsay Shapiro
Judith Sheine
Joy Siegel
David Sirola
Robert Slutzky
Charles Spiess
Richard Sullivan
Michael Szerbaty
Ian Taberner
Keat Tan
Anne Tichich
Ron Walker
William Walther
Warren Winter

## Honor Student Teaching Assistants 1983–88

Ron Albinson
Diana Allegretti
Wayne Alvar
Chris Andron
Kanayo Anekwe
John Angelos
Rhonda Angerio
Dennis Austin
Joseph Bahan
Thomas Baio
Iris Bar-Yehuda
Richard Bartlett
Paul Benoit
Cesar Bettencourt
Christine Bodouva
Gregory Bonsignore
Jose Branco
Robert Braun
Nancy Bretzfield
Gary Burke
Mark Camera
Henry Cantwell
AnnMarie Carragher
Edward Casper
Harold Conyers
Suzanne Couture
Norman Davis
Richard DeCastro
Ernest DeMaio
Daniel Dembling
Luis Diaz
Maria DiNatale
Robert Drake
Ralf Dremel
Michael Duignan
Michael Egan
Lucy Eichenwald

Alexander Eng
Ronald Ervolino
Zandra Fernandez
Robert Fitzgerald
Theodore Floratos
Joseph Franchina
Jeffrey Friedman
Carla Fritz
Maria Furgiuele
Steven Gambino
Cesar Giaquinto
Peter Hagemann
Thomas Haggerty
Lourdes Hernandez
Michael Himelstein
Barbara Hunt
Hugh Isleib
Darryl Ivan
Mark Kaminis
Rosemarie Kloefkorn
Kenneth Koons
Margaret Leporati
Andreas Letkovsky
Andrea Lightman
Bryan Manning
Robert Markovitz
Richard Massa
John Mastropietro
John McGuire
Michael McNerney
Joseph Mottola
William Mullan
Richard Napoli
Christopher Nardone
John Nolis
Mark O'Dell
Seak-Boo Ooi

Guy Page
Kevin Paul
Wayne Plourde
Hubert Poole
Jason Popkin
Joseph Porcelli
Mark Powell
John Power
Maria Quintans
David Resnick
Dianne Rinaldi
Joseph Robinson
George Schramm
Essam Sembawa
Russell Sherman
Irwin Silverman
Clay Smook
Suzanne Sowinski
Richard Sullivan
John Tegeder
Lory Tepfenhart
Thomas Theobald
Alan Topel
Patricia Trifaro
Bart Trudeau
Robert Turner
Peter Van Geldern
Luis Vera
Maria Vera
Mark Warren
James Westcott
Jesse Whiteson
Lois Wilhelmsen
Maria Wilthew
Michael Yacoub
Lawrence Young
Steven Zaweski

# INDEX

## BRIDGE

The nave of the Beauvais Cathedral, when first built c. 1282, fell and collapsed under its own weight, because the medieval builders tried a daring structural form to satisfy their desire to fill a lofty space with light and the energy of religious spirit. To throw a two-ton stone 200+ feet above your head and keep it there, and to make the supporting walls so thin and open that they seemed made more of light than of stone took daring, vision, and technical precision. The means were finally found to achieve what once seemed impossible. Since the Shuttle Challenger explosion, we must again find ways to keep stones of all kinds aloft as a testament to the human spirit.

We inhabit volumes larger than ourselves. Finding ways to put pieces beyond our reach so as to make *room* demands ingenuity in construction. Piling stones like the Great Pyramids in Egypt is a difficult way to create space. To create large volumes, to wrap material around a void and keep it there despite all the forces acting on it, is to make a *span*. Setting stones so as to counterbalance the forces between them can make an arch. The stones of an arch are kept in perpetual low orbit by the skill of the architect. The stones of Machu Picchu are in a higher orbit than the stones of Venice. Resolving the forces in elements that define volumes in space can produce magnificent plastic works. The Verrazano Narrows Bridge in NY Harbor, a great suspension bridge, levitates steel, concrete, highways and trucks like toys high above the sea, as much as half a mile from any support! Even more wonderful are human places like the Pantheon, Hagia Sophia, the cathedrals, the Eiffel Tower, where the economic, elegant and daring use of materials and structures have created wonderful spaces, producing architecture inhabited by both body and spirit!

Just as bamboo or a tree bends in the wind, so does every part of a building respond to the field of forces around it. The ideal static geometry assumed for the study of ARCHITECTONICS must be augmented by an understanding of geometry in motion. DYNAMICS can reveal the forces that act to make spaces and forms. How to think about engineering of materials and structures as design investigations is the subject of the next course, called DYNAMICS. The medium for DYNAMICS includes both the space (solid and void) of ARCHITECTONICS, and *time*.

Where do we come from? Consider the chambered nautilus, a mollusc who seems to create its shell walls from an infinitesimally small origin. How did it begin to make its beautiful form, the logarithmic spiral? Life appears to make a leap, perhaps of faith, creating its reality by growing into the void. Evolution means literally "to turn or spin outward". "Volume" itself comes from the same Sanskrit root, "vol"—meaning "to roll."

We used to be completely anchored to the Earth. Now, however, humankind has succeeded in spanning space not just across the land, but also outward from our planet's center. Bruce McCandless, the astronaut who floated free above the Earth in the Manned Maneuvering Unit was not just "hovering out there in space." His forward thrust kept him falling around the earth as fast as gravity pulled him to the surface. McCandless maintained his position because he was spinning about the center of the earth at orbital velocity, which is 17,000+ MPH. So a picture of this astronaut is not only a still life, but also a movie.

Jonathan Block Friedman is a registered architect who has taught architecture for over 15 years. He is Professor of Architecture and Coordinator of the Design Fundamentals Program at New York Institute of Technology, responsible for over 700 students and 35 instructors on three campuses. He has also taught at the University of Kentucky and the New Jersey Institute of Technology and has been a visiting critic at Cooper Union, Columbia, and Harvard. A National Merit Scholar, he was educated at Princeton and Cambridge, studying with Kenneth Frampton, Peter Eisenman, Michael Graves, and Charles Gwathmey, and has worked for Richard Meier, among other architects. He has won a national architectural design competition and a grant from the New York State Council on The Arts and recently earned Honorable Mention in the National Space Institute's Design Competition for a proposed Earthlight Lodge Lunar Resort and National Park. He has lectured in the US, Central America, Europe, and Australia. His architecture has been exhibited at the Cooper Union and Paul Robeson Rutgers Galleries and in Israel and Japan. He has worked with both New York's Mayor Lindsay and Portola Institute, the *Whole Earth Catalog* group in Palo Alto. He holds several US patents and is listed in Marquis *Who's Who in Computer Graphics*.

The author lives with his wife and son in Glen Cove, New York.